Long Road To Delano

Sam Kushner

D1601516

INTERNATIONAL PUBLISHERS New York

© 1975 International Publishers Co., Inc.
Second Printing, 1976

Printed in the United States of America

Library of Congress Cataloging in Publication Data

Kushner, Sam, 1914-
  Long road to Delano

1. Trade-unions—Agricultural laborers—California—
History.   2. United Farm Workers—History.
3. Agricultural laborers—California—History.   I. Title.
HD6515.A292U58   331.88'13'09794   74-30123
ISBN 0-7178-0423-2
ISBN 0-7178-0424-0 pbk.

Contents

Acknowledgments

American Melodrama: The Presidential Campaign of 1968 by Lewis Chester et al, 1969, Viking Press; *Delano* by John Gregory Dunne, 1971, Farrar, Straus & Giroux, Inc; *Factories in the Field: the Story of the Migratory Farm Labor in California* by Carey McWilliams, new edition 1971, Peregrine Smith, Inc; *Forty Acres* by Mark Day, 1971, Praeger Publishers; *Merchants of Labor: The Mexican Bracero Story* by Ernesto Galarza, 1966, by permission of McNally & Loftin, Publishers; *Sal Si Puedes* by Peter Mathiessen, 1970, Random House; *So Shall Ye Reap* by Joan London and Henry Anderson, © 1971, with permission of Thomas Y. Crowell Company, Inc., Publishers; *Spiders in the House and Workers in the Field* by Ernesto Galarza, 1970, University of Notre Dame Press; *Time of Our Lives: the Story of My Father and Myself* by Orrick Jones, 1973, Octagon Books, Farrar, Straus & Giroux, Inc.

Foreword

In this book, Sam Kushner has outlined the century-long struggle of farm laborers to organize themselves for a better life. Kushner's writing combines a deep personal commitment to social justice with thorough-going journalistic skill and an historian's grasp of the many forces at work in California farm labor history.

The author of this book, who has distinguished himself as the farm labor reporter for the *People's World*, has covered the nine year struggle of the United Farm Worker's Union with more depth and accuracy than any other journalist on the scene, gaining the reputation of an expert through his intimate knowledge of the strike, its protagonists and its broad historical significance.

Long Road to Delano is the story of the endless battle waged by farm workers, activists, radicals and communists to organize the field workers into a powerful union. The book both describes as well as evaluates the historical process wherein many men have been broken, but which has nevertheless resulted in some clear cut victories for the nation's most neglected group of workers.

In digging up many forgotten facts, and more importantly, analyzing and scrutinizing them, Kushner has made a valuable contribution to the understanding of the United Farm Workers' strike begun under the leadership of Cesar Chavez in 1965. He shows the historical roots, both of the farm workers' clash with the power of the U.S. agribusiness as well as the back door agreements and the raiding tactics of the leadership of the International Brotherhood of Teamsters. He tells us why it is important that the Chavez-led union be victorious and what is at stake for organized labor and for all liberation movements, including those of women, Chicanos, Blacks, Native Americans and other oppressed groups.

In addition, he also analyzes aspects of the historical process of liberation among Mexicans and Chicanos in their efforts to resist racist oppression, in their fight against the use of the border and immigration policies as a weapon of division and oppression, and in their struggle for cultural independence. All of these struggles have been deeply related to their fight for a union in the fields.

Luisa Moreno, one of the great Chicana leaders of former years, often described the willingness to sacrifice and die for a just cause as "being in the highest and noblest traditions of the Mexican people."

In this volume the author correctly singles out this dedication in the perennial use, among Mexican working people, of the revolutionary symbols—the black eagle, the red and black flags, the rejection of the international border, and the sacred reverence for Mexico's revolutionary figures—Zapata, Villa and the Virgin of Guadalupe.

Quoting Dr. Juan Gomez-Quinones of the University of California, Los Angeles, he reflects the deeper implications of the farm workers' struggle for those who are struggling for national liberation and socialism in this country.

Long Road to Delano emphasizes another significant historical point, all too often neglected by labor historians—the role of the Chicano and Mexican people in the building and development of the labor movement in the midwestern and southwestern states.

Workers of all minority groups have suffered from the racist character of our American society in terms of meager wages and subhuman working conditions. But for Mexican workers, their struggles in the fields and factories have been an attempt to redress the conquest in 1835 of Texas and in 1848 of the rest of the Southwest.

In these pages Kushner carefully compares the early attempts at farm labor organization with the more recent and successful accomplishments of the United Farm Workers. Chavez's technique, the author writes, is to organize the workers first, then strike later, as opposed to the former strategy of striking and trying to build a union at the same time. The latter strategy often ended in failure, though, as was mentioned earlier, these first attempts provided stepping stones for subsequent victories. Anyone familiar with labor history will recall the comparisions that William Z. Foster used to make about the differences in the 1919 steel strike and the 1937 campaign that proved victorious for the United Steelworkers Organizing Committee of the CIO.

Few significant developments escape the author's attention. For example, he tells of Cesar Chavez insisting, at the first convention of the UFWA, held in Fresno, California in 1973, that all races, nationalities and sexes be represented on the union's national executive board.

The author also tells of another tradition adopted by the UFWA, the general strike, originally inspired by the Wobblies and recently immortalized by the Delano strike song, *Huelga en General*.

The UFWA has been able, in Kushner's words, to make breakthroughs in areas where other farm unions have fallen short. Chief among these have been the widespread public support of the grape and lettuce boycotts and the winning over of important segments of Protestant, Catholic and Jewish religious leadership.

The veteran labor reporter writes of the shady history of the Teamsters' Union leadership in making undemocratic moves in efforts to destroy the UFWA's popularity among farm workers. He also documents the shoddy track record of the conservative and racist leadership of some of the national and international AFL unions. Kushner does this without imputing their corruption to the rank and file membership of either the Teamsters or the AFL-CIO unions. An important chapter of *Long Road to Delano* is dedicated to the important role of Communist party members in organizing farm workers in California. The courageous efforts of these people have been passed over in most books dealing with farm labor history. It is here that Sam Kushner breaks new ground again—yet he tells the story clearly and simply without creating false heroes or heroines and beating drums. I, for one, am glad that at least one chapter of the book was devoted to those organizers and their crucial role in the saga of farm labor.

Seven out of eleven chapters are devoted to the 90 years prior to the 1965 strike in Delano. Those were action-filled periods, and *Long Road to Delano* has captured the events in an exciting and human style. This book offers what many of us have been searching

for—a well researched, insightful, and readable history of the farm
labor movement. Hopefully, this study will encourage other students and writers to uncover even more chapters that have been
passed over by historians, past and present.

Sam Kushner was himself on the scene when the great events of
the Delano grape strike took place. He chronicles this in the last
four chapters of this book. As Dolores Huerta, vicè-president of the
United Farm Workers Union, told the *People's World* banquet on
October 14, 1973, ". . . Brother Sam has done what Cesar Chavez
has accomplished—spreading the whole idea of brotherhood, and
this means getting people together even though we may be different
in terms of our ideologies and practices. It makes me feel good when
I, know that we have hundreds of farm workers and other people
throughout the country who are saying, 'I am working every single
day of my life—and it is a daily grind—to make change.'

"Sam Kushner symbolizes this to me, because I know he often
found it very difficult to write because of the discrimination he faced
from a lot of people—especially when he covered the strike in the
beginning. But that did not stop him—he found a way to make
friends with everyone. We not only respect Sam as a journalist. We
respect him because he has shown us how friends should treat each
other. And when Sam was sick a few years back, and we thought we
were going to lose him, we felt very sad. Were it not for him, a lot of
people would not be working together to help our union."

Dolores Huerta could have said the same thing about Sam
Kushner's relationship with the whole Chicano movement and
other movements he has covered as a journalist.

In recent decades, no book has been written about the farm
workers strike and boycott that compares with *Long Road to
Delano*. Kushner writes with broad strokes yet with scholarly preci-
sion and deep compassion about California's turbulent farm labor
history, past and present. I can affirm that this is the best book on
this subject and it will take another very special work to surpass it. It
stands as a model for those writers who believe in the role of the
participant-observer, combined with diligent research and on-the-
scene reporting, and for those who wish to accurately convey the
inside of a struggle as complex as farm labor.

It is a privilege for me to contribute these few words to the *Long*

Road to Delano, the story of thousands of farm workers who have sweated to build a strong democratic and truly independent union. Their saga is a dynamic part of the story of the entire U.S. labor movement and of the Chicano and Mexican peoples' struggle for liberation and unification. All those who stand for freedom for oppressed people, for peace and socialism and for the final victory of the workers, can be indebted to Sam Kushner for writing this book.

Secretary of C.A.S.A. (Brotherhood of General Workers), a national organization of immigrant workers; professor, Chicano Studies Department, California State University at Los Angeles, former president of the Mexican-American Political Association (MAPA).   BERT CORONA

Preface

Not since the formative years of the CIO has the nation witnessed a labor struggle comparable to that of the grape pickers in the San Joaquin valley.

As one who witnessed firsthand the great campaigns to bring union organization to the auto workers at the Ford Motor Company in Detroit and to the farm equipment workers at the International Harvester plants in Chicago more than 30 years ago, I was impressed by the drama and scope of the farm-labor strike that began in Delano in September, 1965. For much of the last ten years I have covered the developments in the agricultural labor movement and have had the opportunity to witness some of the more dramatic moments in this most recent confrontation between agribusiness and the field workers.

Just as the impact of the early CIO days was felt throughout much of the union movement, so too has that of the farm workers. When the auto workers in Flint, Michigan, decided to sit-in at the huge auto assembly plant, clerks in the five-and-dime stores in Brooklyn, where I then resided, also sat-in during the wave of union organization of that period.

With the farm workers, while the effect of their struggle was somewhat different, it was no less significant. A most important impact of this struggle was described by Prof. Juan Gomez-Quinones in his article in the Spring, 1970 issue of *Aztlan, a Chicano Journal of Social Sciences and the Arts*. He wrote, "On September 8, 1965, what was to become the National (United) Farm Workers Organizing Committee called a strike in the area of Delano, California. It dates a new era for the Mexican-American, reflected above all in the emergence of a militant spirit expressed in new organizational forms and employing different tactics. Though to the uninformed what is shaking the community is without precedent for it, the movement quite clearly taps historical roots and experiences that are unique to the Mexican-American."

Catholic priests, anxious to break the traditional mold in which they had been cast, were among those who came to Delano to assist in the organization of the farm workers as did many Protestant ministers and some rabbis. The impact of the strike on religious life in the United States was considerable.

Also growing out of this union-organizing drive was a cultural movement, initially reflected by the Teatro Campesino. It began as the agitational propaganda weapon of the strikers but in ensuing years the Teatro helped give birth to many similar Chicano theater groups throughout the nation.

Among the numerous contributions that the grape strike made to modern history, probably one of the most significant was the activization of socially conscious forces within the ranks of organized labor. The campaign brought forth forces in the union movement who had long been dormant. For many of the old-timers it was a return to the militant past of labor unionism, and a time for the completion of one of the major unfulfilled responsibilities of labor—organization of the workers in the fields.

The farm workers had paid dearly for the years in which they remained unorganized. We were informed that "the field-worker's average life span is only 46 years as compared to the 69-75 for non-field-workers. . . . The fieldworker is being cheated out of some 25 years of life.."[1] And that farm labor, comprising only seven percent of the U.S. work force, has over 22 percent of all fatalities from work accidents.[2]

When Cesar Chavez and his co-workers in the National Farm Workers Association founded that organization in 1962, they planned an organizing drive in the fields like no other that had ever taken place.

1. Migrant Community Studies Project, Denver Research Institute, University of Denver, November, 1971.
2. According to the foreword of "Farm Labor Organizing, 1905-67," July 1967.

Those who from the very outset viewed the grape strike and boycott as among the most significant labor developments in modern times, as well as the key to vast changes in the Chicano and other movements, were afforded the opportunity to view at close range this unfolding drama. The strike was part of labor's interrupted history in the first half of the 20th century. It was instrumental in playing a major role in unlocking the great potential of the Chicano movement in the United States, which, like that of the Blacks, emerged and affected the public consciousness on a scale never before seen.

It was probably inevitable that I would some day write a book about farm labor. My long period of activity as a labor reporter as well as a union organizer served as an apprenticeship to a better understanding of the latest war in the fields. I did not approach this assignment as an "objective" reporter. If anything I was a partisan, one who was anxious for the newborn union movement to succeed. While attempting to report events as I saw them, I did not view the battle as one between equals. By telling the story of their struggle and of their oppression I was trying to spread the word of this unequal battle to all persons who might be of assistance to the campesinos.

Initially, it was my intention to write a book that would deal mainly with the immediate developments preceding the grape strike and the major events around that campaign. However, since several books had already been published about the strike, its leaders and the union, it seemed more appropriate and useful to place between two covers the continuing history of some of the many campaigns to organize the farm workers. Recently, it seems, the past has become all too obscure—all too unrelated to the latest campaign to organize the grape pickers.

The major part of the first draft of this book actually was begun in the spring of 1972. As I dug more deeply into the rich past of farm labor organizations, it became increasingly clear that a major part of the book should include accounts of these heroic and often unsuccessful efforts. Interviews with many old-timers in the fields reminded me time and again of the old trade-union truism that no strike is really ever completely lost. Each serves as a school in which workers learn to better cope with the difficulties of organization, and every single struggle forces some new concessions out of the growers, no matter how small.

Regardless of the current organizational strength of the AFL-CIO United Farm Workers of America, there is no doubt that the great leap in improving wages and working conditions for a major section of the nation's farm labor force has been largely attributable to its strikes, boycotts and organizing campaigns. The momentary victories or defeats cannot obscure the long-run significance of this movement and the fact that it has given hundreds of thousands of farm workers a new dignity as human beings—not the rented slaves they had been for many decades.

It took a great deal of cooperation from many people to put this book together. First, I am deeply indepted to the *People's World*, on which I worked from 1961 to the fall of 1973. It was with the sympathetic understanding of its editors that I was free to wander the fields to follow and report developments in the most significant and protracted story then taking place on the West Coast.

Beyond all others, the campesinos, young and old, who willingly unfolded their histories, were valuable sources of information and the inspiration for the writing of this book. Cooperation from rank-and-file union members and from UFWA officials was as wholehearted as it was indispensable. In addition, I am also indebted to the many other unionists, communist and movement activists who shared the aspirations of the farm workers as well as their tribulations and experiences and who took the time to discuss them with me.

At the risk of omitting some significant contributors, I would like to express my special indebtedness to Dolores Huerta, Gilberto Padilla and Philip Vera Cruz, all of whom are officers of the UFWA. Also to Paul Schrade, former UAW official, whose support to the farm workers was used by his opponents in his union as one pretext for ousting him from the post of West Coast regional director of the United Auto Workers Union.

As is evident in the text of this book, I have drawn freely on many of the earlier and current works on farm labor. Stuart Jamieson's *Labor Unionism in American Agriculture* (U.S. Department of Labor, Bureau of Labor Statistics) was a volume of source material that was of invaluable assistance, as was Carey McWilliams' indispensable classic *Factories in the Fields.* I also found most helpful, *Roots: An Asian American Reader,* which was a project of the University of California at Los Angeles Asian American Studies Center. Dr. Ernesto Galarza's books on farm labor, most especially his *Merchants of Labor,* made available a scholarly study of a period—the bracero era—about which all too little is known or understood.

Philip S. Foner's complete study of *The History of the Labor Movement in the United States* (volume 4, on the *Industrial Workers of the World 1905-1917*), provided essential material for the chapter on the Wobblies. For additional material in that chapter I am in the debt of an old and dear friend, the late Elizabeth Gurley Flynn, who, fortunately, recalled some of her IWW days in her book, *The Rebel Girl, An Autobiography, 1906-1926.*

Most helpful in developing some of the chapters on the most recent era of farm labor struggles were Eugene Nelson's *Huelga;* Mark Day's *Forty Acres;* John Gregory Dunne's *Delano;* Peter Matthiessen's *Sal Si Puedes* and *So Shall Ye Reap,* by Joan London and Henry Anderson. I was also fortunate in having the use of material in several issues of *Aztlan,* a *Chicano Journal of the Social Sciences and the Arts,* of the Chicano Studies Center, UCLA.

Space will not permit giving thanks to the many others who contributed to this volume and who deserve crediting. However, I would be remiss were I not to mention thankfully the comments as well as the arduous work of typing the manuscript done by my good friend Jan Cords during the time she was the organizer of a UFWA boycott team. And, more than anyone else, my wife Flo, who urged, coaxed and prodded me into finishing this book. It was she who enthusiastically shared in the decision that after what seemed a lifetime as a reporter I should devote my full time and energy towards the writing of this book.

In the spring of 1970, while I was bedridden in Midway Hospital, the subject of several major operations, the first vague notions about this volume whirred through my sometimes befogged mind. Were it not for the successful efforts of several talented and sympathetic surgeons, there is little likelihood that this book would have ever been started, let alone completed.

Because of the vast scope and detail of the subject, the book is unavoidably limited. Its emphasis is on some of the major thrusts that led to the Delano developments and most specifically to those California events which had the most direct historic impact on the farm workers' struggles in the present period.

While the concept of this book was my own, much of its organization and editing was the handiwork of a young journalist whom I first met in Delano, where he was assisting in the production of the farm workers' union newspaper, *El Malcriado*. Bob Dudnick, a talented newspaperman who seems to have touched all bases in his professional career, is presently the president of the San José local of the Newspaper Guild. With meticulous care he went over this manuscript several times and after each reading came up with helpful proposals for its improvement.

As is evident from all of the aforementioned, this book, like so many others, is the total product of the contributions of many people. To the degree that *Long Road to Delano* is a cohesive book about the historic struggles of agricultural labor we are all indebted to them. Its shortcomings, of course, are solely my own.

Long
Road
To
Delano

1 A Century of Strife and Servitude Begins

". . . a history of greed, of perjury, of corruption, of spoliation, and high-handed robbery for which it will be difficult to find a parallel.
Henry George, 1871

For more than a century the great central valley of California has been irrigated by the sweat and blood of countless thousands who were attracted by promises of security and even riches. Instead, a great many became targets of racists assaults and virtually all were impoverished.

No longer are there the winding, twisted roads over which steaming, overheated and overloaded Model T Fords carried more than their full loads of hopeful humanity whose very existence was often as precarious as the hairpin curves over which the rickety wheels rode. These days the main thoroughfare into the lush San Joaquin Valley from the bustling Los Angeles basin is a multilaned, well-graded interstate highway. But for many of the farm workers that is just about all that has changed since the days of Ma and Pa Joad.

When the Joads came to California, they crossed a river and a desert, drove over bare mountains and stopped and looked at a great valley glimmering in gold and green as far as their dusty vision could reach. That was in the depression; the days of the *Grapes of*

Wrath. Today. driving north from Los Angeles on Interstate 5 —
old Highway 99 — you can see the same valley, reaching also to the
limits of your vision. Little has changed over the years in that
breathtaking sight of nature's wonders. Off the Grapevine, a few
miles north of Lebec, the valley stretches out, silent in the oppres-
sive midday heat and at other times still under the heavy sleep
blanket of morning fog. You get the feeling of vastness looking down
on the valley floor as the highway goes straight and clean as the road
to Life and Hope. So too did it look to the Joads and countless
others.

The great valley is the heart of the state; the rest came later.
Here, in this valley, the work is done to feed the cities of much of
the nation and the fruit of the land is harvested by the laborer but
kept by the rancher.

You stop in Mcfarland, about 20 miles north of sprawling Bakersfield, and you buy some gas, a bottle of coke or a cup of coffee. The
land now has changed subtly. Behind you are the oil rigs and the
cotton fields. Off to the side you have passed towns like Arvin and
Weedpatch, little known to the passing traveller but well known to
the migrant farm workers. They are among the many communities
in which bitter battles to organize the farm workers have taken
place.

If it's winter the country lies like a work-weary old woman in a
grey shawl of fog. The vines huddle low, for you are in grapes now.
And if it's September, the sun is bright and the grapes are as tall as
man and taller.

You are but five miles from Delano where, in 1962, Cesar Chavez
and a handful of hopeful organizers, unnoticed and unheralded, met
to plant the seeds of the National Farm Workers Association.

Agribusiness

California agriculture, more appropriately and accurately described as agribusiness, is the largest industry in a state which
boasts many other giant industrial complexes, including the huge
aerospace firms.

Agribusiness is no newcomer to the top of the economic ladder in
this very large state. It has been there a long time. Billboards
proudly proclaim the exalted economic position of this industry.

They have been placed there by those who own the wealth that begets the green fields in the valleys, on the cultivated hills and even on mountain sides. They seem to warn the populace not to tamper with this golden-egged goose.

Agribusiness is not modest, nor necessarily truthful. What can be seen from the highway in no manner reflects the hundred-year struggle in these fields. There are no public tributes to the fieldworkers—Chinese, Japanese, Mexican, Filipino, Black and Anglo—whose backbreaking labor over the years provided the sinew and sacrificed the lives of men, women and children to build the agribusiness empire.

Here and there a dilapidated deserted building stands, reminder of bygone strikes. One such remains standing near Arvin, no longer the bustling center it was during the strike movement in the late 1940's. Nowadays farm labor unionists and others who know of its existence point it out and speak with reverence of the struggle it symbolizes.

Hidden from view are the camps, the homes and union centers from which were generated the long' bitter and often bloody struggles against oppression and near-slavery that have more often than not characterized the uprisings in the fields.

In the late 1960's, the red and black huelga (strike) flag of the United Farm Workers, utilizing the traditional colors of the Mexican labor movement, appeared to be more symbolic of past struggles than anything else that met the naked eye. Red, traditional color of workers in revolt, serves as a reminder of the blood shed in the seemingly never-ending struggle for a modicum of social and economic freedom. The black reflects the earlier influences on both sides of the Mexican border of the anarcho-syndicalist movement.

Eighty years earlier, in 1880, Karl Marx considered the California phenomenon to be of special interest. It aroused his curiosity and he wrote to his journalist friend in the United States, Friedrich Sorge:

"I should very much be pleased if you would find me something good on economic conditions in California. California is very important for me because nowhere else has the upheaval most shamelessly caused by capitalist centralization taken place with such speed." (K. Marx and F. Engels, *Letters to Americans*, 1848-1895 — New York: International Publishers, 1953)

Setting the stage for this "capitalist centralization" that attracted the attention of Marx, half a world away, was the end of the main thrust of the gold rush in 1860, by which time the "mining barons," as Carey McWilliams described them, had pushed aside the adventurous easterners and midwesterners who had come to mine the California gold.

Also by 1860 the immense California acreage had passed into the hands of a comparatively small number of people, who immediately set about the task of extracting as much profit as they could from the products of the soil. This came about as a result of one of the largest land swindles ever recorded. Henry George in 1871 described the expropriation of the rich land through the utilization of the Mexican land grants as "a history of greed, of perjury, of corruption, of spoliation and high-handed robbery for which it will be difficult to find a parallel."

The gold rush had attracted hundreds of thousands to California, and there was a need to feed this great new multitude of humanity. In the decade between 1850 and 1860 the population of the state had increased more than four-fold, from 92,000 to 380,000. The transcontinental railway, which could bring food into the state from other fertile areas, was almost a decade away, not completed until 1869. The need for a local food supply was urgent, and just as the mining barons owned the rich lode so did the new land barons own the land.

Wheat and the Indians

Wheat was the get-rich-quick crop which needed little care and a relatively small labor force. Between 1860 and 1880 annual wheat production jumped from 6 million bushels to 29 million. Ten years later, California became the second highest wheat-producing state, producing 40 million bushels in 1890.

In his classic book on earlier farm labor developments, Carey McWilliams in *Factories in the Field* reports that "the only cheap labor then available in California was Indian labor, and Indians were promptly recruited in the fields." (Carey McWilliams, *Factories in the Field: The Story of the Migratory Farm Labor in California* — Santa Barbara and Salt Lake City, Peregrine Smith, 1971. First published in 1935.)

Contemporary accounts relate that during the Spanish mission period Indians received half the wages that were paid to Mexicans or Anglos. Also during the period that the Mexicans dominated the land in California, it is reported that the owners refused to honor Indian pueblo rights on soil included in their land grants. The Mexicans, however, McWilliams explains, did not dispossess the Indians but permitted them to continue "to work on ranchos as more or less vassals."

But once the Anglo land barons took over they put an end to all this. The Indians were uprooted from their native land and driven further back into the mountains. When employed, they were paid only a semblance of wages, or none at all. On occasion a bottle of whiskey was all they got.

Mechanization of the huge wheat fields, far more extensive in California than in the Middle West, rapidly reduced the need for manual labor—and for Indians.

Land Grab and Early Rebellion

One of the earliest recorded rebellions by workers in the fields took place in 1871, when more than eight-and-a-half million acres of land were owned by only 516 persons in California. In Fresno County alone 48 owners each held more than 79,000 acres and throughout the state 16 landowners each controlled 84 square miles.

Millions of acres lay idle with no humans living on the land or tilling the soil. Yet there was no land for the people who had come in response to the promise of California land. Many who refused to accept the validity of the Spanish grants under which much of this land was claimed, and sometimes settled, became known as "squatters."

Hundreds of so-called squatters in the Sacramento area banded together in an attempt to prevent dispossession from lands claimed by Captain John Sutter, who had acquired them under a Mexican grant. On August 22, 1850, the rebellious settlers took over Sacramento, now the state capital, and marched through the streets in military formation. After a day or two of what some historians describe as "rioting," the National Guard arrived and drove farmers from their vantage points. Those who could not, or would not, pay the price demanded by the land barons were evicted. "The land barons won," McWilliams reports, and thus there was established a pattern that prevailed for more than a century.

The land barons, holders of the wheat-producing properties, also were sharply affected by the effects of the economic crisis that engulfed the nation in the 1870's. Mines were shut down, banks closed and many newer business enterprises went bankrupt. Simultaneously. there was a rapid decline in profitability from the wheat fields.

Competition from new grain areas of Russia and the fertile Mississippi Valley, high freight rates and gyrations in world prices all contributed to the difficulties of the wheat growers, who by 1880 averaged a return of about four percent. With the end of wheat as its main crop—and having done much to exterminate the Indians in genocidal exploitation—California agriculture was in need of new crops and new people to again work the soil. Soon both were found.

In the 1880's the transcontinental railroad had been completed, and refrigerated cars were being developed. These changes made a considerable impact on still developing California agriculture. Simultaneously, agronomist Luther Burbank experimented with fruits and other farm products, thereby laying the basis for further enrichment of the farm growers. Also at this time there occurred a most important development, the beginning of intensive irrigation.

The state was set for the new bonanza for the owners of California's fields.

The Chinese

And suddenly there emerged a plentiful supply of foreign labor to till the fields and pick the crops—the Chinese. They were seen by the growers as the "perfect solution" for their immediate needs. On June 10, 1893, the *Pacific Rural Press* said, "The availability of cheap Chinese labor gave the fruit growers hope. They extended their operations and the Chinese proved equal to all that had been expected of them. They became especially clever in the packing of fruit; in fact, the Chinese have become the only considerable body of people who understand how to pack fruit for eastern shipment." With minor variations in their racist rhetoric the growers were later to say much the same about the Japanese, Filipinos, Mexicans and the Hindu Indians.

There was one thread that ran through all of the successive work forces which predominated in the fields—they were all from outside the border of the United States and therefore more easily exploited. Beginning with the Chinese, there developed the growers' own special adaptation of the concept of imperialism. Instead of physically participating in the seizure and exploitation of foreign lands and people, the growers utilized the land in the United States that they or their ancestors had seized, often illegally, with imported and shamefully exploited foreign labor.

Either way the results were the same—enrichment as a result of the labor of a relatively helpless and subjugated foreign work force. Having full control of the state machinery in the United States was fully comparable to utilization of the armed forces of the United States in distant or nearby lands.

Chinese people had been brought into this country to work the California mines and to perform the equally backbreaking work necessary to build the transcontinental railroad. In addition, they were employed in miscellaneous menial capacities in San Francisco. By 1870 they constituted 10 percent of the work force on California farms, and 16 years later seven out of eight farm laborers in the state were Chinese. Refuge in the farms was sought by Chinese workers who tried to escape legal and extralegal attacks on them in San Francisco and in the mining towns, as well as unemployment. Upon completion of the transcontinental railroad 10,000 were put out of work.

Deprived by racist laws from having families in the United States, they lived in substandard housing while working on the farms. Yet, despite all of the privations and exploitation, Chinese workers proved to be the initial foreign-born saviors of California agriculture. Not only were they excellent workers, but "By and large," McWilliams declares, "it is correct to state that, in many particulars, the Chinese actually taught their overlords how to plant, cultivate and harvest orchard and garden crops."

With unemployment on the rise among white workers, a hue and cry was raised against the continued employment of the Chinese in the fields. Joining in this demand were small farmers as well as organized labor, a small but vocal force.

The large growers, determined to hold on to their cheap labor force, ignored the chauvinist outcry as well as many state and federal laws enacted specifically against the Chinese. Their motives were by no means altruistic. "We cannot pay the wages demanded by the whites," they insisted.

Still another economic crisis in the United States—in 1893—brought this struggle to a head. It sharply affected California, where 27 banks failed by June. Throughout the state large-scale riots took place, and the Chinese workers were literally driven from the fields. Once again a pattern was being set.

During periods of major unemployment, the foreign workers became the target of racist attacks. In later years the Japanese, Filipino and Mexican workers were also among the nationalities who felt the brunt of similar massive racist assaults.

So desperate was the economic plight of unemployed white workers that after they had succeeded in eliminating the Chinese from the fields, the growers hired the whites for far less pay than the Chinese laborers received. The white unemployed workers who marched on Fresno to take the place of the ousted Chinese were paid 75 cents a day and board to work the fields. On the same jobs Chinese workers had been getting $1.40 a day.

By 1882, Congress had passed its first Exclusion Act, aimed at the beleaguered Chinese people, who were already the victims of discriminatory legislation in California as well as of attacks throughout much of the nation. Stanford Lyman, in his documented article, *Ethnic Conflict in California History*, which was later reprinted in the University of California, Los Angeles publication titled *Roots: An Asian American Reader*, declared:

"By 1880 the drive to exclude Chinese, which started in California and moved eastward to the Rockies, had spread throughout the nation and laid the basis for America's first bill to restrict immigration on the basis of race. In 1870 Chinese laborers had been shipped from California to North Adams, Massachusetts, to break a strike of shoemakers. Hailed at first by those opposed to the striking union, the Knights of St. Crispin, the Chinese were subsequently the objects of anti-coolie meetings held in Boston to protest the reduction of American labor to the standards of 'rice and rats.'

"In 1877 another gang of Chinese coolies were imported from

California to break a cutlery manufacturing strike in Beaver Falls, Pennsylvania. . . . Ohio papers protested against the use of Chinese labor in the cigar-making industry, the industry whose union leader, Samuel Gompers, was to become a lifelong foe of the Chinese and one of the most potent forces in denying them equal opportunity in craft work. America's labor unions fulminated against the Chinese and demanded their exclusion from the nation and their expulsion from the labor force."

Later, Lyman, who was on the faculty of the Department of Sociology, University of California, San Diego, reports that:

"By the turn of the century the Chinese were isolated, neglected and demoralized. Located inside Chinatowns of American cities they achieved some sense of cultural freedom, a relaxation of tensions and precarious independence. Some found a new sense of freedom in giving support to Sun Yat-sen's liberation movement for China; a few prospered as merchants and gained political and social power in the ghetto, but most remained homeless and trapped, too poor to return to China and too oppressed to enter fully into American society.

"Sojourners without wives, they could not procreate a second generation which, had it been born, might have succeeded like the second generation of other immigrant groups. Only after 1930 were there enough Chinese women present in America to guarantee that a new generation of significant proportions would develop in the next two decades. The much vaunted Chinese family remained but an idea in Chinatown for eight remorseless decades."

The Japanese

Even while the battle was taking place in the fields and elsewhere on the right of the Chinese to work, there appeared a new crop and, of course, the need for a new supply of labor. Preferably, from the growers' viewpoint, this new labor force would also be of foreign extraction and one which was reputed to be docile, uncomplaining and obviously alien in a land of predominantly white men and women. The crop was beets and the labor force was Japanese.

The growers had been preparing for this situation for a long time. When Congress enacted the Exclusion Act aimed at the Chinese, it was largely ignored by the desperate Chinese work force as well as by the exploiting growers. At that time there were 132,300 Chinese in California and less than 100 Japanese.

Wary of the strong anti-Oriental sentiment in the state during the 1890's, but still desiring foreign labor, the growers began a low-key campaign to recruit Japanese for the arduous hand-labor in the beet fields. By 1903 approximately 30,000 Japanese workers were employed within California. Once again the growers seemed to strike gold on their fertile farms. The industrious Japanese, beset by all of the same problems which had been the bane of the Chinese, formed associations through which they found work and which between seasons seemed to disappear.

Through their ingenuity and hard work the Japanese workers helped to reclaim major areas of wasteland. In Fresno County alone it was estimated that 3,000 Japanese lost their lives in the bitter struggle to reclaim the land because water and sanitation were bad.

When the Japanese began working fields, they seemed to be ideal employees from the growers' viewpoint. Many worked for as little as 35 cents to 40 cents per day and in addition provided their own transportation and board. Once they became the dominant group of farm workers in the state, the Japanese capitalized on their position. On occasion they would demand a major increase in wages in the midst of a harvest, and get it. Work stoppages were part of the arsenal of the Japanese work force.

The *Los Angeles Times,* then one of the major land-owning corporations, said in a racist editorial on January 17, 1920, "Japanese labor is not cheap labor. The little brown traders know how to get as much for their product as the traffic will bear." Large ranchers were especially irritated that some of the Japanese farm workers acquired sufficient capital to purchase land of their own. And when they became small ranchers they hired Japanese almost exclusively to work their properties. The big growers did not welcome this kind of competition.

Attempts to deprive the Japanese of the right to own land were legalized with passage of the Alien Land Act of 1913 and in similar legislation enacted in 1919. In 1924 new federal restrictions on Japanese immigration were promulgated. The specter of organization has always haunted the California growers and the Japanese had a built-in system of organization because of their closely knit working units. In some measure it was controlled by their uniting for the available jobs. Also it related to their desire for union organization, despite the racist attitudes of the nation's union leaders.

The growing disenchantment of California growers was bluntly voiced at the 1907 California fruit growers convention, where it was said:

"The Chinese when they were here were ideal. They were patient, plodding and uncomplaining in performance of the most menial service. They submitted to anything, never violating a contract. The Japanese now coming in are a tricky and cunning lot, who break contracts and become quite independent. They are not organized into unions, but their clannishness seems to operate as a union would. One trick is to contract work at a certain price' and then in the rush of the harvest threaten to strike unless wages are raised."

This was indeed a strange characterization, coming as it did from an organization of growers that was part and parcel of the historic system of racism and exploitation which had already treated the Indians, the Chinese and the Japanese as inferior people fit only to work the fields at the lowest wages and in subhuman conditions.

Passage of the Alien Land Act and restrictive immigration laws prevented the Japanese labor force from replenishing itself and also had the effect of expropriating land owned by them. Summing up the era of large-scale Japanese employment, McWilliams said, "The Japanese have made their peace with California but at a heavy price."

After the era that McWilliams analyzes, there came the greatest of all injustices against the Japanese in the United States. That was their internment in the concentration camps in 1942, following the outbreak of World War II. All persons of Japanese ancestry on the West Coast—citizens as well as aliens—were placed in barbed-wire internment camps. They left behind them their churches, their lands, their possessions and all their accumulations.

The Filipinos

For the greatest part of the past 50 years California growers have mainly relied on Chicanos and Mexicans to work the fields. It was also during this period that a large number of Filipinos were hired to work the fields, many of whom had been recruited in the Philippine Islands. Filipinos are playing a special role in the present history of the farm labor movement but their past significant struggles have been obscured in some recent accounts. To some degree the influx of Filipinos and Mexicans into the fields overlapped.

In part stimulated by Japanese labor strikes in California and a labor shortage in the state in 1924, the growers began to draw heavily on Filipino workers who had migrated earlier to Hawaii. The large-scale employment of Filipinos had resulted from a major plantation strike there which resulted in a large scale recruitment for the struck island farm.

Soon many of the Filipinos who had come to Hawaii in search of employment moved on to the continental United States. Even though the Filipino population in Hawaii (in 1930) probably exceeded that in the United States, the seemingly perennial panic in the United States over Asian labor once again became evident. The influx of Filipinos in the fields as well as in the cities was seen by many as the third successive invasion of Asians into the domestic labor force.

Unlike the Chinese or Japanese, the Filipinos were not considered to be aliens. They were "subjects" of the U.S. government who were nevertheless ineligible for citizenship unless they had served three years in the United States Navy.

The racist theme of the growers was heard once again in regard to the Filipinos as farm workers. "Growers at first considered Filipinos to be highly desirable laborers, as they were even more docile, low-paid and hard working than the more Americanized Mexicans." (*Labor Unionism in American Agriculture*; U.S. Department of Labor, Bureau of Labor Statistics Bulletin No. 836 by Stuart Jamieson.)

A report of the California Department of Industrial Relations gives us some other indications of the reasons the growers advanced for hiring Filipinos.

"At times the growers prefer the contractor employ a mixture of laborers of various races, speaking diverse languages and not accustomed to mingling with each other. This practise is to avoid labor trouble which might result from having a homogeneous group of laborers of the same race or nationality. Laborers speaking different languages and accustomed to diverse standards of living and habits are not as likely to arrive at a mutual understanding which would lead to strikes or other labor troubles during harvest seasons, when work interruptions would result in serious financial losses to the growers." (California Department of Industrial Relations, *Special Bulletin No. 3; Facts About Filipino Immigration into California*, San Francisco, 1930).

For the growers the Filipinos seemed ideal. The new recruits into the field were predominatly young, male, and for the most part, unmarried. They were mobile and mainly employed as "stoop labor" in asparagus and lettuce. Many were also employed in berries, tomatoes and grapes.

But the Filipinos turned out to be far from the docile workers that the growers expected. In fact, their militant history did much to lay the groundwork for the organizing drive that began in 1965 and led to the most successful farm-labor organizing drive in the history of the United States.

Carey McWilliams in *The Nation*, September, 1935 wrote: "The Filipino is a real fighter and his strikes have been dangerous. In August 1934, about 3,000 Filipinos went out on strike in the valuable lettuce fields near Salinas, California. On September 3rd a union of white workers (Vegetable Packers Association Local No. 18211) employed in the packing sheds returned to work under an agreement to arbitrate. In fact they were told to return to work by Joseph Casey, AFL official. But the Filipino workers refused to call off the strike."

Jamieson, in reporting on the outcome of the same strike of the Vegetable Packers Association, says that the white workers came out of that struggle with improved working conditions, shorter hours and higher wages. But there was an additional factor which was indicative of the division in the fields over the years. Jamieson said that "In leaving the Filipino union members unprotected and subject to attack from vigilantes, however, the organized white shed workers had lost the good will of non-white field workers and reduced the chances of winning sympathetic strike support from them in the future."

Despite low wages of about $2.50 a day in 1930, and terroristic race riots throughout much of the West Coast, the Filipino workers in the main remained a steadfast pro-union group. As was the case earlier with the Chinese and Japanese, the racist AFL leadership was a strong early opponent of Filipinos in the fields, especially during the depression years of the mid-1930's.

One of the earliest recorded attacks on the Filipinos took place in Yakima on September 19, 1928. Like a prairie fire the attacks spread to California's Exeter in October, 1929; Watsonville, January, 1930, and to Stockton, where a Filipino clubhouse was bombed. Nor were the attacks limited to the West Coast. In July 1932, Filipinos working in Florida vegetable fields were assaulted.

Among the Filipino farm workers who travelled the West Coast from the canneries of Alaska to the lettuce fields of Imperial Valley were Philip Vera Cruz and Larry Itliong, activists and leaders of the AFL-CIO Agricultural Workers Organizing Committee.

Vera Cruz, who started working in the Delano grape vineyards and thereafter called this city his home, tells of the life of Filipinos in Delano.

"Filipinos in Delano have worked in the grape vineyards for a long time. Some of them told me the common practice of hiring during the depression years. They said that, in the pruning season, a grower required new employees to get to the labor camp for two or three days, or more, for training without pay. In the training and practice period, those new help were charged 75 cents for board a day. . . . Then after those recruits learned the job, they were paid 10 to 15 cents an hour.

"In those depression years, Filipinos were blamed for taking the Anglos' jobs. Racist growers and politicians picked on the Filipino minority as a easy target for discrimination and attack. Filipinos were harassed and driven from their jobs. But the sad thing was they didn't have anywhere else to go. They were pushed to the wall and the whole town was against them. The police made false arrests and threw them in jail. In certain cases the courts imposed excessive fines. Those poor unwanted people risked their lives even just to go and buy their groceries. In those race riots staged in their camps, some were hurt and one was shot in bed."

Discriminated against by the growers and by other workers in the fields, the Filipinos banded together even tighter than did other farm workers. Deprived of normal family relations, many lived in the camps. Exploited and oppressed by labor contractors, they sought refuge in union organization, which by the middle of the 20th century was primarily expressed through membership in the AFL-CIO Agricultural Workers Organizing Committee.

Despite the fact that some of the growers followed a policy of elevating Filipino workers to the position of foremen, overseers over Filipino and Mexican workers, the more militant Filipinos, some of whom had a radical background as a result of their participation in struggles throughout the Northwest and in Alaska, continued the battle for unionization in the fields. There appeared to be no alternative, according to Larry Itliong, Philip Vera Cruz and others, who later were to become leaders of the United Farmworkers Union after it merged with AWOC.

One example of the radical impact on Filipino farm workers is given by Jamieson. He said:

"The Communist Party strengthened its following among the agricultural workers also, by upholding the rights of racial minorities. Filipinos in particular were being subjected to mob violence from whites in a series of race riots in California and other states. The *Daily Worker,* as spokesman for the Party, condemned the outbreaks. After a riot in the Salinas-Watsonville area in January 1930, the paper announced that the agricultural workers' section of the Trade Union Unity League (which was led by Communists) would begin an organizing drive in the Pajaro Valley in order to combat race conflict.

"Representatives of Workers International Relief and International Labor Defense were sent to Watsonville to help Filipinos who had been arrested and beaten during the disturbances. Protest meetings . . . were organized in San Francisco, Los Angeles and Oakland. Mexican and Filipino beet workers and asparagus cutters were reported attending meetings of the Agricultural Workers Industrial League."

The Mexicans

In the early part of the 20th century, the California growers, ever in search of a work force that would be available at cheap wages during the harvest seasons, while not being a burden on them or the communities in which they lived during the rest of the year, once again believed they had found a "perfect solution." Between 1920 and 1930 the number of Mexican-born persons in California more than tripled—from 121,176 to 368,013. It should be kept in mind that it was also during these years that the border scarcely resembled its present appearance. Movement across the U.S.-Mexican boundary was more widespread and the restrictions which now exist were either largely absent or ignored.

Once again the growers crowed with delight over the influx of labor into the fields. In describing the Mexican worker, Dr. G.P. Clements, manager of the agricultural department of the Los Angeles Chamber of Commerce, in November 1929, said, "No labor that has ever come to the United States is more satisfactory under righteous treatment. He is the result of years of servitude, has always looked upon his employer as his padron, and himself as part of the establishment."

But the Mexican labor force in the fields also found that the so-called righteous treatment included mass deportation and tightening of border controls during the periods of economic stress when Anglo workers, such as the dust bowl refugees in the 1930's, were willing to work for even lower wages.

As was evident in the Oxnard strike, as well as many other recorded instances, Mexicans had been in California and other fields for a long time. However, it was during the last world war, still another period during which the U.S. growers were in need of foreign labor, that the greatest influx took place.

Government statistics on the number of Mexican workers within the boundaries of the United States have long been suspect. Chicano scholars and activists, especially in recent years, have questioned the reliability of official statistics in computing the number of Mexican farm workers as well as of urban Mexicans.

Nevertheless, while the official figures undoubtedly understate the magnitude of the migration across the border, they do provide some basis for measuring employment trends.

By 1920 it is reported that farm publications referred to the "Mexican harvest," which is interpreted to mean that more than half the migrant workers in the fields were Mexicans. San Joaquin Valley growers, in early 1926, ignoring the protests of the Central Labor Council, began large-scale importations of Mexicans. This was some

ten years after the Imperial Valley growers brought in thousands of
Mexicans to relieve the labor situation.

The *Pacific Rural Press*, February 13, 1926, reported that S.
Friselle Parker was sent to lobby Congress "to get us Mexicans and
keep them out of our schools and out of our social problems."

An average of 58,000 Mexicans were brought in annually to work
the fields between 1924 and 1930, according to this growers' publication. McWilliams reports that "in the decade between 1920 and
1930 the Mexicans were unquestionably the largest single element
in the 200,000 agricultural laborers in the State (California.)"

McWilliams sums it up well in saying that "during this decade,
1920 to 1930, the farm industrialists were enchanted with the Mexicans. The Mexicans were available in large numbers (at least
150,000 worked in the fields during these years); they were good
workers; unorganized; and at the end of the season, 'hibernated.'
Time and again, in their deliberations, the growers have emphasized the fact that the Mexican, unlike the Filipino, can be
deported."

In effect, the border was used by the growers and the government agencies over which they exercised great influence, if not
actual control, in much the same manner as a sluice gate on an
irrigation ditch. When there is an ample supply of water, the canal
is shut down. This happened in the case of fieldworkers of Anglo
descent, when there was an ample supply available because of U.S.
joblessness, the border was tightened.

It was also during this period that the growers with multinational
work forces separated the workers into individual camps. Mexicans
were kept separate from the Filipinos and the Filipinos were isolated from the Anglos. The announced reason was that food habits
were different and the workers wanted to live among "their own
kind."

As has been evident throughout the recent history of farm labor
organization, the aim of the growers was other than what they said.
Segregation was, in the first place, a convenient means of exercising
control over sections of the work force through the utilization of
foremen, contractors and favored employees, who often were of the
same nationality as the workers. Secondly, it was a most convenient

way of isolating workers from each other. The racism of the growers utilized nationalism among the workers to prevent the one thing the growers feared most of all—unity that would lead to union organization.

Early Strikes

One early example of the basic reality of such fears took place in Oxnard, California, early in 1903. More than 1,000 Mexican and Japanese workers, toiling in the beet fields where the Chinese had been previously employed, struck for wages and better conditions. They organized the Sugar Beet and Farm Laborers Union of Oxnard and elected Kosaburo Baba president and J. M. Larraras secretary.

Included among strikebreakers were Japanese from San Francisco. In a shooting fracas, a Mexican striker was killed and four others injured. Following the traditional pattern in the farm communities, police arrested all of the union officials.

A representative of the California State Federation of Labor, AFL, was sent to the scene and aided in the defense. Finally, the unionists were released and the strike was won. "This was the first instance of the AFL aiding any Japanese." Karl Yoneda reported in his book, *Japanese Labor History in the U.S.A.* (published in Japanese in 1967).

But these events did not reflect any change of policy by the AFL toward the Chinese or Japanese workers. When Larraras wrote to AFL President Samuel Gompers for a charter, Gompers responded: "Your union must guarantee that it will under no circumstance accept membership of any Chinese or Japanese."

To which Larraras responded with the union's position. Yoneda describes the reply as "a historically beautiful document of solidarity and brotherhood." Larraras said, in part: "I beg to say in reply that our Japanese here were the first to recognize the importance of cooperating and uniting in demanding a fair wage scale. They were not only with us, but they were generous when one of our men was murdered by hired assassins of the oppressors of labor.

"They gave expression of their sympathy in a very substantial form. In the past we have counseled, fought and lived on very short rations with out Japanese brothers, and toiled with them in the fields and they have been uniformly kind and considerate. We would be false to them and to ourselves and to the cause of unionism if we now accepted privileges for ourselves which are not accorded to them. We are going to stand by men who stood by us in the long, hard fight which ended in a victory over the enemy.

"We therefore respectfully petition the AFL to grant us a charter under which we can invite all the sugar beet and field laborers of Oxnard without regard to their color or their race. We will refuse any other kind of a charter except one which will wipe out race prejudice and recognize our fellow workers as being as good as ourselves."

Ignoring the experience and demands of the Oxnard workers, the 1904 AFL convention, after listening to another of Gompers' anti-Japanese tirades, passed a resolution which declared that "Japanese were as difficult to assimilate into the American culture as were the Chinese."

(When the United Mine Workers in 1907 admitted 500 Japanese, Gompers instructed UMWA president John Mitchell to exclude them from membership, saying, "It was unthinkable that Orientals sat in the same lodge room with whites and that the union demands the same wages for yellow men as for the whites.")

Worried by the possible unity of teamsters, longshoremen and farm workers, following a draymen's strike in San Francisco in 1901, growers began talking about the need for a "general law prescribing a closed season for strikers during the gathering and moving of staple crops."

Sixty years later, the growers, using almost the same language as their predecessors, inveighed against the efforts of the United Farm Workers Organizing Committee and called for legislation to il-legalize harvest-time strikes.

Growers continued to combat every move toward unionization, no matter how moderate. The president of a San Jose-based fruit workers union tried to reassure the growers that his was indeed a most conservative organization. He assured the growers that his union's demand was a very simple one, for two dollars a day. In an attempt to assuage the feelings of the growers, he also said, "I am at liberty to state that not a member has ever ventured such a radical suggestion as an eight-hour day for every worker in the fruit indus-try."

These assurances failed to get the union any widespread response from the farm workers, even though there were reports that it had gained some strength in the San Jose area; nor was it looked upon with any favor by the growers.

Nevertheless, rebellions continued in the fields, most of them sporadic strikes for increased wages. Some were successful; most were lost. Japanese workers, because of their own built-in system of organization as a result of living together and having cohesive work crews, were the most successful in applying economic pressure at harvest time and thereby successfully negotiating wage increases. By the beginning of the 20th century, the stage was set for large-scale organized opposition to the growers.

2   The Racist Ingredient

"It will be a few years before the farm workers can start having membership meetings, before we can use their ideas in the union."
Einer Mohn, Director of the Western
Conference of the Teamsters, 1973

The California growers displayed the customary talents of budding profit-hungry capitalists. Opportunistic to an extreme in shifting from one money crop to another, and ruthless in its exploitation of ever replenished human resources, agribusiness also followed another lucrative course, on which it was to remain for more than a century and which it is still pursuing. It was this path of super-exploitation that made possible the riches that filled the coffers of the new breed of capitalists who have remained at the top of the economic pile in California for over a hundred years.

Even as the nation in the post-Civil War era was beginning to evaluate the high cost of racism as reflected in the system of slavery of persons of black skin, the growers were embarking on their own "Southern strategy." This included full use of persons of color as workers in the fields but it did not require that the employers of such labor feed and house these workers while they were not employed in the fields. In this respect the California growers went their southern slaveholder cousins one better.

The racism in the fields was in numerous instances reflected in the actions of white workers, also oppressed by the capitalist system, who were temporarily turned against workers of different skin color. This prejudice was intensified by the desperate competition for jobs, especially during periods of economic stress, and was supported by reactionary union officials, many of whom had been mere echoes for the employers.

Over the years capitalism has constantly sought new pools of workers for the lowest paying, most backbreaking and dirtiest jobs. It was these workers who were destined to be the most exploited of all. In large measure, it was this successful search for new workers that accounted for the giant waves of immigration on both coasts. As each wave of immigrants organized and utilized its acquired skills, these workers moved up the economic ladder and the exploiters of labor sought out replacements.

Where the immigrants were of the same color and of similar religion to that of the exploiters, sooner or later some found their way to middle rungs and a few even to topmost positions on the economic ladder, while American Indian, Chinese, Japanese, Filipino and Mexican and Black workers were generally held down.

As has already been described, some of the Japanese field workers did manage to become owners of some of the relatively smaller ranches, and in later years they, too, as in the Los Angeles County celery strike of the 1930's and the San Joaquin Valley grape strike of the 1960's, bitterly opposed union organization of the workers on their property. But one would be hard put to find a Japanese among the bankers and financial overseers in agribusiness. The ladder of capitalist advancement went only part way for them, after which they ran into the solid racist wall. No matter how much Japanese and other non-Anglo entrepreneurs adopted the ways of their former exploiters, they were never fully accepted as equals by those who dominated agribusiness.

More often than not, the Mexican and Filipino field workers who one way or another escaped from field work ended up as labor contractors rather than as ranch owners. Among the Mexican workers the contractors were referred to as "coyotes"—hated exploiters of those who worked in the fields, at the mercy of the contractors for their economic existence.

While the basic policies for the fields emanate from the aseptic board rooms of banks, which own a large part of the fertile lands on which farm workers labor, their effect is reflected daily in the fields. The grape strike of the 1960's provides ample examples of what has happened over the years to some of the people who had come to the grape fields to work and who in the course of the years found themselves in an entirely different role.

One story had its beginning a long way from the San Joaquin Valley of central California. It started in Yugoslavia, to which the coal barons of the East looked longingly when they were in need of workers for the hazardous coal-mining operation. Young, strong and hopeful persons of Slavic descent came across the Atlantic in response to promises of riches and a glorious new life.

For many of these immigrants it was a complete changed way of life. They had come from farming families and had lived in temperate climates in their native lands that were not unlike that of California. But the recruiters for the mine owners had enticed them to work in the bowels of the earth, far beneath the sun-drenched land.

Like so many other promises made to immigrants, those of the mine owners were spurious, and soon the Slavic workers found themselves involved in bitter struggles in the mining camps of western Pennsylvania and in other coal mining areas. During one of the struggles, a Slavic family deeply loyal to the United Mine Workers union was brutally evicted from the only home it had, a company-owned mining-camp shack. The mine owners retaliated against the militants in the coal fields in the 1930's by driving them from the shacks that were home to them.

Among those who were blacklisted by the owners was a Slavic family that ultimately made its way to the San Joaquin Valley, where it settled and eventually became the owners of a grape ranch. One of the owners of this ranch in September, 1965, at the time of the grape strike, was the son of the former miner, who still vividly recalled how he and his family, including his young son, had been driven from the company town.

When the father, now retired and still retaining his traditional loyalty to the union movement in which he had been a participant, challenged his son's eviction of Filipino and Mexican workers from the camp on their ranch at the time the Delano grape strike began in 1965, the son responded, "This is different—they're Mexicans and Filipinos."

Perhaps more than any other single incident, this seemed to express the essence of the racism which had pervaded the fields and poisoned those who owned the ranches—even those who had emerged from the working class and who themselves had been earlier targets of exploitation.

One no longer sees signs in the farm communities that read "No Dogs or Mexicans Allowed." They were commonplace throughout the Southwest during the youth of Cesar Chavez, president of the AFL-CIO United Farm Workers of America. Neither is it stylish these days to relegate Mexican workers to the theater balconies, as was the case in Delano as late as the early 1960s; or even to segregate burials, as was largely done in that same farming community of about 15,000.

In commenting on the killing of three strikers in Pixley and Arvin during a strike of the Canning and Agricultural Workers Union in the 1930s, Peter Matthiessen in *Sal Si Puedes* writes: "Vigilantism, a kind of unorganized mob rule that has characterized California racism since 1859, was easily turned from the 'yellow peril' to the 'Reds'." In the late thirties, vigilantism was organized by the growers behind a front called the Associated Farmers, which made no secret of its admiration for the fascism in Europe and engaged in open terrorism of strikers." (Peter Matthiessen, *Sal Si Puedes*—New York: Random House, 1970)

There are those who dispute this "unorganized mob rule" characterization, contending that they were carefully planned and executed.

While growers are circumspect about how they talk about the Mexican workers, at least to reporters, once in a while they appear to slip and reveal their true feelings. Such an occasion, it seems, came when Matthiessen interviewed Delano grower Bruno Dispoto in 1965.

"Mr. Cesar Chavez is talking about taking over this state—I don't like that. Too much 'Viva Zapata' and down with the Caucasians, *la raza,* and all that. Mister Cesar Chavez is talking about *revolución.* Remember California once belonged to the Mexicans, and he's saying, 'Look, you dumb Mexicans you lost it, now let's get it back!' "

In the same colloquy Dispoto was asked if he would agree to a face-to-face meeting with Chavez. He replied, "It would be of no use to me to talk with Mister Cesar Chavez! If we talk to a union it's going to be the Teamsters or somebody!"

Even though Dispoto was one of the 29 Delano growers who had to swallow his words and agree to a contract with "Mister" Chavez on June 29, 1970, the echo of his phrases was around for a long time. On January 11, 1973, William F. Spalding, senior partner of top-level big industry law firm of Gibson, Dunn and Crutcher, told a Town Hall forum of businessmen in Los Angeles about his view of collective bargaining with the Farm Workers Union led by Cesar Chavez. It was a most revealing speech, preceding by several months the announcement of the major California growers that they were not renewing their contracts with Chavez's union and were instead negotiating contracts with the Teamsters.

"It is generally recognized that a UFWOC (United Farm Workers Organizing Committee as it was called at that time) is not merely a labor organization. It is basically a union of Mexican American nationals who organized for the purpose of improving the lot of that group. . . . This nationalistic, social aspect of the movement is the thing that most characterizes it."

Spalding, a top labor relations spokesman for West Coast business interests, is a proponent of "a businesslike atomsphere" in labor-management relations. Workers in some industries might well appreciate negotiations such as those between managements and the farm workers union. The "businesslike approach" has gotten many of these union members little more than pitiful increases and intensified speedup.

It was appalling to Spalding that under the contracts signed between 1967 and 1970 by Chavez's union with the growers that "Employment is through hiring halls," and he complained that the union "can't deliver workers as needed. Usually the halls are manned by untrained people and lack good seniority records, telephones and any staff organization."

But more significant was his complaint about the new status of the farm workers. "There is no control of the worker by the field boss and owner. This has resulted in a complete loss of discipline, excessive labor costs, and poor quality of work as evidenced by inferior pack quality vis-vis non UFWOC packs." Ommitted from Spalding's talk that day was any mention of growers' profits during the time of the union contracts—among the highest in the industry's history.

Union representatives, the suave attorney charged, "have no interest in developing a businesslike atmosphere with the employers whose workers they represent." A revealing description of the negotiations, albeit a highly exaggerated one, according to UFWOC representatives, was given by the company lawyer in his talk. Here is how he saw the negotiations from the vantage point of the employers' side of the bargaining table:

"The negotiation of these agreements is in an atmosphere that is conducive to uproar rather than any agreement—no time limits for meetings and a large, unwieldy, Spanish-speaking group often consists of 60 persons. The union insists on round-the-clock sessions unbroken by breaks for meals, rest, or conferences. The process is further complicated by the inability to conduct any off-the-record discussions with the union officials. This makes it extremely difficult to find exactly what the bargaining objectives of UFWOC really are."

While the farm workers union representatives in certain instances no doubt had yet something to learn about the finer points of the bargaining process, which had so long been denied them by reactionary employers, more often than not they were guided by skilled attorneys and negotiators who chartered them through the rough waters of complex labor laws. The newly born union knew what it wanted: fair and equitable agreements, openly arrived at, in full view of the union members. For the farm workers, the initial discussions with the managements were part of the educational process. Over the years, for many who had been in other unions, what had been struggled for on the picketlines had all too often been lost at the bargaining table. The farm workers were not taking any chances this time. They wanted and got a wide-open operation.

Not only was this irritating to the growers; it was incomprehensible. Virtually all other unions in the nation had by then been straight-jacketed by the employers into a form of negotiations that militated against rank-and-file participation. In this they were assisted by countless government regulations. That the farm workers union, which in the 1960's chartered a new historic path in organizing, should seek a different but time-honored approach to collective bargaining—one that would fully involve its membership and expose the growers and their representatives to the thinking of the farm workers and not to just a select small group of union negotiators—was fully understandable to many people but not to the growers.

While farm workers, most of whom were Mexican Americans, daily encountered the blatant prejudice of the growers and their agents, and had come to expect the more sophisticated racist terminology of their high-priced attorneys, they were most appalled by the racist language and actions within the ranks of the labor movement. On this score the Teamsters Union has the longest and most ignominious record.

"I'm not sure how effective a union can be when it is composed of Mexican-Americans and Mexican nationals with temporary visas," said Einer Mohn, Director of the Western Conference of Teamsters, in an interview on February 5, 1973.

"Maybe as agriculture becomes more sophisticated, more mechanized, with fewer transients, fewer green carders [foreign nationals with work permits for employment in the U.S.] and as jobs become more attractive to whites, then we can build a union that can have structure and that can negotiate from strength and have membership participation," the top Teamsters Union official on the West Coast also said in that interview.

When asked about what would happen to workers displaced by mechanization and whether the Teamsters Union had any protective agreement for them, Mohn responded:

"No, that isn't a problem to solve in this way. Shortage of jobs is the problem. If there weren't such a shortage of jobs, Mexican-Americans could get jobs. I don't know what will happen to the Mexican-Americans. After all you can't expect whites to step aside and let Mexican-Americans and Negroes have the [machine] jobs they have had for years."

Mohn insisted later that he had been misquoted in some parts of the interview that he had granted to Jane Yett Kiely, a graduate student at the Theological Union in Berkeley, California. Ironically, she was making a study of "the current labor crisis in the lettuce

fields" for top executives of the Safeway Stores, Inc., with which the
United Farm Workers of America was embroiled in a bitter battle
over the sale of non-UFW produce. She had been referred to Safeway management through the Montgomery Street's Center program (San Francisco) for theology students' internships in business.

In commenting on Mohn's statement that "it will be a couple of
years before they (farm workers) can start having membership meetings, before we can use farm workers' ideas in the union," Ms. Kiely
said that "worker voice in the union would demand protection
against job loss for the current, predominantly Spanish-speaking
work force."

Shortly after Mohn's views were made public, Henry Winston,
chairman of the Communist Party, U.S.A., was in Los Angeles to
address a public meeting, and while in that city he was invited to
appear on a talk show on television station KHJ. He had not been
previously informed that his protagonist (by phone) would be a labor
official, Sigmund Arywitz, secretary-treasurer of the Los Angeles
County Federation of Labor, AFL-CIO.

When Winston denounced Mohn's comments as "racist," it was
Arywitz who came to the Teamster official's defense. He said that he
was a long-time friend of "the respected Teamster's leader on the
West Coast" and to his personal knowledge Mohn was not a "racist."
The touch of irony in this instance was that the UFW, an AFL-CIO
affiliate, was embroiled in a bitter dispute with the unaffiliated
Teamsters at a time when Arywitz was "called upon" to come pub-
licly to Mohn's defense.

The open record of racist comments by Teamsters Union representatives goes back a long way. For example, one teamster who
was part of a convoy of five carloads of Teamsters Union members
escorting two truckloads of cement workers through the picket lines
of CIO Cement Workers Union, Local 536, in Concord, California,
in 1937 exposed the official racism of the Teamsters in that dispute.

In testimony before the grand jury this Teamsters Union member
told of the guns, baseball bats and iron clubs used to beat the CIO
members. He was paid $6.00 a day, he said, plus bonuses paid to
him and other Teamsters for each person beaten. The rates were
quite revealing. For each CIO organizer beaten the bonus was
$25.00, for news photographers, $50.00, and for slugging the
Japanese CIO organizer the rate was $75.00.

Five years later, April 1942, the National Labor Relations Board ordered the Cowell Cement Company to reinstate the 171 CIO union members who had been locked out in July 1937 with back pay and full reinstatement of their seniority. The company union which had been established by the Teamsters was ordered dissolved.

Over the years, Teamsters Union officials have broken many strikes, especially in farm labor where Spanish-speaking workers have sought to build unions of their own choice. These were part of the perennial power plays that pockmark the history of this union, especially on the West Coast.

In the October 27, 1937, Washington State *Labor Herald* it was reported that the then Western Teamsters Conference Director Dave "Beck showed quite clearly his 'war' is directed against workers by promising the banker-industrialist Associated Farmers he will make no attempt to organize the viciously exploited farm drivers." This reportedly took place at a meeting of the Western Conference in Los Angeles.

Developments in the canneries probably afford a good example of Teamsters Union leaders' exploits at the expense of the workers. There was an upsurge in organizing in 1936, and cannery workers were no exception to the rule. In preparation for the forthcoming and inevitable drive, the employers in December 1936 organized the California Processors and Growers, aimed at coping with the expected problems with organizing workers.

J. Paul St. Sure, top man in the new industry organization, said, "We had very definite ideas about the kind and shape of union we'd like to deal through." He soon made it clear that the "shape of the union" he favored was the Teamsters.

In the first three months of 1937, cannery workers were being organized by 15 AFL locals, and by April six strikes were in progress. Meanwhile, the Stockton (California) Central Labor Council authorized Agricultural Workers Union No. 20221 to organize the canneries in that city.

Also in April, 1937, Colonel Walter Garrison led a shotgun assault of Associated Farmer "minute men" in what became known as "the Battle of Waterloo Road." It was that attack which broke the back of that cannery strike.

A labor reporter for the *San Francisco Chronicle* saw some possi-

ble conspiratorial arrangement between the cannery owners and the
Teamsters in the fact that Teamsters Local President Vincent
Dunne and Paul St. Sure were close personal friends as well as
fraternity brothers. In addition, it might be noted that Gene Ben-
nett was one of the attorneys who represented the canners. In later
years he became a member of the law firm of Pillsbury, Madison
and Sutro, for many years representatives of Safeway Stores, which
has had a vested interest in the progress of union organization of the
fields and canneries.

In spite of the fact that the California Federation of Labor, reportedly in conjunction with the Teamsters Union official (Charlie Real)
and canners, had revoked the charters in the cannery drive of all
locals except that of the newly established Stockton local, the strike
against three canneries in April 1937 was effective mainly because of
support from the warehousemen in the AFL International
Longshoremen's Association.

Charlie Real, under instructions from Teamsters Union President
Dan Tobin, ordered the members of Local 70 to go through the
picket lines established by the cannery workers. By a 175-to-35 vote
the rank-and-file Teamsters voted to respect those picket lines. The
president of Local 70, Clifford Lester, said, "Nobody has the right
to order men to become strikebreakers. We don't want any part of
the fight between the Teamsters International and the ILA."

Tobin and his West Coast director Dave Beck then removed all
incumbent officers of the local with the exception of Real, and appointed Joe Casey to administer the affairs of Local 70. The ousted
officers responded with a rally of their own outside the union building from which they were barred, and voted confidence in their
elected officers. It was reported that between 500 and 700 Teamsters Union members attended that Local 70 meeting.

By early May, Beck came up with a "package deal," including
wage increases for Local 70 members. The membership bought it,
and this cleared the way for breaking strikes at California Packing
Company, California Conserving Company and Hunt Brothers
Company. The Teamsters deliveries broke the back of those picket
lines.

It was small wonder that the Teamsters Union was not the favorite labor organization among cannery workers. When the AFL in 1945 granted the Teamsters Union full jurisdiction in the canneries, the workers resisted to the point of striking. The protesting workers called on the Sailors Union of the Pacific (SUP) to come into the picture, but the SUP was told by the AFL that the jurisdiction in the canneries belonged solely to the Teamsters. Many of them appeared before the National Labor Relations Board (NLRB) to oppose the Teamsters.

The CIO Food, Tobacco and Agricultural Workers of America (FTA) in August, 1945, began its campaign in the canneries and signed up enough workers to be able to obtain a representation election.

From all indications, the Teamsters Union officials did not enter into this controversy with any reluctance. Nevertheless, the FTA *News* in a contemporary report said that, "While the Teamsters are not anxious to take on this extra load (representing cannery workers) which the AFL has willed to them, the Teamsters have not hesitated to send their goons in to prevent the workers from joining the FTA." The October 10, 1945 representation election showed 6,067 workers voting for the FTA and 4,701 for the Teamsters. Only 90 workers cast their ballot for "no union."

In February 1946 the NLRB nullified the election, and FTA President Donald Henderson accused the Teamsters of "political pressure exerted upon the NLRB to modify a decision consistent with the Wagner Act." In May of that year, some of the Teamsters beat up FTA representative Jack Montgomery, who said, "It's no surprise that Teamsters have to use strong-arm stuff—they have no base among rank-and-file cannery workers. Fear is all they have to fall back on."

Despite an NLRB order that no contract be negotiated before a new election was ordered and that no union be favored over the other, the canners on March 25 signed contracts with the Teamsters Union and placed full page ads in many California papers that day announcing their deed. FTA organizers were barred from the plants and Teamsters Union representatives were welcomed. It was estimated that about 500 FTA supporters were blacklisted.

Such was the atmosphere in August 1946 when the second election took place and the Teamsters won. And Paul St. Sure, chief cannery negotiator, brazenly declared that "We supported the Teamster position."

The decades-long policy of discrimination persists. Even as late as 1973 it was shown in a lawsuit brought by 14 Teamsters Union members from cannery locals in Modesto, California. Teamsters Local 748 and seven cannery managements were charged in a Federal Court suit with practicing racism and sexism in employment. On the job and in promotions the companies were accused of favoring Anglo males over other workers. Among those who brought the action were former Teamster officials, Frank Corrola, Cerfino Anchondo and Dionicio Acuna, who were trying to win back their jobs as Teamsters Union organizers. They claimed that they were fired from their union positions because they had filed a large number of complaints by workers charging discrimination with the Federal Equal Employment Opportunities Commission.

Carolla's wife Leonora stated that she had been fired from her job as an office worker in the local because she spoke with workers in Spanish, in violation of an order by Teamsters Union director of Agricultural Workers Organizing Committee, William Grami, who forbade discussions in any language other than English.

Early in 1971, workers of Mexican descent filed six complaints with the federal agency in the first six months of the year. No women filed complaints during the same time span. In the second half of that year, largely as a result of Chicano union officials making known to the workers that they might have legal redress against discriminatory practices, 106 men of Mexican descent filed grievances with the federal government agency and 138 women did likewise. After the local officials were removed from office, the complaints fell off drastically.

Also in December 1973 seven UFWA farm workers in Coachella Valley, according to *El Malcriado*, the union newspaper, filed "a massive $100-million lawsuit claiming racism and union-busting tactics by the International Brotherhood of Teamsters and 44 Coachella Valley grape growers." Among the charges made by the UFWA farm workers was "that Teamsters discriminate against them because they are Mexicans and Filipinos," according to the same union newspaper report.

Einer Mohn, the Western Conference of Teamsters Director at the time the lawsuit by Coachella workers was filed, has a long record of union-busting in the fields, according to Ernesto Galarza, director of the National Farm Labor Union (AFL) organizing campaign in the fields in the early 1950's. In an interview in April 1973, he related Mohn's role in smashing the strike of 1,200 tomato pickers in Stanislaus and San Joaquin Counties during the 1952 strike. He said: "In 1952 we struck the tomato fields in Stanislaus and San Joaquin Counties. It was a very effective strike. I was in that strike from beginning to end and at first the Teamsters respected our picket lines, creating a major crisis for the growers.

"One day, midway through the strike, we had a visitor (Mohn) from San Francisco. He made his presence known to us. After a day or two he went to the gates of the Heinz plant where trucks were backed up for perhaps half a mile. They refused to cross our picket line. Mohn, without any word to us, waved the trucks through the picket line. We knew then that the strike was over."

Prior to Mohn's strike-breaking visit, Chicano Teamsters local officials from Stockton displayed considerable sympathy towards the walkout of the farm workers. On occasion some of them even addressed meetings of the striking farm-workers union. Following Mohn's visit all cooperation from local Teamsters officials and rank and filers, including Chicanos, came to an end.

Probably no racist attack by Teamsters Union officials matched in severity and scope that of the Coachella Valley in the spring of 1973. One of those assisting Chavez's United Farm Workers of America was Francisco (Pancho) Medrano, a member of the national staff of the United Auto Workers. In a interview in May, 1973, he said that "on Thursday May 10, 1973, at approximately 1 p.m. I was present in the park at Vine and Fifth in Coachella across the street from the UFWU office at 722 Vine. At least three cars full of Teamsters and two pickup trucks full of Teamster goons arrived and circled the park and then made two U-turns in the middle of the street. . . .

"The car stopped right in front of the UFWU office. Some of the thugs had a Mexican flag that they were playing with, sort of pretending to be cleaning their truck with the flag as a rag. There were a group of students from Mexico City who were present and became very upset at this show of disrespect for their country, and they

tried to have the flag returned. The thugs were shouting and generally acting very rowdy. The language they used was not the kind of
language that civilized people use in normal everyday conversation.

"After the thugs played with the flag and saw how upset the
Mexican students became, they began to hit them. Then all confusion began. More goons appeared, more foul language was used,
and at least three or four students were hit. Even worse, the thugs
were carrying guns. All told, I know I saw at least three (guns)
myself."

Probably the best overview of the rampant racism among Teamsters officials was provided by Mauricio Terrazas, a Los Angeles
rank-and-file member of the Teamsters Union for almost a quarter
of a century, who was so incensed by 1973 developments, especially
the attack in Coachella on Chavez's union, that he joined in a legal
action to enjoin his own union from expending union funds on
further attacks against the AFL-CIO United Farm Workers of
America.

Terrazas was a long-time supporter of the drive to organize the
field workers. During the early years of the Delano strike, he
helped rally union as well as community support for the striking
farm workers. On June 11, 1973 he said that "Teamsters support
came from the local level. Many rank and file members were anxious to support working people in the field. It has always been clear
to me, and I'm sure to my fellow union members, that my wage and
benefit level is the result of working in an industry that has been
unionized for some time. Farm workers, on the other hand, lag way
behind in wage levels and job protection because unions have con-
tinually been destroyed by powerful grower opposition."

He recounted with pride how he helped get (Los Angeles) Teamsters Joint Council 42 to help finance the renting of a bus for use in
the historic Easter march in 1966 from Delano to Sacramento.
"However," he said, "at the point the Western Conference of
Teamsters intervened in the dispute between the Farm Workers
Union and the DiGiorgio Corporation, the Joint Council was forced
to back out of the agreement. This was one of a number of examples
where high union officials within the Teamsters organization had
determined for reasons that are never explained to the Teamster
membership, to undercut and destroy the United Farm Workers
Union."

Also Terrazas said that "the racist statement by Einar Mohn (previously cited in the Kiely interview) gives a clue to the racist nature
of his leadership. It is not the first time that I have heard that Mohn
is a racist and would prefer little or no influence of Mexicans within
the Teamster organization. I know what it is like to be discriminated
against because of my race. For 15 years I was the only Chicano
driver for Safeway Markets. I was a member of Local 626 at the
time. On one occasion it required my filing and winning a grievance
against Safeway before I was allowed to have equal standing with
Anglo drivers."

Terrazas then added that "For Mohn to say he wants a union with
less Chicano influence and that the Chicano field workers who the
Teamsters are forcing into locals will not be allowed full participation for at least two years, does a great deal of harm throughout the
Teamsters Union. Chicanos have always been prevented from being
a part of the Teamster leadership. Racist remarks like those of
Mohn's definitely stimulates division among racial groupings within
locals all over the country. It weakens, at the same time, our ability
to negotiate contracts with fair employment clauses in them."

He also charged that the Teamsters' drive against the AFL-CIO
Farm Workers Union "serves to inflame the public against Mexicans" and that it pictures the UFWA as a "Mexican Union that is
violent, dishonest, subversive and incompetent. These are racial
stereotypes that have been used for years to discredit Chicanos."
(Statements of Mauricio Terrazas were made in his deposition as
part of a suit which he and a fellow teamster, James Dycus, brought
against his union's leadership. It was filed on June 11, 1973 in the
Superior Court of the State of California for Los Angeles County.)

The concern over the racist policies in the fields, which were still
very much part of the national scene in 1973, aroused clergymen as
well as trade unionists in and out of the Teamsters' Union. On June
30, 1973, the 300 delegates to the California and Western Conference of Black Elected Officials, meeting in Los Angeles, expressed
alarm over the "unmerciful assaults by hired members of the Teamsters in the vineyards of Arvin (Kern County) and Coachella Valley
of California."

While hailing the UFWA as "one of the few movements in this
country to carry on the non-violent ideals of the late Dr. Martin
Luther King, Jr., the Black elected officials called for "impartially

supervised free and secret ballot elections in the vineyards." In addition, the Black legislators demanded "those responsible for these reprehensible crimes [in the fields] upon a movement of people be brought to justice."

3 First Major Radical Challenge

"It's for the kids we're doing this."
Richard Ford, Wobbly organizer, 1913

There was a new dimension to the resistance in the fields early in the 20th century. The sporadic battles, mainly limited to one or another ethnic group in an earlier era, were no longer the pattern of workers' strikes in the fields.

The farm workers, assisted by radical organizers who believed in the unity of all workers in a single labor organization regardless of craft or ethnic origin, came up with their own solution to the problems of those working the fields. This was their response to the long-time divide-and-conquer policy of the landowners, who had repeatedly and successively claimed that the Chinese, Japanese, Filipino and Mexican field hands had each provided them with the "perfect solution" for cheap and available field workers. This hitherto successful time-tested formula was about to undergo a new stress and strain.

The first widespread union movement among agricultural laborers that succeeded in attracting national attention to the plight of the field workers was led by members and supporters of the International Workers of the World (IWW), commonly known as Wobblies. It was organized in 1905 because the existing labor movement, craft-dominated in structure and conservative in leadership, failed to meet the needs of the most oppressed workers. The Wobblies set out to build "one big union" which would encompass all those who worked for wages.

In top AFL circles they were called "trade-union smashers and rammers from without" and were accused of trying "to divert, pervert and disrupt the whole labor movement." Philip Foner gives a different perspective on the organization of the IWW. "Among the factors influencing its appearance was the existence of great masses of disfranchised immigrants and floating workers, the widespread corruption of American politics that turned workers away from it, the reactionary policies of the AFL which disgusted progressive unionists, and the growing conviction among left-wing Socialists that neither reform legislation nor votes for socialism seemed to make much headway in gaining immediate benefits for the workers or bringing closer the day when the Socialist Republic would be established." (Philip S. Foner, *History of the Labor Movement in the United States*, Vol. 4—New York: International Publishers, 1965)

For the Wobblies the instrumentality was "one big union"; the major tactic, the general strike; and the ultimate goal, the downfall of capitalism.

While the utopian view of the IWW was simplistic, especially in retrospect, its organization of industrial unions and the attraction it held for such militant unions as the Western Federation of Miners were enough to arouse the hatred of entrenched AFL leaders like President Samuel Gompers. On May 13, 1905, he wrote that, "There is no better work which our special organizers can do right now than counteract the effect of this proposed industrial movement."

The most prominent person of Mexican descent participating in the 1905 founding convention of the Wobblies in Chicago was Lucy Gonzales Parsons, wife of the famous Haymarket martyr Albert R. Parsons. In Foner's account of that convention, it was noted that she joined with those who saw participation in the voting political process as alien to the revolutionary aims of the new organization.

The Wobbly convention was taking place simultaneously with the general strike of the Russian workers, and it was Lucy Gonzales Parsons who gave eloquent voice to the need for international solidarity with the embattled Russian workers, then on the verge of their first (1905) revolution. She told the delegates: "You men and women should be imbued with the spirit that is now displayed in far-off Russia and far-off Siberia where we thought the spark of manhood had been crushed out of them. Let us take example from them."

In response to her appeal and that of "Big Bill" Haywood, the delegates hailed the "mighty struggle of the laboring class of far-off Russia against unbearable outrage, oppression and cruelty and for more humane condition for the working people of that country" and also voted to "pledge our moral support and promise financial assistance as much as lies within our power to our persecuted, struggling and suffering comrades in far-off Russia."

It is a somewhat ironic footnote of history, especially for those who look upon international May Day observances as a latter-day communist invention, that the first IWW convention voted that the first day in May of each year should be "designated as the Labor Day of this organization." (May Day originated in the United States. It had its origin in the battle for an eight-hour work day in 1886. In 1888, The American Federation of Labor voted to rejuvenate the movement for the 8-hour day and designated May First, 1890 as the day to witness a nation-wide strike for the shorter workday. In July 1889, the Second International meeting in Paris, inspired by the example of the workers in the United States, voted to make May First a day for international demonstrations.)

But for the farm workers, especially those of Mexican descent, the convention action covering IWW membership, spelled out by "Big Bill" Haywood at a meeting ratifying the convention's work, emphasized what was probably its most meaningful decision. He declared it "did not make a bit of difference whether he is a Negro or a white man. It does not make any difference whether he is American or foreigner."

Adopting the slogan that "An injury to one is the concern of all," the Wobblies declared that membership was open to all, regardless of race, creed, color or sex and that any immigrant with a valid union card was eligible for membership. This was in marked contrast to many of the existing AFL unions which discriminated against Black workers and immigrants.

Many years later—in 1918—a Chicago journalist, Carleton H. Parker, perceptively wrote that "The IWW's deepest strength lies in the fact that it extends the red hand of fellowship to the lowliest of workers, that it has made itself the special champion of those who are paid the least and work the hardest."

Unlike so many other organizations, the Wobblies practised what they preached, and preach they did. When called upon by the local civic leaders in Redding, California, to assist in ousting the Chinese workers from that community, the IWW responded, "If you want to raise the wages of the Chinese, we'll help, but we won't kick anybody off their job because of color."

Also in 1910 the Porters Union in Spokane, Washington, sought IWW cooperation "to eradicate the brown men from competition." The IWW publicity castigated that union in its publication, *Industrial Worker*. The porters' organization was told that if it "were but half as class conscious as the average Japanese worker, there would be better conditions for the porters than the wretched ones they are now forced to submit to." Then, for further emphasis, it was declared that "It must be understood that the IWW will turn down any effort to discriminate against our Japanese fellow workers."

The Wobblies, in addition to bluntly rejecting racist philosophy and practises by employers and old-line labor organizations, also took on the Socialists on the West Coast, accusing them of swallowing the "capitalist bait." On September 10, 1910, the *Industrial Worker* said, "All workers can be organized regardless of race or color, as soon as their minds are cleared of the patriotic notion that there is any reason of being proud of having been born of a certain shade of skin or in an arbitrarily fenced off portion of the earth."

The IWW categorically rejected the "yellow peril" concept which was then being echoed by some Socialist candidates for office on the western seaboard, reflecting the accepted racist view that the Japanese and Chinese workers were inferior to whites and that they would lower the standard of living for all. It was paradoxical, the Wobblies noted, that the Socialists wore buttons showing clasped hands and inscribed with Karl Marx's historic slogan from the Communist Manifesto, "Workers of the World, Unite!"

These Socialists were reminded by the Wobblies that when Marx wrote his slogan he certainly did not mean "all workers, except the Chinese and Japanese. He included the Negroes, the Hindus, and the Asiatics in the revolutionary call."

In its publication, the IWW pointedly made reference to the Japanese, Chinese and Filipinos, who were members of many of its local organizations. The recognition that the Wobblies also practised what they preached in regard to the Black workers came in a tribute to that organization from a most unusual source. Mary White Ovington, a wealthy white New Yorker, was one of the founders of the National Association for the Advancement of Colored People (NAACP). In 1913 she wrote in an article on "The Status of the Negro in the United States" that one of the two organizations that cared about the fate of the Negroes in the United States was the IWW. She said that the "IWW has stood with the Negro." The other organization that merited her praise was the NAACP.

Increasingly respected by farm workers, up and down the West Coast, because of its principled stand in behalf of the workers who were so blatantly discriminated against by industry, labor organizations and even Socialists, the IWW was also winning admiration because it embarked on a large number of free-speech fights that rocked much of the nation. These free-speech battles were particularly effective on the West Coast and made a very significant impact on the laborers in the fields.

About sixty years after the Socialists and the Wobblies participated in a successful free speech fight in Seattle, the farm workers in Delano, California, successfully challenged restrictions on their rights to free speech in the fields. And just as the Wobblies filled the jails of city after city in their determined battle for the right to speak up, the farm workers—in 1973, members and supporters of the United Farm Workers Union—filled jail after jail throughout California in violation of employers' injunctions, many of which made picketing of the fields virtually impossible.

The right to speak on street corners may not seem too important to generations reared in the age of the electronic media, but in the early 1900's it was the very lifeblood of any movement seeking to communicate with the workers. Foner explains that, "By passing ordinances suppressing the IWW's right of free speech on the streets, the city officials, acting for lumber, agricultural, mining

interests, and other employers, were convinced that they could
crush the organizing drives and destroy the movement."

Further he relates: "The issue for the IWW was clear: The right
to speak meant the right to organize, and the Wobblies rallied their
strength across the continent to break down the attempt to stifle this
right, convinced that in their battles to smash gag laws, they were
upholding the constitutional rights of all people."

The knee-jerk reaction of city administrations in farm communities to labor organizers has been similar over the decades. For
instance, as late as 1965, the Delano City Council, after first ignoring the development of the strike movement around its city in the
quaint hope that it might just go away, passed a law barring parades
without permits on its city streets. But on that occasion, when
United Auto Workers Union President Walter Reuther, followed by
a galaxy of farm workers, newsmen and others, blithely violated this
law, the local police acted as traffic guardians for the so-called law-
breakers instead of as jailers.

It was the Missoula, Montana, battle for free speech in the summer of 1909 that set the pattern for a long series of similar IWW
battles and helped create the atmosphere for some of the fiercest
union challenges to the owners in agriculture. It was in this industrial town, gateway to lumber camps and mining towns and
thoroughfare for migratory workers, that Elizabeth Gurley Flynn
and her husband Jack Jones came to organize the migrant workers.
In that battle for free speech, during which Flynn through her fiery
street-corner speeches exposed the role of the employment agencies and brought many a migrant worker into the Wobblies, she was
arrested and Jack Jones was arrested and beaten in jail. (Elizabeth
Gurley Flynn, the famous Rebel Girl, later joined the Communist
Party of the United States. Elected National Chairperson in 1961,
she served at this post until her death in 1964. ed.)

Displaying the intuitive ingenuity that seems to be part of every
major labor struggle, the Wobblies timed their meetings for just
before supper time so that when they were arrested they had to be
fed in jail. When the police tried to release those jailed before
breakfast, the Wobblies refused and, according to Elizabeth Gurley
Flynn, "They had been arrested. They demanded a trial, and individual trials and jury trials at that."

Backed by Butte Miners No 1, the largest local union in Montana, Senator Robert M. La Follette and university professors, the battle of the Wobblies for free speech grew. Townspeople were disturbed by the notoriety of their town and were also disturbed by the mounting costs of feeding those jailed. One of those who carefully observed the free speech fight was the AFL organizer in Missoula, C. O. Young, who forbade the local AFL to support the IWW. When it was over, he made his report to AFL Secretary-Treasurer Frank Morrison. He said: "The 'won't works' have tried the game here of filling the jails so full that the officials of the city would have to capitulate, and they have succeeded in forcing the local authorities to quit. Encouraged by their success at Missoula, they are publishing broadcast that they will do the same to any other city that denies them the privilege of using the streets for speaking."

Spokane, then the largest western center for migratory labor, in 1909 was in the process of building the largest IWW local in the nation. On November 16, 1909, the pregnant 19-year-old Elizabeth Gurley Flynn also came to Spokane, where she was forbidden by the Wobbly leaders to speak on street corners, but she did address a meeting in the Municipal Courtroom, in which she lambasted the newspapers, police, judges and others and then took up a collection of $25.

Despite the fact that she did not speak on street corners, she was among the Wobbly leaders arrested in Spokane, and the IWW started flooding many cities with leaflets relating the story of the jailing of the "Joan of Arc of the IWW." On March 5, 1910, the city authorities in Spokane surrendered, and the June 28, 1910, edition of the *Spokane Inland-Herald* reported, "For the first time in two years police-sanctioned street meetings occurred Saturday night. The free speech advocates could be heard for blocks, while nearly 1,500 gathered to listen to contesting orators."

Among those who had been jailed in the course of this struggle was William Z. Foster, who had come to Spokane to report on the battle for *The Workingman's Paper* (formerly *The Socialist*). Foster was picked out of the crowd, arrested and served 60 days in jail. (William Z. Foster, was later one of the great labor organizers in U.S. history and a world Communist leader. Foster was Chairman of the Communist Party of the United States for many years and later was Chairman Emeritus to the time of his death in 1961.)

The success of IWW Local 66 in Fresno set the stage for the next free speech fight, the one which probably had the biggest impact on subsequent developments in the fields. Mexican laborers, brought into Fresno to build a dam outside the city, were organized by the Wobblies; and Local 66 leadership also led a strike of workers in the Santa Fe electric power plant. Alarmed by the success of the Wobblies, employers pressured the police to forbid IWW street meetings.

In the course of the free speech fight in Fresno, a mob of over 1,000 vigilantes, on December 9, 1910, burned to the ground the tent headquarters of the Wobblies (they were unable to rent any hall in the city), beat up many of its speakers and marched on the county jail, where they threatened to break in and lynch the imprisoned Wobblies. A hunger strike inside the jail was the response of the prisoners, who had been put on bread and water after protesting the police manhandling of a drunken prisoner. The prisoners went on a fast and were hosed down by the police, precisely as was done a half-century later, in the summer of 1973, when members of the United Farm Workers Union fasted inside the Fresno jail to protest mistreatment and overcrowding of prisoners.

The six-month struggle for the right of free speech in Fresno set back the Wobblies less than $1,000. On March 2, 1911, Fresno officials, following a meeting of city officials and Wobblies in prison, rescinded their ban against street meetings, and three days later all prisoners were released. They announced that "solidarity won in Fresno." A month later, Local 66 of the IWW had moved into a new hall and wrote to the union's newspaper, "We are holding street meetings twice a week, which are well attended."

Thereafter, the mere threat of the Fresno formula brought about free-speech victories for the Wobblies in San Jose and Marysville in California as well as in Tacoma, Washington.

E Street between Fourth and Fifth in San Diego was traditionally set aside for street meetings. Single taxers, socialists, Salvation Army preachers and evangelists were among those who vied for audiences that at times numbered in the thousands. While customarily there was no interference with the Wobblies, when IWW Local 13 organized Mexican workers at the San Diego Consolidated Gas and Electric Co. and provided the leadership for a successful strike for higher wages and shorter hours, there was some reaction.

Attempting to capitalize on its victory, Local 13 began holding nightly meetings with speakers in English and Spanish. When the Wobblies tried to hold a memorial meeting for the Haymarket martyrs, the police closed up the rented hall and the Wobblies transferred the memorial meeting to the free-speech area. There the speakers were jailed, fingerprinted, photographed and then released. After a short period of harassment, the Wobblies were able to continue their meetings, and in May, 1911, street meetings were being held three times a week.

In early 1912 the City Council upon recommendation of the Grand Jury ordered the traditional free-speech area closed down. The IWW, AFL unions, the Socialist Party and church organizations established the California Free Speech League, and on February 8, the first day the new ordinance went into effect, 38 men and three women were arrested for violating it.

Violators of the new ordinance were beaten, crowded into cells which were jammed with two-and-one-half times their normal capacity and given meager food twice daily. So brutal was the police mistreatment that a protest march on February 26 was organized by the Free Speech League in conjunction with the AFL Central Labor Council. The five-abreast marchers stretched for two miles, and on March 10, 5,000 persons who had come to the county jail to protest the brutality were themselves given a taste of the abuses they were protesting. The police sprayed the crowd that had come to the IWW-sponsored protest rally with a three-inch spray of water.

Labor protests against the brutality in San Diego spread through labor circles in many parts of California. Joe Hill (Hillstrom), IWW songwriter who was later framed and shot in Salt Lake City, was among those who addressed a Los Angeles rally sponsored by the central labor body of the AFL to protest the San Diego terror. Among the central labor bodies that protested the police attacks was the San Francisco AFL, the most powerful in the state. The San Francisco labor body sent a committee to San Diego to investigate the charges levelled by the free-speech advocates and, while critical of some of the Wobbly policies and tactics, the investigating committee reported that "their acts are part of the workers' struggle for better conditions and brighter lives."

The committee reported that, "Outside the jail not a single act of violence or even of wantonness has been committed! Not a blow has been struck; not a weapon used; not a threat of any kind made by an IWW or other sympathizer with the free speech movement. Such patience with the most infamous and galling inhumanity and injustice speaks well for the discipline by the leaders of such men."

By the summer of 1914, despite the still existing ordinance against free speech, Wobblies were holding meetings in the circumscribed area. There was general admiration for the Wobblies throughout the ranks of the working people, and the official journal of the San Francisco building trades unions reported that "the fight in San Diego has made the IWW famous."

It was largely as a result of these battles, as well as others for free speech in San Francisco, Oakland and in other locations, that the Wobblies became known and were admired throughout the state, especially among migrant workers. Locals had been established in Fresno, Bakersfield, Los Angeles, San Diego, San Francisco and Sacramento.

These were the jumping-off points for the ever travelling Wobblies. While their numbers in 1913 in California were reportedly relatively small—about 5,000 paid members, accounting for less than ten per cent of the migrant labor force—their impact was great. Many of their farm strikes were successful, and the colorful, highly class-conscious Wobbly songs could be heard in many fields and camps.

At the Durst Brothers hop ranch in Wheatland, California, in 1913, the prevailing conditions were typical. For decades, California farm workers had worked under similiar conditions. But the difference in the summer of 1913 was that the Wobblies, dedicated organizers and spokesmen for the poor, came on the scene.

Following the usual grower practice, Durst advertised widely throughout California, southern Oregon and Nevada for pickers. He needed about 1,500 workers but advertised for at least 3,000.

During the opening days of August, 1913, 2,800 workers were camped on a hill near the ranch. Of those, 1,500 were women and children. More than half were aliens. Seven interpreters had to be used and there were 27 nationalities in a single work crew of 235.

Those who could afford it lived in tents—rented from Durst at 75 cents a day. Many slept in the open fields. There was a water shortage, and only nine outdoor toilets for the 2,800. Jim Durst, a cousin of the owner, had the lemonade concession and charged five cents a glass. Workers rarely earned $1.50 for working a 12-hour day. Work for all, including hundreds of children, began at 4 a.m., and by noon the temperature had risen above 100 degrees.

Working and living conditions at the Durst Ranch were not accidental, as was revealed by a later California State commission of inquiry. The widespread advertising was deliberate and aimed at forcing wages down. The filthy living conditions were likewise planned—to encourage workers to leave before the season was over, thereby forfeiting the 10 per cent of their wages which Durst held out. Wages averaged between 78 cents and a dollar a day, depending on the available labor supply.

Included among the 2,800 in the Durst camp, were about 100 card-carrying Wobblies, among whom were veterans of the previous battles in Spokane, San Diego and Fresno.

About 30 of these Wobblies organized a local and began urging the hop-pickers to take action. At a Saturday night August 2 mass meeting the workers set up a committee to present ten demands to the Durst Brothers. Ralph Durst promised, in vague terms, to improve camp conditions but refused to budge on the wage demand for $1.25 per hundred of hops picked. Instead of granting the demands, Durst fired the leaders of the committee. When the employer was warned that there would be a strike unless he agreeed to the wage demand and improved conditions, Durst struck Ford, the committee spokesman, with a heavy glove and called in the local constable, who, gun in hand, ordered Ford off the ranch.

At the mass meeting on August 3, Richard (Blackie) Ford, an experienced Wobbly organizer, addressed a meeting of 2,000 workers and, lifting a sick child from its mother's arms and holding it aloft, shouted, "It's for the kids we're doing this." More than 50 years later in Delano I heard farm union organizers address rallies and use almost the same words in describing the long-range nature of their battle.

The protest rally had already concluded when the sheriff and some of his deputies moved in to arrest Ford. They were accompanied by the district attorney, who was also Durst's lawyer. A deputy fired a shot and a melee ensued in which the district attorney, a deputy sheriff and two workers were killed. Four National Guard companies were immediately dispatched by the governor. They surrounded the ranch and arrested more than 100 workers. The Burns Detective Agency was also called in and 100 of its operatives were deputized.

"There followed one of the most amazing reigns of terror that California has ever witnessed," McWilliams said in describing the aftermath of August 3. Eight months after the Wheatland attack, Ford and Herman Suhr, who was not even present when the riot took place, were convicted of murder and sentenced to life imprisonment. Their conviction was sustained on appeal.

Wheatland has been described "a spontaneous revolt" of migrant labor. Carey McWilliams also said "It stands out as one of the significant episodes in the long and turgid history of migratory labor in California."

So great was the impact on organized labor in California of the Wheatland strike that when the IWW again struck the Durst ranch the following year the walkout was endorsed by the AFL councils in Sacramento, Fresno and San Diego. And Japanese workers, who were among those who struck, left the strike zone so as not to endanger support from the traditionally anti-Oriental AFL; they put ads in the Japanese-language newspapers calling on their countrymen to stay away from the Durst ranch until Ford and Suhr were released and the strike demands granted. Yoneda has described this action as "a meaningful gesture of working class solidarity and should be remembered by all of us." (Karl Yoneda, *Japanese Labor History in the U.S.A.*, published in Japanese, 1967)

Although the Wobblies did not accomplish their immediate goal to win the release of Ford and Suhr, they did succeed in mounting a strong movement in their behalf. Ford was not paroled from Folsom prison until September 11, 1925 and Suhr on October 26, 1926.

The jailing of Ford and Suhr was costly to the growers in actual money terms as well as in the resentment of many fair-minded persons who were convinced that the Wobbly leaders were framed. By 1917 the Wobblies estimated that the conviction of their two leaders had cost the growers $10 million annually. At the same time, the growers, while not agreeing with the Wobbly estimate, admit-

ted that the convictions had cost them between $15 and $20 millions. The Wobblies did not cease their agitation for the freedom of
the two imprisoned leaders until they walked out of the prison
gates.

Although the impact of the Wobblies on agricultural labor lasted a
relatively brief time, it was nevertheless very significant. President
Woodrow Wilson's Federal Commission on Western Labor found
that in March, 1914, the IWW had 40 California locals with five
full-time paid organizers and hundreds of part-time organizers. In
the view of Dr. Carleton Parker of the University of California, a
member of a special committee of the California Commission on
Immigration and Housing, which had probed the Durst strike and
its aftermath, the Wobblies had ushered in "a new and momentous
labor epoch" in the fields.

"While the results of these years of activity did not loom large in
terms of the size, strength, and permanency of the unions established in these industries [lumber, construction and agricultural in
which migratory labor predominated] they left an imprint which
could not be erased," Foner wrote. "The free speech fights and
strikes associated with the IWW's drive to better the living conditions of these exploited workers, neglected by the AFL, and the
solidarity established during these struggles among men and
women of different races, religions, and nationalities laid the foundation for still others to come later."

While the organizing efforts of the Wobblies in the fields did not
fit in with concepts of traditional trade-union organizing as we now
know them—obtaining collective bargaining contracts, etc.—they
did address themselves to some all-important points that the IWW
wrapped into a single campaign. They united the workers to fight
against the most blatant injustices inflicted on the fieldworkers by
the growers.

But the Wobblies' campaigns in the fields were often on a hit-
and-miss basis, because they disdained any relatively tight structure. In this respect, they did not differ from other left-wing movements in that era. Raids by vigilantes and government agents, legal
persecutions for allegedly violating wartime laws and other forms of
abuse were all inflicted on the IWW in September 1917.

About three-fourths of the Wobbly membership was unemployed

as a result of the depression of 1913-15, which was especially heavy in its impact on the West Coast. In effect, this spelled the end of the Wobbly movement in the fields but its lingering effect, the strength of the defense movement it had generated and the example of united struggle it had given to the laborers in the fields as well as in other industries made it a target of repression for many more years.

Of the more than 500 arrested following the initiation of federal prosecutions on September 7, 1917, in Sacramento, Wichita, Kansas and Chicago, 42 were brought to trial in California. Five of the Sacramento defendants had died in jail while awaiting trial, reportedly from influenza. Those who stood trial became known as the "Silent Defenders" because they issued a pre-trial statement that they had been prejudged and that they could expect no verdict other than guilty. Their silence was dramatically broken when the verdict was announced. They arose in the courtroom and sang "The Internationale," the revolutionary working-class song.

The raids had been preceded by many newspaper articles about alleged sabotage in the fields, all attributed to the Wobblies. On September 2, 1917, the *Fresno Morning Republican* reported on the kind of "sabotage" that was being attributed to IWW organizers. Haystacks had been burned and raisin trays had been dumped and covered with dirt, the newspaper said. Four days later the IWW headquarters in Fresno was raided and 19 persons were arrested. These arrests followed by 24 hours similar raids in Hanford, Stockton and elsewhere. In the preceding days IWW organizers had been urging workers in these communities to strike for better conditions.

Meanwhile, the U.S. Justice Department opened an office in Fresno with a special agent in charge "because of the hotbed of the IWW," the Los Angeles Times said on September 11.

The tandem relationship between the growers and government agencies was perhaps most clearly demonstrated by the September 2 bulletin of the Twelfth Federal Reserve Bank, which decried the rising cost of farm labor as hampering "the effectiveness of this country's [war] efforts."

Growers went about cutting labor costs in a most systematic manner. Federal agents in farm towns manned "labor bureaus" to which reports were made on union agitation. Meanwhile, profits continued to mount.

The quest for farm labor continued, and the growers demonstrated that they were as imaginative as they were ruthless. After singing hymns and patriotic songs, squads of detention home children were marched to work in the fields at 5 a.m. But the youngsters were not even fortunate enough to keep all of their miserable earnings, between $20 and $59 for a season's work. The detention homes got 40 percent of their earnings and the children got the rest. Lest the impression be given that the growers sought only "bad boys," it should be noted that recruits were also sought and gotten from the Boy Scouts and the YMCA.

And the organization of the Woman's Land Army of America, California Division, also resulted in recruiting young women to work the fields for 25 cents an hour. They, of course, were expected to pay all their own expenses and board out of this. One grower hailed this organization as one which gave its members an opportunity to "do their bit" for the war effort. Another rancher, however, more accurately reflected grower sentiment when he said, "These women and girls will help curb the rapacity of certain foreign alien elements in their demands for higher wages." But when the women started talking about an eight-hour day, overtime, camp inspection and other conditions, the growers dispensed with them.

The growers longed for Chinese and Mexicans to work the fields. Pressures mounted on Washington to permit the admission of 40,000 Chinese laborers.

In June, 1918, a grower representative was sent to Mexico to arrange for several thousand laborers. Growers also urged the U.S. government to provide them with armed guards to insure that the Mexicans would work. So onerous was the work, and so low the pay, that many Mexicans apparently left the fields at the first opportunity. "I know of one firm who are making a group of their imported Mexicans work for ten and twelve hours a day, handcuffing them at night to prevent their escape," said a University of California professor at an April, 1918, symposium at the Commonwealth Club of California, in San Francisco.

When the workers struck in the postwar period, as they did in the southern California citrus fields in early 1919, the press called the walkouts "Russian strikes" and the strikers were arrested wholesale.

So devastating was the effect of the repression in the wake of the mass arrests and vigilante actions following the end of World War I, that between 1919 and 1934 one cannot find a single mention of farm labor in the proceedings of the California Federation of Labor. There were some momentous struggles in the fields in the late 1920's and early 1930's but they were not mainly of the AFL variety.

While the growers were reaping their profits and congratulating themselves on the relative absence of union organizations, a new force was emerging that was to provide the leadership and militancy for some of the most sustained labor struggles in the California fields. Also to be challenged was the American Federation of Labor, which in the 1920's had all but foresaken the organization of farm labor.

4   Communist Organizing

"The CAWIU made history . . . there is, in fact, no parallel in the history of the American labor movement for its spectacular record."   Carey McWilliams, 1935

While the 1920's were relatively quiet, they were far from entirely so. When farm workers were hard pressed, as was often the case, they attempted to organize.

There are indications that in September, 1922, Mexican grape pickers in the Fresno area were attempting to organize and a union was formed in the Imperial Valley city of Brawley during the cantaloupe season. However, the inability of farm workers to form stable unions did not inhibit them from engaging in sporadic work stoppages.

Some historians persist in minimizing the role of Communists in organizing farm workers during this period. Some of them labelled the Communists as "opportunists" seeking to capitalize on strikes initiated by others. Jamieson, on the other hand, indicates that the participation and influence of Communists on farm labor organizing predated the formation of the Trade Union Unity League and, influenced some of the Mexican unions in the late 1920's.

"Radical labor organizers," Jamieson reported, "appear to have been working within the Mexican mutual aid societies during the late 1920's. Most of their organizing was sporadic and individualistic until the policy of revolutionary dual unionism was put into practise by the Communist Party in the early 1930's, when the Cannery and Agricultural Workers Industrial Union (CAWIU) of the Trade Union Unity League (TUUL) was formed."

In November, 1927, a stable organization which included farm workers was organized in Los Angeles by a committee of the Federation of Mexican Societies. It called on the many mutual aid and benefit organizations in the barrios to give financial and moral support to organizing Mexican workers in unison. Shortly thereafter, a number of local unions were established in Southern California and combined to organize the Confederacion de Uniones Obreras Mexicanas (CUOM)—Federation of Mexican Workers' Unions—patterned after the union movement in Mexico. It was the most important among Mexican labor organizations.

Jamieson noted that "its principles reflect in part the influence of American leftist organizations such as the IWW and the Communist Party." Among the principles it adopted were the restriction of immigration and abolition of employment agencies and commissaries. It adopted the concept of class struggle and came out in support of "integration into a single union of all labor in the world to combat international finance."

Partly because of the migratory nature of the work force, CUOM—which at its peak had between 2,000 and 3,000 members in twenty locals—was reduced to an organization of a few hundred within 18 months.

At the same time organizing of the unorganized was taking place on other fronts. One such effort began in 1925 by a group of southern California members of the Communist Party who organized the Japanese Workers Association. Since one of the main aims of the Communist Party was to organize the working people, including agricultural workers, this newly established group concentrated its efforts in this direction.

Two years later, in 1927, this association organized the Southern California Organizing Committee (Japanese) with Karl Yoneda, then a newly recruited member of the CP, as one of its key organizers. Yoneda, who was born in 1906 on a little Glendale farm near Los Angeles, had been taken to Japan at the age of 7 in order to get his

education there. His schooling in Japan was not that anticipated by
his family. In his third year of high school Yoneda was a "drop-out"
who joined the Japanese labor and student movements. In 1925 he
assisted in organizing the Hiroshima Printers Union and the following year was fined for publishing, without the permission of the
Ministry of Home Affairs, a monthly magazine called Tsuchi
(Earth). "By then, I was already familiar with 'kusai meshi' (stinking
rice) — in other words jail and police brutality," he later recalled.
(Interview with Karl Yoneda, 1974).

As an active anti-militarist who opposed the rule of the emperor,
Yoneda, at age 20, refused to report for the draft in the Japanese
Imperial Army and escaped to the United States where he joined
the Communist Party and played a key role in organizing agricultural workers as well as in other struggles. He was among the more
than 25 Communist Party members in southern California who
were organized into what was then known as the "Japanese frac-
tion."

For four years, 1926 through 1929, economic struggles were organized throughout southern California among workers of Japanese
descent. Other Communist Party members of Mexican and Filipino
background also carried on organization among agricultural workers. Yoneda recalls the organizing done by many different groups of
Communists as they worked side by side. In 1930 all of them joined
into the Agricultural Workers Industrial League (AWIL).

Yoneda, as was the custom among many workers, used a
pseudonym. His name was Goso Yoneda. He adopted his first name
from Karl Marx. His name on the membership books he got from
the Japanese Workers Association and the Agricultural Workers
Industrial League was Karl Hama. (In Japanese Hama means
"beach.")

During this period he met Eugene Dennis who was later to become the general secretary of the Communist Party of the United
States. At that time Dennis was working with the "Pacific Sec-
ratariat" of the World Communist Movement and was very familiar
with the developments in the Communist Parties of Japan and
China. "Whenever it was possible for him to do so, Dennis undertook working with the Japanese agricultural workers," Yoneda said.
(On March 23, 1942, Yoneda was among the "volunteers" to go to

Manzanar, the first of ten concentration camps for Japanese on the
west coast. He "volunteered" in order to build a camp suitable for
the Japanese people." Imprisoned there with 10,000 others, he later
volunteered to join the United States Army. He served two years in
the Pacific theatre of war under General Joseph Stilwell. "We
Japanese faced a bitter choice between the racism of U.S. imperialism and Japanese fascism and militarism").

Aside from the continuous activity of Communists among field
workers during the 1920's, there were some important factors they
had going for them when they began the intensive period of farm
labor organizing. By their work among the unemployed the Communists had come in contact with large numbers of seasonal workers
who were among the hardest hit in the depression. In this respect,
the Communists emulated the Wobblies, who had made many of
their initial contacts with migratory labor in the lumber camps and
on construction jobs where these workers sought employment in
between field jobs.

Communists also waged a public fight on all forms of racism
against Filipino and Mexican workers. The continued activity
throughout California and in other states by representatives of
Workers International Relief and the International Labor Defense,
both closely allied with the Communist Party, enhanced the prestige of the Communists.

The instrumentality which was to rock much of the state of
California and the nation was the Trade Union Unity League, organized principally by the Communist Party, following the 1928
Sixth World Congress of the Communist International. That international meeting of Communist Parties concluded that many of the
existing organizations in the capitalist world, including old line unions such as the American Federation of Labor, were no longer
viable instruments in pursuit of work class and revolutionary
goals.

Referring to the establishment of the TUUL and its aim of organizing farm workers, Stuart Jamieson said, "It was the first
nationwide labor union in agriculture to be established since the
demise of the Industrial Workers of the World." (The IWW, however, remains organizationally alive today and has even attempted·
to organize shops as late as 1973. But Jamieson is correct in the

wider sense that the Wobblies had by that time ceased to be a significant force in labor, industrial or agricultural.)

The TUUL organized drive in the fields touched off a series of similar organizing campaigns during the greater part of the following three decades. Not all of these efforts, by any means, were under Communist leadership. Involved in these successive drives were the Congress of Industrial Organizations (CIO), the American Federation of Labor and many independent unions, especially among Mexican workers. Some of the latter were either organized by Mexican consuls or aided by them.

Organizing efforts in the fields in the latter part of the 1920's followed the pattern utilized by the Japanese Communists. The demands were relatively simple, for wage increases and recognition of the ranch committee. The main economic demand was to raise hourly wages from 20 to 25 cents. In highly seasonal ranches, such as strawberries, the workers usually won their complete demands. However, most of the strikes were against small growers, who themselves were often at the mercy of the large produce merchants.

In the course of other struggles of that period the Communists had some indication of the repression that would face them in future major struggles in the fields. In 1929, protesting the presence of Japanese imperialism in the San Pedro harbor, Yoneda and another Communist, Tetsuji Horiuchi, were arrested. They were both held for three days on suspicion of violating the criminal syndicalism law of California. By the time they were released the Japanese naval training ship had left port.

Later, at a meeting of Communist trade unionists there was agreement on who would go to Imperial Valley to assist the large number of agricultural workers to organize. At that time, Yoneda recalls, there were 7,000 Mexican workers there. In addition, there were an estimated 1,000 Japanese and several hundred Filipinos. Very few Anglos were then employed in the Valley.

Indicative of the composition of the Communists who went to the fields to organize were the persons later arrested there on charges of criminal syndicalism. They were Horiuchi, Danny Roxas (a Filipino), Braulio Orosco, Eduardo Herrera, Lawrence Emery, Oscar Erickson, Frank Spector and Carl Sklar.

Initially, in the early months of 1930, the TUUL succeeded in

establishing the Agricultural Workers Industrial League with headquarters in Brawley, California, in the heart of Imperial Valley. This
industrial union of workers in the fields embraced all farm workers
— Mexicans, Filipinos and Anglos. Shortly thereafter it became the
Agricultural Workers Industrial Union and the following year a new
name denoted its enlarged jurisdiction: Cannery and Agricultural
Workers Industrial Union (CAWIU).

The early years of the great depression were a most difficult time
for strikers. Nevertheless, Jamieson reports, TUUL affiliates were
involved in a majority of farm strikes and in all of the large ones. In
January, 1930, he reports, TUUL was involved in a strike of 5,000 in
the Imperial Valley. The following month the Communist-led union
movement participated in another Imperial Valley strike. This one
affected 700 lettuce shed workers. In July, 1931, TUUL led a strike
of 1,500 cannery workers in Santa Clara County and the following
year it participated in another California strike, that of the 1,500 pea
pickers in San Mateo County. The TUUL affiliate was also active in
the strike of 400 fruit trimmers in Solano County at about the same
time.

During the January and February, 1930, Imperial Valley strikes
TUUL succeeded in enrolling hundreds of farm workers despite the
fact that its organizers were constantly harassed, kept under surveil-
lance and arrested on trumped-up charges during the work stoppages. At the conclusion of those strikes which failed to win the
objectives of the new militant union, a conference was scheduled in
El Centro for April 20 to map further union strategy in opposition to
the contract system, speed-up and unemployment.

To prepare for this important meeting a rank and file conference
was called for April 14 in El Centro, which was attended by more
than 100 Mexican, Filipino, Black and Anglo workers. Among those
in attendance was Frank Spector, Los Angeles District Organizer of
the International Labor Defense and a charter member of the
Communist Party, who was among those subsequently arrested on a
charge of criminal syndicalism and sentenced to a 3 to 42 year jail
sentence in San Quentin Prison. In an article in the (ILD) Labor
Defender of December, 1930, written while he was serving his
sentence in prison Spector gave a vivid account of that meeting as
well as other developments in Imperial Valley. His description also

underscored the important role played by the Communists in the Imperial Valley's bitter battles at the time. In describing the April 14 meeting, he said:

"One after another the workers spoke, each in his own language. They told of starvation and sickness of their wives and children, of constant wage-cuts, of the long hours of bitter toil under a scorching sun. Each one spoke of the readiness of the workers to fight under their union's militant guidance. Suddenly the door burst open. Into the hall rushed an armed mob of policemen, deputy sheriffs and privately hired thugs, with revolvers and sawed-off shotguns which they trained upon the assembled workers. Out of this mob stepped Sheriff Gillette, chief gunman of the Imperial Valley bosses. Ordering the workers to throw up their hands, a frenzied search of the 108 workers was put through; then they were chained in groups. Then the mob, with a brutal display of force, threw them into huge trucks. The entire 108 were then hauled under heavy guard and thrown into the El Centro County jail."

During the ensuing two months some of the Mexican workers were deported, others released. It was a time, Spector wrote, when the Imperial Valley "assumed the appearance of an armed camp. Along the railroad tracks, packing sheds, bridges, warehouses, in the fields and on the ranches, before the government offices, armed guards were placed. Newspapers told fantastic stories of 'plots' to blow up bridges, sheds, railroads."

Such was the atmosphere on this front of struggle, one of many throughout the nation at that time, for the revival of prosecutions under California's Criminal Syndicalist Law, under which 32 workers in "recent strikes" were being charged. Between its passage in 1919 and the middle of 1930 about 500 Californians had been arrested for violation of this law.

Bail for each of those held on criminal syndicalism charges in Imperial Valley initially was set at $40,000. Following grand jury indictments the authorities were forced by various pressures to reduce the number of persons charged and to lower bail to $15,000 each.

Tetsuji Horiuchi, a TUUL organizer and Carl Sklar, organizer for the Los Angeles Communist Party, were found guilty and sentenced to 3 to 42 year terms in Folsom Prison. Guilty verdicts and

similar sentences were imposed on Oscar Erickson, national secretary of the Agricultural Workers Industrial League, Lawrence
Emery of the Marine Workers Industrial Union, Danny Roxas,
Filipino secretary of the AWIL in Imperial Valley and Spector.
They were sentenced to San Quentin. Two Mexican workers, Eduardo Herrera and Braulio Orosco, originally held for deportation,
were later imprisoned at San Quentin to serve 2 to 28 year sentences.

Spector declared that "The indictment returned was drawn up on
the testimony of three stool pigeons, all operatives of the scab-
herding Bolling Detective Agency, in the hire of the growers. The
trial was conducted with a frenzy of prejudice and class hatred,
fanned by tales of 'plots.' Needless to say, the defendants were
convicted and railroaded to prison, on the basis of a 'guilty' verdict
brought in by the jury of ranchers and business men."

In their appeal to the U.S. Supreme Court on June 14, 1930 the
Imperial Valley prisoners, as they were popularly known, spelled
out the case against them. They said, "eight of us, of whom all were
members of the Trade Union Unity League, some of whom were
members of the Communist Party and some not; rank and file
members of the Agricultural Workers Industrial Union as well as
those who were organizers of any of the above mentioned organizations in the Imperial Valley—all were convicted of nothing less than
the intended overthrow of the present government of the United
States and the entire existing economic system—this to be accomplished by using the workers of the Imperial Valley as a lever."

They charged that "it made no difference that outside of the
testimony of three under-cover men who were paid for their testimony nothing remained in evidence of fact to substantiate the wild
charges that were made." They further claimed that not a scintilla of
evidence was turned up against them despite "the criminal inven-
tiveness and ingenuity of the anti-labor spies. . . ."

Roxas and Herrera distributed leaflets and copies of the *Daily
Worker* and *Labor Unity*, the defendants reminded the U.S. Supreme Court. Orosco was shown to be present at some meetings at
which cited literature was kept and sold, and Sklar was placed as
being in Imperial County.

Such was the nature of the testimony at the trial of the Imperial Valley Eight.

Another view of the same trial was given in a speech by F.A. Thaanum, then commander of El Centro American Legion Post No. 25. He said, "The way to kill the Red plague is to dynamite it out. That's what we did in Imperial County. The judge who tried the Communists was a Legionnaire, 50 per cent of the jurors were veterans. What chance did the Communists have?" (*Labor Defender*, December 1930)

Why did the Communists concentrate a major effort on the Imperial Valley fields? In the first instance many of the workers in these fields who had contacts with the Communists in other areas, such as the unemployment movement and in battles against racist discrimination, sought out Communists they knew and called on them to assist the farm workers in their struggles. Then there were the objective conditions; the short seasons of big lettuce yields in January and February, cantaloupes in June and July and watermelons in July and August led to brief intensive work seasons, with the speed-up followed by long periods of unemployment. While the majority of workers were Mexican, there were also many Filipino, Black and Hindu workers among the estimated 10,000 harvesting the crops. Packing and shipping jobs in the packing sheds was done almost entirely by the 2,000 Anglo migratory workers.

The Communists also saw the growing resistance of the workers in Imperial Valley as further vindication of their policy of establishing radical unions among the most oppressed people, since the established labor leadership failed to react to demands for help.

Wages were between 25 and 35 cents per hour and housing accomodations in company camps forced large families to live in a single tent or shack with a brush covered roof. The irrigation ditches were a source of drinking water as well as for washing up and the stench from the ditches on the edge of the camps that were the only available toilets was unbearable. Disease and a high mortality rate were the common fate of the field workers.

It was conditions such as these that generated many strikes in the Imperial Valley. Especially brutal terrorism put down the strikes in 1917 and and 1922. The 1928 strike and those in the first half of 1930 "were the most significant in point of number of workers, as well as in their militancy," Spector commented.

It was the January, 1930 lettuce pickers strike that saw the entrance of the TUUL into Imperial Valley. Following the unsuccessful lettuce picker strike, during which hundreds were jailed and many were beaten while incarcerated, the shed workers struck, also unsuccessfully, against increased speed up and wage cuts.

The terror of that period extended far beyond the agricultural communities. In Gastonia, North Carolina, 7 militants faced a total of 117 years in jail, and in Atlanta, Georgia, 6 organizers faced possible electric chair execution, charged with "inciting to riot and insurrection." Attempts in Los Angeles and elsewhere to protest these unbelievable persecutions were met with equally severe police attacks against those demanding the release of the jailed.

More than four decades later, the California Supreme Court ruled the Criminal Syndicalism Law unconstitutional. The last of the jailed Imperial Valley organizers to be released from San Quentin was Lawrence Emery on Feb. 21, 1933. For many years afterward he was a Marxist journalist.

Also active in the 1930 Imperial Valley strike was Eugene Dennis, then a TUUL organizer, who later became general secretary of the Communist Party, USA.

Dorothy Ray (Healey), who began her activity in the labor movement as an activist in the CAWIU and who later became chairperson of the Southern California District of the Communist Party, said that in the early drives of the CAWIU organizers came in to help lead strikes that had been initiated by Mexican unions. This was true of the 1930 Imperial Valley strike, she said, despite contrary accounts by virtually all historians who, long after the strikes had taken place, alleged that the Communists had tried to displace the indigenous leaders of these walkouts. Even McWilliams in his *Factories in the Field* writes about how the TUUL "seized upon the strikes as an occasion to attempt the consolidation of the agricultural workers into a union."

As a matter of fact, the Mexican workers in many areas had already formed unions of their own, some of which worked very closely with the CAWIU' and often came to either the Communist Party or the TUUL seeking assistance.

A 20 percent wage cut at the California Packing Company in San Jose provoked a walkout at one of the company's plants on July 30, 1931. This was the first strike in a cannery since 1919 and it was the second CAWIU strike.

Like so many other members of the Young Communist League, Healey, then a 16 year old high school student, joined with the workers in their struggles. She went to work at Cal-Pac and was among those who struck the plant in that early CAWIU strike. Alex Norel, also a Communist, was one of the strike leaders. (He later became active in the left-led unemployment organizations.)

Like so many other CAWIU strikes, this one ran into brutal opposition from the police. Strike meetings of representatives of various canneries were held in the union headquarters but there was no hall large enough for the union to hold mass meetings of all the strikers. Every time the union called a membership mass meeting in St. James Park the police would attack with tear gas and beatings.

The union was demanding 40 cents an hour, 10 cents an hour more than pre-strike wages, plus time and a half for overtime, free transportation, union recognition and rehiring of all employees without discrimination against strikers.

The strike was lost because of the inability of the leadership to keep in touch with the workers as a result of the police brutality that prevented membership meetings.

The San Jose strike was followed by one in Vacaville, Solano County, under CAWIU leadeership. It began in November, 1932, with a walkout from the ranch owned by U.S. Congressman Frank Buck, spread to other farms and in a short time 400 Mexican, Filipino and Anglo workers were out.

Orrick Johns, in his book, *Time of Our Lives*, describes one of the many vigilante attacks against the Vacaville strikers.

"In the first week in December, when the strike was a few weeks old, a masked mob of 40 men in a score of cars, took six strike leaders out of the Vacaville jail, drove them 20 miles from town, flogged them with tug straps, clipped their heads with sheep clippers, and poured red enamel over them." (Orrick Johns, *Time of Our Lives: The Story of My Father and Myself* — New York, Octagon Books, 1937)

When the Communists organized a defense committee that came to Vacaville, 180 deputized armed vigilantes were in town and strikebreakers were given lead pipes and pruning sheers. McWilliams reports: "Although the Vacaville strike was broken, the stiff resistance put up by the workers indicated that the time was ripe for organized action."

The mood of that time seems to be accurately reported by Johns, who said that one worker told him, "We would have to starve working so we decided to starve striking."

About 3,000 pea pickers struck in the De Coto-Hayward area in Alameda and Santa Clara counties in April, 1933. The wage rate was about 12 cents an hour. The usual violence by the deputy sheriffs occured. Johns, after describing a strike meeting in the fields, says, "A few days later the strike was settled, with definite (economic) gains for the pickers but one man was dead and many injured."

Wage increases followed other CAWIU strikes, but always the price paid in human sacrifices was high. Pat Calahan who, together with Caroline Decker, was among the leaders of Mountain View and Sunnyvale cherry pickers strike of 1,000, was severely beaten and had his jaw broken. And then, as was customary, he was arrested. Gains were also made following a peach strike at Merced, Sacramento and Gridley, and a grape strike in Lodi and Fresno.

One of the most complex and highly publicized strikes under CAWIU leadership in the 1930's was the El Monte berry strike, which at its peak involved almost 6,000 workers. While most were Mexican (about half U.S. citizens) there were also sizeable Filipino and Japanese work forces. Many of the owners against whom the strike was initially called were Japanese. Also, in the course of this strike there was the direct intervention of the Mexican consul, who, on his second try, got strike leaders and the membership to act independently of the CAWIU. Involved in this complicated strike were the Mexican and Japanese consulates, the labor and political movements of Mexico and an assortment of governmental agencies. As a result of the strike, sizeable wage increases were won, and in the San Joaquin Valley jobs were obtained for some of the berry-pickers who no longer had jobs to return to at the end of the season. The presence of these union members in the San Joaquin Valley strengthened the stand of the union when it called the cotton strike. Therefore, in part, this important strike was a prelude to the huge San Joaquin Valley cotton strike, which began in October.

Two important CAWIU-led strikes in August, 1933, also helped set the stage for the cotton strike. In Santa Clara County, 1,200 workers went out on strike in the peach orchards, demanding a 30 cents-an-hour scale, 10 cents more than they had been getting. The union won 25 and 27½ cents an hour and, after striking four days, all workers, united in the CAWIU, marched back together to their jobs.

Meanwhile, unrest was evident in Fresno County, where 130 Mexican workers, after striking for a two-cents-an-hour increase, struck the peach orchards again, demanding an additional five cents hourly raise on ranches near Parlier and Selma. In 1970, Selma was the location of one of the main headquarters of the United Farm Workers Organizing Committee.

In adjoining Tulare County, CAWIU organizer Pat Chambers, a Communist, had succeeded in organizing the 700 workers on the important Tagus Ranch. In this battle, two major protagonists met head on. Chambers, whom McWilliams describes as "a small, quiet-spoken man, but a person of great courage and genuine ability as a leader," was leading the challenge against one of the largest ranches in the state, owned by the reactionary Meritt family. The 700 Tagus Ranch workers struck and so did 2,000 employed in the orchards in Merced County owned by the California Packing Company. By mid-August an estimated 4,000 peach pickers had struck.

The first to capitulate was Cal-Pac, which agreed to raise wages to 25 cents an hour, a 7½ cent raise. The Tagus Ranch and Fresno County growers soon followed suit. In the presence of government officials, the growers signed an agreement for wages with the union and agreed to take back all strikers without discrimination.

Strikes swept over much of California in the wake of these victories. An especially violent one took place in the grape fields of Lodi and Fresno. But these were only forerunners to what was to come in the cotton strike in the San Joaquin Valley and in the lettuce and other strikes in Imperial Valley.

Jamieson, who was often critical of CAWIU strike organization, describes the cotton strike that began in October, 1933, as the "largest, most sensational, and most ably organized of all strikes led by the CAWIU."

During the depression cotton growers had drastically cut wages. Choppers who were getting $1.46 an acre in 1930 were down to 66 cents an acre in 1932 and 72 cents in 1933. Picking, which had paid a dollar per hundredweight in the late 1920's, dropped to 40 cents in 1932. Taking into account the militancy of the workers and a possible labor shortage, the growers reached an agreed-upon price for the 1933 season of 60 cents per hundredweight. In preparation for the strike, the CAWIU had trained a corps of Mexican, Black and Anglo organizers and established a network of 19 new locals throughout the cotton region. The locals demanded a dollar per hundredweight, abolition of labor contractors, and union hiring without discrimination.

A historic union rally took place in Corcoran, where 5,000 cotton pickers voted to strike. The strike shortly involved up to 18,000 workers and the picket lines stretched for 114 miles up and down the valley. The growers reacted swiftly and predictably. They ousted the workers from the camps, and immense emergency colonies of strikers were set up in McFarland, Porterville, Tulare, Wasco and Corcoran.

In Corcoran the union set up its headquarters on a rented 40-acre farm.

The strikers got extensive outside aid from Communist-organized relief agencies. Locally, small growers who had their own beefs against the wealthy cotton gin companies and their usurious practices, also supported the strike. McWilliams indicates the temper of the times when he reports that a local minister, who carried a union card as well as a card in the Communist Party, told the workers to hold out. His slogan was, "We'll win this fight, by the aid of God and a strong picket line."

Strike relief also came from a most unexpected source, the California Emergency Relief Administration. It is believed that this was the first time that a public agency, under federal direction, provided relief in a large strike. Yet Pat Chambers had been arrested in Tulare at the beginning of the strike because he led a march for relief for strikers.

In the hot noonday sun, a group of workers were leaving the Pixley union hall after a meeting on October 12, 1933. A large number of men had pulled their cars up outside the hall, stepped out and riddled the building with rifle fire. Two strikers fell dead and others were wounded. And in nearby Arvin, still another worker was shot down.

Eleven ranchers were arrested and charged with murder. The trial was a travesty. The murderers, who were positively identified, were acquitted. The strikers, 3,000 of them, mournfully marched through the streets of Bakersfield at the funeral of their brothers.

George Creel, World War I jingoist and propagandist, was sent as a government emissary to try to convince the strikers to return to work. They rejected his pleas. Boos from strikers greeted the similar plea of Enrique Bravo, the Mexican consul, who warned of "grave international complications" if the strike continued.

Finally, Governor James ("Sunny Jim") Rolph, appointed a fact-finding committee headed by Dr. Ira B. Cross of the University of California. The committee recommended a 75 cents-per-hundredweight scale and simultaneously criticized the violation of the civil rights of the strikers.

With the government cutting off relief supplies as a means of increasing pressure on the strikers, and growers threatening to increase the number of strikebreakers, the union reluctantly agreed to the new wage rate, thereby bringing to a close the historic but costly strike. In 1944 McWilliams wrote that "The strike, the largest of its kind in American history, lasted for 24 days."

Despite this success, CAWIU failed to consolidate its position —largely because the workers moved on to other crops after the conclusion of the cotton season. By year's end, headquarters in Bakersfield, Delano, Shafter, Corcoran, Hanford and Fresno were among those abandoned. Only a skeleton office in Tulare remained.

Writing in the Spring, 1970, issue of *Aztlan*, a Chicano journal, Ronald W. Lopez sums up the 1933 union drives in agriculture in his article on the El Monte berry strike:

"In 1933 California was swept by a series of agricultural strikes unprecedented in size and number and not matched since. There were at least 37 strikes between April and December, practically affecting all of the major crops in the state. Altogether, approxi-

mately 65 per cent of the state's entire crop for 1933 was involved. .
. . There were nearly 50,000 workers in the combined strikes that
involved an estimated loss of 700,000 working days. The longest,
largest and most highly publicized of the many strikes was the cotton pickers' strike in the San Joaquin Valley. It lasted 27 days . . .
involved somewhere between 12,000 and 18,000 strikers, affected
four counties, and at least three strikers were killed and six of the
strikers' children died of malnutrition. . . . In 1933 the CAWIU was
the predominant force in the 37 recorded strikes, having provided
leadership in 24 of the strikes, accounting for nearly 80 percent of
the total number of workers involved in strikes that year. In this
instance, as in preceding ones, the majority of the workers were
Mexicans."

Frank Nieto, a Chicano communist who was a leader of a group of
Mexican workers in the Imperial Valley, came to Los Angeles one
day in December, 1933. He headed straight for the offices of the
Communist Party and the Young Communist League. He had come
to enlist help in organizing the lettuce fields of Imperial County,
which adjoins Mexico. In the months gone by, in the fall lettuce
season, they had tried to organize and then had seen their efforts fail
as a result of the terror unleashed by the growers and the police.

Nieto was a distinctive man in many ways. His left hand was
missing and his trademark was a glove where the hand should have
been. Healey recalled that "He was one of the most important
Mexican leaders of the (CAWIU) union all during the 1930's, an
enormous organizer and a totally selfless dedicated man who followed the crops and organized wherever he went."

Another active leader in the Imperial Valley strike of 1934 was
Ishmael (Smiley) Rincon, one of the many Chicano workers who
joined the Young Communist League during that struggle. (Rincon
later fought in the Abraham Lincoln Brigade in defense of the legal
government of Republican Spain. During World War II Rincon was
killed in the Pacific war zone).

Imperial Valley is a land-locked island of irrigation with expanses
of desert to the east and west, Mexico to its south and the Salton Sea
on its northern end. There agriculture is the way of life; there is
virtually no other. And the labor force that continues to this day to
pour across the border, as through a sieve, is the lifeblood of that

industry. In the early 1970s thousands of farm workers who toiled in the Imperial Valley lived in Mexicali because the cost of living there was considerably less than at Calexico on the U.S. side. In 1934 the situation was considerably more difficult for the field workers.

On New Year's Eve, at the time of a great flood in Los Angeles, communists and others from the CAWIU began what was to be a most fateful mission to the Imperial Valley to help organize a strike. Unsuccessful strikes in the fields in 1928 and 1930 resulted in a major deterioration in wages. In 1929 and 1930 wages had ranged between 35 and 50 cents hourly. By the Spring of 1933 wages had dropped to 15 cents an hour with irrigators getting a penny and a half more.

Conscious of CAWIU successes elsewhere, growers agreed with the Mexican Field Workers Union to a minimum hourly wage of 22½ cents for harvesting lettuce and no less than five hours pay for any worker taken into the field that day. Even though this agreement, like many others with Mexican unions in that period, had been reached with the assistance of the Mexican consul, it was violated within weeks, and on November 17, 1933 workers staged a one day protest stoppage.

From all indications, CAWIU members in the Imperial Valley, led by Nieto and others, won over the majority of the workers to seeking the assistance of the militant, Communist-led union. A major battle was shaping up in the lettuce fields in the opening days of 1934, and the workers apparently believed they needed union leadership that would be militant and effective.

In the 1934 lettuce strike, which began on January 8, the majority of workers were Mexicans, although there were a significant number of Filipinos, some Blacks and even fewer Anglos. In the pea strike the following month, which centered in Calipatria, most of the workers in this CAWIU strike were Anglos, refugees from the Dust Bowl. Because author John Steinbeck has so graphically and truly depicted their hardships in books such as *In Dubious Battle* and *Grapes of Wrath*, they have sometimes been referred to as "Steinbeck's people."

In the cotton and other CAWIU strikes, Pat Chambers had become a prime target of the growers, the press and the police. He stayed in the background during much of the Imperial Valley lettuce strike, working out of El Centro, about ten miles south of Brawley, the main strike center. There Dorothy Ray Healey and Stanley Hancock, a 23-year-old San Diego newspaperman who also was a Communist, were among the union organizers.

"In every strike we went into we made no bones about our Communist affiliation," Healey recalled. "We'd start by telling the workers that some of us were Communists and why—and what it represented. It made no difference as far as the workers were concerned. All they wanted to know is, would you lead honestly? Were you effective?" (Interview with Dorothy Healey, January 1973.)

Mobilization of the rank and file for full strike participation was a prime task for CAWIU organizers. Almost immediately they set up a strike committee, relief committees and other committees to handle food, the kitchen, publicity and the many other tasks that are part of every well-run strike.

"What you saw was the enormous flowering together of native talents of human beings who never before had a chance to work together. There was the development of leaders and of orators," Healey said.

All this happened in an atmosphere in which "incredible police attacks" took place and where, faced with a largely hostile press and with few means of communicating with the rest of society, the strikers and their leaders felt, Healey said, as if they were on "an island on which you felt totally isolated."

While the most publicized brutality of that strike was the kidnapping of Abraham Lincoln Wirin, noted civil liberties attorney, almost unknown "were the terrible police raids on the colonias (Mexican community)." Vigilantes, instrumentalities of the anti-union Associated Farmers, were all Anglos who brutally broke up picket lines and union-sponsored parades. They came into the colonias and beat up the workers.

But they did not succeed in terrorizing the strikers. The strike spread to Calexico as well as to Hemet, El Centro, Holtville, and many other surrounding communities.

(The union at that time little realized that the growers were seeking to cut back on their planted acreage under a California version of the federal Agricultural Adjustment Act (AAA), under which farmers were paid for not growing products at a time when millions throughout the nation were ill-fed.)

The workers were striking for much more than wages — at issue was their right to live as human beings. Even official government studies, such as the *Annual Report of the Imperial County Health Department* (1931), revealed "cases of the members of one family drinking ditch water directly below where another family was polluting it." Also in this report, which did not cover migrant workers, it was disclosed that the death rate in Imperial County was consistently 50 percent higher than that of the rest of the state during the previous decade. In the 1928-30 period, all but 100 who died of tuberculosis were Mexicans and fewer than 60 were white. In 1930, 134 out of each 1,000 children died within a year of birth. In the state as a whole the death rate was less than 59 out of each 1,000 born.

"The only water to drink in the hot sun of the Imperial Valley, where the temperature went up to 120." Healey recalled, "was the irrigation water and that was used for everything. It was used for toilets and it was used for washing. It was also used for drinking. That was the thing that was most indignantly resented—even more than the horrible wages."

About twice a week the CAWIU leaders crossed the Mexican border into Mexicali (directly across from Calexico) where they met with Mexican union leaders to coordinate activities. "There was always the warmest feeling, the fraternity was enormous and there was a mutual regard and acceptance." This relationship between U.S. and Mexican unionists has prevailed in many of the union organizing efforts in the United States in succeeding years.

Even the daily terror in the colonias and on the picket lines was surpassed one day when the police launched an attack on the Azteca (union) hall. The events that followed were not unique; throughout the history of farm labor struggles one hears similar stories.

When the police, claiming they had an arrest warrant, demanded that the strike leaders surrender, the workers in the hall—about 2000—refused to comply. The police barricaded the hall and threw tear gas through the small windows.

As the workers, many were women and children, left the hall

they were beaten over the head by police and sheriff's deputies. Meanwhile the workers had spirited out the strike leaders and hid them from the authorities. A $10,000 reward was offered for their arrest. The workers hid and protected the union leaders for more than a week.

Latter-day historians who contend that Communists "provoked" the violence in the Imperial Valley by their very presence are just giving off with "nonsense," Healey contends. She cited the Calipatria pea strike as a case in point. The strike was spontaneous and no Communists were involved during its early days. Yet the vigilante attacks against these strikers were as brutal as those against the strikes publicly led by Communists.

John Steinbeck, in his book, *In Dubious Battle*, not only offers an excellent panoramic view of the bitter struggles in the fields but also expresses the view that as far as the vigilantes were concerned anyone seeking five cents an hour more in wages was a Communist. This view stands up better in the light of history than does the viewpoint of those who have been trying to rewrite it.

Were there meetings among the farmworkers at which the role of the Communist Party was discussed? Obviously there were. "The Mexican and Mexican-American (Chicano) workers were, in part, the product of the 1910 Mexican Revolution, and also reflected a strong anticlerical feeling which was so dominant in Mexico in the 1930s." One night a meeting took place in a Chicano's home by kerosene lamp. Healey had been invited to speak on the role of the Party. After her talk the farm workers said, "We are already revolutionaries!"

By March the lettuce and pea strikes had been smashed. Lawyers who had come to the valley to defend workers were arrested and so were those who had been in charge of bringing relief to the strikers. It was a time for teaching the persons who had struck, and their leaders, a lesson. That was the belief of the growers. And for the workers it was a time to be staunch, to demonstrate that even in defeat they were not without courage.

The trial, presided over by a justice of the peace with no legal training, was "like a Roman carnival." Growers, their families and supporters took up almost all of the seats in the courtroom while hundreds of workers, disdaining the terror of the vigilantes and their legal counterparts, massed outside the courthouse to hear the proceedings over loudspeakers. Healey and Hancock acted as their own attorneys in light of the persecution of lawyers in earlier cases.

At one point, when Healey was on the witness stand being questioned by Hancock, she was asked to describe the food in the camps where the workers lived. The foreman of the jury arose in the courtroom and blurted out, "This is a lot of nonsense. When I was in the AEF (American Expeditionary Force of World War I) we ate beans three times a day and it it was good enough for us it was good enough for these dirty Mexicans." The same foreman could not contain himself as the trial dragged on for a week, and again arose to address a question to the court. "Do we have to waste our time listening to these people? We already know whether or not they are guilty."

Efforts by the defendants to dissuade field workers from testifying were unsuccessful. From the outset, it was obvious that every farmworker who testified would be arrested. They were arrested for deportation or on vagrancy charges upon stepping down from the witness stand. Then the police or vigilantes—it was hard to tell one from the other—would ransack their homes, leaving them in shambles.

Nevertheless, six Mexican field workers insisted on testifying. Rather than permit the farce to continue with more Mexican workers victimized for their courageous stand, the defendants cut short the trial. They were found guilty and were sentenced to the maximum sentence, six months. Earlier courts had also sentenced Pat Chambers and Emma Cutler, who headed the strike relief program. They received similar sentences.

Even after they began serving their sentences in the El Centro jail on May 14, they were not immune from terror. One night the road camp where the men had been taken was attacked, a cross burned, a grave dug with a nailstudded cat-o-nine tails and a noose in it, and a note proclaiming, "This is what is going to happen to you reds."

Elmer (Pop) Hanoff, was the California Communist Party's trade union advisor in many of the farm struggles. During the Imperial Valley battles he holed up in an El Centro hotel where he was often consulted by Communist forces in the fields. His presence in the

Valley was not, however, completely unknown to the growers and
to the police. When the police came to grab him, he succeeded in
eluding them by jumping from his hotel room on to a passing hay
wagon and escaped arrest.

The Imperial Valley strike of agricultural workers came at a time
when the Communist Party in California was in the midst of major
activities on several fronts. While agricultural labor was a major
Communist Party concentration for five years preceding the 1934
strike, the Party was also deeply involved in trying to organize the
unemployed, as well as assisting in organizating the new industrial
unions. 1934 was also the year of the great San Francisco general
strike. Defense of the victims of the farm labor strikes became a
major part of the work of the International Labor Defense and of the
Communist Party. The Party spent a considerable part of its funds
and organizing ability to assist the farm workers throughout the
United States. Especially notable was the great 1932 Colorado beet
field strike, organized by Communists, in which an estimated
25,000 workers participated. That strike, led by El Comite Frente
Unico de los Trabajadores Agricolas, resulted in the recruitment of
more than 200 Chicano agricultural workers into the ranks of the
Party according to Pat Toohey, veteran Communist Party organizer
who was then the editor of *La Voz del Obrera*.

In that same year in San Antonio, Texas, pecan shellers struck.
One of the leaders in the historic walkout was Emma Teneyuca,
who later became the chairperson of the Communist Party of Texas.
More than 10,000 persons were involved in this strike. In the course
of that very bitter battle Emma was beaten by the police, tear
gassed and arrested.

Both of these strikes contributed in a major way to the formation
of the United Cannery, Agricultural, Packing and Allied Workers of
America of the CIO. In subsequent years leaders of the AFL-CIO
United Farm Workers of America recognized the contribution that
these and other fighters in the fields had made to the strikes they
had been leading. The lessons of past struggles were required "reading" for the leaders of the new union of agricultural workers.

During its short, hectic and militant life the CAWIU often
worked with the Mexican unions in the field. One of these was
CUCOM, Confederacion de Uniones de Campesinos y Obreras del

Estado de California which in June, 1933, claimed 10,000 members.

One of the last CAWIU strikes took place in Contra Costa County, where 1,000 apricot pickers walked out of the orchards in support of demands for 35 cents an hour, an eight-hour day and union recognition. One hundred and fifty pickets were arrested and dumped across the county line and 13 strike leaders were arrested. The traditionally anti-labor *Oakland Tribune* called it a "round-up and deportation of undesirable agitators," while the San Francisco Labor Council viewed it as "outrages by mobs of farmers aided and abetted by state highway police."

The last CAWIU strike, in Hayward in July, 1934, called for wage increases as well as removal of troops from the San Francisco waterfront, where they had been summoned to smash the historic dock strike.

On July 20, 1934 the CAWIU headquarters in Sacramento was raided. The attackers had sawed-off shotguns, blackjacks, rubber hoses, riot clubs and assorted other weapons. Nineteen CAWIU leaders were arrested on criminal syndicalism charges. The trial lasted more than four months, one of the longest in the state's history. Eight were convicted. After serving almost two years their sentences were reversed on appeal.

This trial, the second one on criminal syndycalism charges, aimed at smashing the militant agricultural workers union. It was part of a wholesale assault on working people at that time. It was the time of the Pacific Coast Maritime Strike and the San Francisco general strike. Pat Chambers, Caroline Decker, Martin Wilson, Jack Crane and Nora Conklin were sentenced to five years each. Albert Hagourdy was sentenced to three and one half years and Norman Mini to three. Lorene Norman was releases on bail shortly after her imprisonment.

Lorene Norman was pregnant at the time of the arrests and her child, born after her release, died in birth. She had been released on bail from the Tehachipi State Prison, which at that time was an institution for women.

Elaine Black Yoneda, who was the western vice president of the International Labor Defense, recalls the difficulties in getting the most elementary justice for Communists organizing in the fields. On one occasion Louis Yamomoto, a Communist organizing in the fields, was among those arrested and held on high bail. He was held in the Stockton jail.

"We went to bail him out. Pat Chambers was with me at the time. We were stopped at a road block by a group of vigilantes who were there to make sure no one got through to the local Justice of Peace to post bail. They were there with their shotguns. So we told the vigilantes that we were going to see the Justice of the Peace to get married. They waved us through and when we walked in the Justice's office and told him we were there to post bail for Yamomoto he was stunned. Chambers was being held on charges on unlawful assembly and resisting arrest. They had no alternative but to release him to us and we drove away through the vigilante road block."

In the massive campaign for freedom for those convicted in the Sacramento case, large scale labor support for the California Conference for Repeal of the Criminal Syndicalism Act was expressed. Among the unions which joined in its support and activity were 7 Central Labor Councils, 3 Building Trades Councils, the Maritime Federation of the Pacific, the International Longshoremen's Association, 85 local unions, 34 unemployed unions and 31 political groups, including the Communist and Socialist Parties and various Democratic Party groups.

Rallies throughout the state were held in behalf of those convicted. One of them took place in Mission Dolores Park in San Francisco, where Elaine Black Yoneda was among those arrested. Also arrested at the 1934 rally was Leo Gallagher, the ILD attorney in the case. His arrest, ironically, necessitated some additional delays in the appeals since he was at the moment busy defending himself.

In the interim between the first agricultural workers criminal syndicalism trial in Imperial Valley and that in Sacramento, the Communist movement had succeeded in mobilizing major labor backing for the organization of farm workers, as well as against the vicious laws used by the growers, and others, to exterminate the unionization drive.

None of the contemporary commentators minimize the contribution that the CAWIU made to the history of farm labor organizing. Jamieson said:

"The CAWIU, during it s brief span of less than four years, led dozens of strikes, large and small. Some were spectacular successes, others were dismal failures. Though in the end the union was crushed, its campaign was not without lasting effects. Wages were raised in all major growing areas of the state as a result of the upsurge of 1933 . . .—perhaps more important, the CAWIU's organized agitation served to attract sympathetic public attention to some of the more pressing problems of agricultural labor in California. State and federal government agencies, in time, undertook various measures to ameliorate some of the worst hardships suffered by farm workers in the state."

McWilliams in his *Factories in the Fields*, declares:

"The CAWIU, however, made history during the period of its existence. There is, in fact, no parallel in the history of the American labor movement for its spectacular record."

The arrests, plus the series of violent sttacks on the union, effectively smashed it. But for many of the workers and relatively unbiased observers, the CAWIU was remembered as having made a most significant and lasting contribution to the long history of farm labor battles.

5 Past as Prelude

"For more than thirty years I have been in strikes in the fields. I think we are going to win this one, but whether or not we win, the growers will know they have been in one hell of a fight." A Filipino farm worker, 1965

The above were the words of a weary but determined Filipino farm worker, then in his sixties, who had been among those who had walked out from the grape ranches near Delano on September 8, 1965. His back bent from toiling in the fields, his leathery skin dark from the years of labor in sun-drenched farms throughout the nation's western states, he nevertheless typified the fighting spirit of the many farm workers who had walked countless picket lines under the leadership of many unions in the long attempt to organize the seemingly endless number of ranches. Yet he had confidence that somehow this one would be different, that this walkout would have a lasting effect and would result in winning more than just some temporary gains.

The scene was the Filipino Community Hall in Delano, which was then serving as a combined office, meeting hall and soup kitchen for workers who were members of the AFL-CIO Agricultural Workers Organizing Committee (AWOC).

He was but one of many whose lives had been deeply affected by the long history of strike struggles. While he was one of those whose history reached back to the days when he was a member of the CAWIU, there were others, younger workers, tied to other past strikes in the fields through the experiences of their fathers, mothers, uncles and aunts.

One of these was Cesar Estrada Chavez.

In San Jose in 1930, a debate was raging among the members of the AFL Dried Fruit and Nut Pickers Union over whether the local should affiliate with the CIO Warehousemen's Local 6, which was under militant and radical leadership. Among those who argued was Cesar's father, Librado (Liberty) Chavez, and among those who listened in attentively to these debates was a youngster, only 12 years old, Cesar Chavez. He heard his father and uncle argue for the CIO position, which eventually was adopted by the AFL local membership.

"Sometimes the men would meet at our house," Cesar Chavez later recalled, "and I remember seeing their picket signs and hearing them talk. They had a strike and my father and uncle picketed at night. It made a deep impression on me. But of course they lost the strike and that was the end of the union. But from that time on my father joined every new agricultural union that came along—often he was the first to join—and when I was 19 I joined the National Agricultural Workers Union (successor to the AFL National Farm Labor Union). But it didn't have any more success than any of the other farm worker unions."

Later Chavez walked the picket line near Corcoran as a member of the NFLU.

In 1971, sixty-seven-year old Philip Vera Cruz, one of the oldest members of the United Farm Workers Union, recalled with pride his brief term as the first president of the Delano Chapter of the National Farm Labor Union in 1948. He, too, participated in a large number of the earlier strikes in the fields.

Dolores Huerta, who became the top negotiator for the United Farm Workers Union, had long been an articulate advocate for farm-labor rights in California political circles. But she served her trade-union apprenticeship as an organizer on the staff of the Agricultural Workers Organizing Committee.

By far the most extensive history of the struggle in the fields of all the initial officers of the United Farm Workers Union was that of Larry Itliong, second in command to Cesar Chavez during the formative years of the union.

Itliong got his baptism in the U.S. labor movement in 1930 when he was among 1,500 workers who walked out of the lettuce fields near Monroe, Washington. In 1933 he was assisting in the organization of Salinas Valley spinach cutters, and a few years later he became involved in organizing Alaska cannery workers. He was elected vice president of the large Local 7 of the CIO United Cannery, Agricultural and Packinghouse Workers of America (UCAPAWA). Later he joined the staff of the Agricultural and Workers Organizing Committee, in effect heading up that campaign when the Delano strike broke out. When AWOC merged with Cesar Chavez's National Farm Workers Association, Itliong became assistant director of the new United Farm Workers Organizing Committee, now called the United Farm Workers of America, AFL-CIO.

These were but a few of the links between the founders and leaders of the AFL-CIO United Farm Workers of America and the historic struggles of other unions in the fields. Many of them had lived through difficult depression years. They knew first-hand the terror unleashed by the growers organized into the Associated Farmers following the demise of CAWIU.

Toward the end of 1934, when Hitler had seized power in Germany and the fear of fascism was increasing, the Los Angeles Committee Against War and Fascism put out its own indictment, *California's Brown Book*, which declared:

"Fascism is rule by violence and terror, in the interest of a minority, to hold down the masses. Such terroristic rule as that now scourging Germany may seem very far away, yet this fascism, which stamps out every last vestige of civil rights, is now showing itself throughout America—with the state of California one of the areas of greatest intensity."

The sharp condemnation of official and unofficial vigilantism, especially in the rural areas, was voiced by many besides Communists and their supporters. Dr. Simon J. Lubin, commissioner of California's Immigration and Housing Department, who was one of the three members of a federal investigating committee established by the National Labor Board in 1934, did much to call public attention to the plight of the farm workers in his report.

"They (the authorities) forbid free speech and free assembly —even by ordinance"! he said. "Brutally they break up public meetings conducted in private halls. They interfere with the organization of labor, and deport representative committees fairly elected. Indiscriminately they arrest innocent men and women under fake charges, and through the use of the suspended sentence, hold them in constant fear. They fix exorbitant bail. They threaten to ruin a few residents brave enough to show sympathy with unfortunate workers. They scoff at our federal courts. They threaten to prevent, by bribery or force, the feeding of starving women and children by federal agents. Their so-called peace officers do the bidding of their masters with the able assistance of pistols, machineguns, tear gas bombs, hard wood sticks. . . ."

John Steinbeck, who was born and brought up in Salinas, added his indictment to those of previous observers. He, like Lubin, made a major contribution to a fuller understanding of the plight of the farm workers when he organized a committee of liberals and others to support the organizing efforts of farm workers. In his widely circulated 1936 pamphlet, *Their Blood Is Strong*, (John Steinbeck, *Their Blood Is Strong*–Simon J. Lubin Society of California, Inc., 1938) he spells out how the growers deported militant Mexicans and Filipinos who led battles in the fields in previous years. But in so doing he falls prey to some chauvinist concepts that picture the "American" workers standing up to the growers because of their heritage.

In 1938, Steinbeck was quoted in the preface to the pamphlet as saying, "As a whole, probably conditions are worse than they ever were due to the constant flow of people into the state and the increasing mechanization of agriculture."

By 1938 there were 250,000 homeless migrants in the California fields, 30,000 had come in that year, and more were on the way. In 1936 they numbered only 150,000. The depression had produced a bumper crop of migratory workers.

"The attitude of the employer on the large ranch," Stenbeck wrote, "is one of hatred and suspicion; his method is the threat of the deputies' guns. The workers are herded about like animals. Every possible method is used to make them feel inferior and insecure. At the slightest suspicion that the men are organizing they are run from the ranch at the point of guns. The large ranch owners know that if organization is ever effected there will be the expense of toilets, showers, decent living conditions and a raise in wages."

With the demise of the CAWIU, which was formalized on March 17, 1935, by the decision of the TUUL to instruct its affiliates to rejoin the AFL—a move which did much to lay the groundwork for many of the CIO unions later organized in agriculture as well as in other industries—there came a period that McWilliams describes as "the rise of farm fascism."

The instrumentality of the growers was the Associated Farmers, which was organized jointly by the State Chamber of Commerce and the Farm Bureau. They extended state-wide the policies of the growers in Imperial County—described by some as "the cradle of vigilantism"—where the Associated Farmers was first organized.

In ensuing years, strike after strike was smashed by this industry-sponsored movement. In Santa Rosa, American Legion officials and members, a member of the State Legislature, the mayor, motorcycle policemen and the head of the local Chamber of Commerce were among the identified leaders of mob action against Communists and farm workers. This attack on August 23, 1935, was preceded by several others aimed at striking terror into those fighting on behalf of farm workers.

Earlier in 1935, Herman Cottrell, Associated Farmers official and organizer of its paramilitary California Cavaliers, declared, "We aren't going to stand for any more of these organizers from now on; anyone who peeps about higher wages will wish he hadn't." One of the announced purposes of the California Cavaliers was to "stamp out all un-American activity among farm labor."

A strike by 2,000 pickers and packinghouse workers took place in the Santa Rosa area apple orchards in the summer of 1935. On August 1, two Communist Party officials, Jack Green and Solomon Nitzburg, were addressing a rally of strikers when 250 vigilantes invaded the hall and broke up the meeting. Three weeks later, the mob of vigilantes seized both of them plus three others and dragged them through the streets of Santa Rosa. The three others were released by the mob after they publicly kissed the American flag and promised to leave town.

Nitzburg and Green, refusing to comply with the mob's demand, were beaten, tarred and feathered and were then paraded around the court house. The public reaction to this attack was widespread and sharp. Twenty-three business and professional men were indicted. They were acquitted in short order. Later, when Nitzburg and Green sued for damages, the court decision was for the defendants.

The Santa Rosa pattern also prevailed in farm strikes that took place near urban centers. Similar developments took place in the celery strike in Los Angeles County in 1936, where an army of 1,500 armed guards, policemen and sheriff's deputies battled hundreds of strikers. But these strikes in the celery fields were unique for other reasons.

They had been called by the Federation of Agricultural Workers Unions of America (FAWUA). This was an outgrowth of the National Committee for Unity of Agricultural and Rural Workers, which was largely under left leadership. Its plan was to establish federal AFL locals which would eventually unite into a viable state-wide organization of field workers. However, the high initiation fees of the AFL and the relatively expensive dues inhibited the success of such a plan. (Federal locals were directly chartered and administered by The American Federation of Labor and not by any specific international union. Most of them either folded or affiliated with the internationals, although federal locals still do exist.)

Confederacion de Uniones de Campesinos y Obreros Mexicanos (CUCOM), the militant union of Mexican fieldworkers, had a long record of successful organization as a result of its work with the CAWIU as well as with unions made up of workers from other nationalities. Therefore, CUCOM provided most of the leadership and a great part of the rank and file for the temporarily organized Federation, which held its first convention in Los Angeles in January, 1936.

Joining this new united organization were several independent Mexican unions, Filipinos and the recently organized Japanese

Workers Union of America. In the spring of 1936, 11 unions affiliated with the Federation drew up a set of demands which called
for a minimum hourly wage of 30 cents, union recognition, and
time-and-a-half for all Sunday and holiday work. The celery strike
that followed involved more than 2,000 workers. The Southern
California Farm Federation, composed mostly of Japanese growers,
refused to meet with union representatives because they charged
the union was "Communist-dominated."

Nevertheless, the FAWUA claimed that 386 growers had bowed
to the union demands by July, 1936. The U.S. Department of Labor
mediated the remaining strikes by getting the growers to agree to a
minimum 30 cents an hour wage and 60 percent union preference in
hiring.

Simultaneously, strikes in strawberries, beans and citrus broke
out in Orange County, adjoining Los Angeles. Jamieson wrote:
"The methods of suppression corresponded closely to those used in
the Los Angeles celery strike. Large numbers of strikers were
evicted from their homes; 400 special armed guards were recruited
by growers to patrol fields and protect strikebreakers; highway
police disrupted strikers' parades and picket lines; some 200 people
were arrested and jailed in a stockade; and numerous strikers were
injured when growers (to quote the *Los Angeles Examiner* of July
11, 1936) 'commissioned bands of armed men, armed with tear gas
and shotguns to conduct open private warfare' against citrus strikers."

The Associated Farmers blamed the strike on Communist leaders
in the FAWUA. This in no way deterred local police from arresting
AFL officials, state and local, who had come there to investigate the
strike. Jamieson indicates the multinational aspect of the citrus
strike. Velarde and Avila were Mexican leaders, Mensalves was
Filipino and Deguchi was Japanese.

During this same period, the AFL had achieved some success in
organizing shed workers and those employed in canneries. But
many in the AFL were becoming increasingly alarmed by the blatant anti-union attacks in the farm areas, which were also being felt
in the cities. Others were also greatly disturbed by the terror which,
under the pretext of anti-communism, violated the civil liberties of

all. Nor did the sponsorship of anti-Semitic lectures by the Associated Farmers lessen any of these fears—at a time when Hitler was on the rise in Europe.

Several attempts by the Confederacion de Uniones de Campesinos Y Obreros Mexicanos (CUCOM) and other unions to win AFL approval for a new national union nevertheless failed. In an article in the May, 1936, issue of the *American Federationist*, Donald Henderson called for support of a national union of agricultural labor. In it, he argued that a viable year-round organization could be organized that would assist its members with their problems during the slack season and would also work for the establishment of unemployment benefits for its members. (Donald Henderson was leter elected as the first president of the United Cannery, Agricultural, Packing and Allied Workers of American at its first convention in Denver, 1937 where it received a charter from the CIO.)

In arguing his point, Henderson appealed to the self-interest of the already organized workers by pointing out that the unorganized agricultural workers provided an all-too-available strike-breaking force in industry. Furthermore, he contended, impoverished workers could not possibly be customers of the goods coming from unionized industries.

In presenting his thesis to the leaders of the American Federation of Labor, Henderson was reflecting the growing movement in California and other fields for a united organization of farm workers within the AFL. Two hundred delegates and observers met in conference in Stockton, California, on June 6 and 7, 1936, with the aim of setting up an AFL affiliated federation of cannery, agricultural and packinghouse workers. The delegates adopted a program that called for a three-dollar daily minimum wage, an eight-hour day and overtime pay. It also called for a guarantee of 20 hours work weekly.

Predictably the conference was viewed with alarm by the Associated Farmers, which issued several statements while the delegates were in session protesting that a daily wage of three dollars would bankrupt agriculture, the largest industry in California. The reaction of Edward D. Vandeleur, executive officer of the State Federation of Labor, was anything but sympathetic to the farm workers. He said, "We will not tolerate any sort of organization but an orderly one."

Responding to the pressures from farm workers, many of them already affiliated to the AFL as federal locals, the State Federation sponsored a conference in San Francisco on February 27 and 28 which could conceivably establish a state-wide organization of agricultural labor, which would call on the AFL to organize a new International Union of Agricultural Workers. On March 21, 1937, the continuations committee from that conference met with the executive committee of the State Federation of Labor in Sacramento and submitted its organizing plan.

While Harry Bridges, at that time one of the vice-presidents of the State Federation by virtue of his leadership of the Longshoremen's Union, was in favor of approving the plans of the agricultural workers, the majority of the AFL leaders in California turned down the proposal of the field workers' representatives. Instead, they reaffirmed the earlier inadequate policy of chartering federal locals for farm workers with the proviso that such locals be under the strict control of the State Federation.

Rank-and-file attempts to get national AFL approval for a united union of farm workers in spite of the opposition of the top leaders of the California AFL were unsuccessful. Jamieson noted that many of the representatives of the National Committee of Agricultural, Cannery and Packinghouse Union had displayed sympathy towards the incipient Committee for Industrial Organizations, predecessor of the Congress of Industrial Organizations. This was especially true, he said, of those previously associated with the TUUL.

The organization of the CIO—first as the AFL's Committee on Industrial Organization in 1936 and finally as the Congress of Industrial Organizations in 1937 (formalized in 1938)—raised hopes throughout the unorganized section of the working class. The farm workers, splintered in a myriad of small unions or completely unorganized, were no exception.

When the CIO United Cannery, Agricultural, Packing and Allied Workers of America (UCAPAWA) held its first convention in Denver July 9-12, 1937, most of the Mexican and other farm unions sent delegates. They also came from the Pecan Shellers Union in San

Antonio and from the Rio Grande Valley in Texas. From the deep South, there came delegates from the Southern Tenant Farmers Union.

UCAPAWA's national scope was reflected in the local unions represented at its Denver founding convention. Included among these were Local 20471, Alabama Agricultural Workers Union, Birmingham; Local 19115, Arizona Fruit and Vegetable Workers Union, Yuma; four cannery and citrus workers locals in Florida, and agricultural workers unions in Michigan, Ohio, Tennessee and Texas.

The largest single contingent came from the State Executive Committee of the California Federation of Cannery and Agricultural Unions, representing thirteen AFL federal locals plus a number of others, including Mexican and Filipino unions. From Colorado came representatives of ten AFL locals representing workers in the beet fields and in other crops. Delegates from the Camden cannery local joined with representatives of four agricultural workers' unions in New Jersey to comprise that state's delegation. Also there were most of the nine cannery locals from the Pacific Northwest.

While organizing field workers has never been easy, it took on added negative features in the late 1930's when the fields were flooded with poverty-stricken Anglos, the dispossessed from the Dust Bowl, who sought desperately to find any kind of work.

Once again the grower-government combination went to work with wholesale deportations of brown-skinned workers. Whether they were born in Mexico or in the United States seemed to be entirely irrelevant to the immigration authorities, according to eyewitness reports of these raids. With an adequate supply of cheap domestic labor, the growers had no need for either imported Mexican workers or those born in the United States. The old pattern was once again repeating itself, this time at the expense of the Mexican and Mexican-American farm workers.

This development only further emphasized the difficulty in organizing field workers by the newly formed UCAPAWA. It was the foreign-born workers and their U.S.-born brothers and sisters who had long carried the banner of unionism in the fields. The Anglos, many of whom had been brought up to believe in "rugged individualism," were not as amenable to union organization. Even so, their bitter experiences educated many of them quite rapidly and they, too, were among those who joined in some of the struggles of those days.

Despite the difficulties, there were several important factors that UCAPAWA and other unions organizing farm labor had going for them. The establishment of a committee of liberals to aid agricultural workers, headed by John Steinbeck and including such prominent personalities as Helen Gahagan Douglas, did much to keep the spotlight on the farm workers and to some degree inhibited some of the more blatant attacks on union organizations.

Also, by that time the Federal Farm Security Administration, responding to the widespread exposure of subhuman conditions in many of the grower-owned and operated labor camps, had established some farm labor camps. Here the workers were permitted to elect their own administrative representatives—at least one element of self-government. More important from the union point of view was the fact that organizers were allowed in the camps. They could legally talk with the workers. Of course, this in no way resolved the immense problem union organizers had in trying to reach the many workers employed on small farms.

Nevertheless, the agricultural workers were not covered by the National Labor Relations Act (NLRA), as a result of political maneuvering in Washington, where the growers exerted great pressure. Representative Vito Marcantonio, staunch anti-fascist left-winger in Congress, who was there as a result of the upsurge of the American Labor Party, unsuccessfully opposed the exclusion of farm workers from NLRA coverage.

Even though UCPAWA got substantial financial help from the other CIO unions, like many other unions it found that organizing in the fields is a costly, time-consuming process—one that could easily endanger the financial stability of a labor organization. This was one of the big problems that UCAPAWA faced. The fact that NLRA coverage of canneries and food-processing plants made it easier to win victories also militated against concentrating on organization in the fields. Later in its history, UCAPAWA was faced with the problem, as were other unions, of losing some of its most experienced organizers to unions in the basic mass production industries, where the CIO was winning contracts.

In its first two months, UCAPAWA chartered 76 local unions and in its first year-and-a-half had 124,750 dues-paying members, which made it the seventh largest CIO union. It had 300 functioning locals at that time. During its relatively brief span of existence the union had among its officials and organizers many well-known Communists, and it maintained close relations with such important Left organizations as the Congress of Spanish Speaking People, the first national assemblage of persons of Mexican descent. Among the Communists active as officials and rank and file leaders of the UCAPAWA were Luisa Moreno, Herschel Alexander, a Black worker organizing in the cotton gins, Dorothy Healey, Pat Callahan and Clyde Champion.

One of the charismatic leaders of UCAPAWA was Luisa Moreno, a talented Chicana organizer and articulate representative of her people. She was an organizer for the Congress during much of the time that she also functioned as a union organizer. Additionally, she was a teacher of Marxism to many who sought answers beyond those provided by the trade-union movement or the organization of the Spanish-speaking workers. In an interview, she recalled that she was the first woman to serve on the executive board of the UCAPAWA. Also, that at the first Congress of the Spanish Speaking People, Anglos such as Donald Henderson, the first president of UCAPAWA, were among those present.

At UCAPAWA's second convention, Dorothy Ray Healey was elected as one of the vice-presidents of the new organization, also serving as an international representative. She, like so many others on the staffs of emerging CIO unions, was among those who were on the payroll of John L. Lewis, the president of the CIO, whose united Mine Workers Union was a bastion of the new federation of trade unions.

In spite of its largely unsuccessful campaigns to unionize the California fields, UCAPAWA claimed 40,000 dues-paying members among field workers—particularly in specialty crops in Colorado, Wyoming, Florida and Arizona. One of its main bases was among fish-cannery and sea-food workers in the Pacific Northwest and South Atlantic regions. In California, where the AFL had effective control of the trucking industry, UCAPAWA did not succeed in a major way in organizing the food process industry.

By 1940, UCAPAWA was no longer a viable union among field workers and in large measure its place had been taken by AFL federal locals and independent farm labor locals. (In 1944, UCAPAWA changed its name to the Food, Tobacco and Allied Workers of America [FTA], formalizing its withdrawal from any significant organizing of field workers.)

The decline of UCAPAWA during the 1940's was rapid, accelerated by the anti-Communist hysteria that gripped much of the nation and affected the labor movement, especially after World War II.

More than 100 locals of the Southern Tenant Farmers Union broke away from UCAPAWA within a year. While the apparent issue revolved around the centralization demanded by UCAPAWA, there undoubtedly was also a major area of ideological difference between H. L. Mitchell, who headed the STFU, and Donald Henderson, UCAPAWA president.

It was differences such as these, in which STFU leaders were uneasy about, or openly opposed, unity with Communists in future organizing. Mitchell, who later headed the AFL National Agricultural Workers Union that merged into the AFL Amalgamated Meat Cutters and Butcher Workmen of America, ended his labor career as an official of the Amalgamated.

Many of the UCAPAWA locals later found their way into the CIO. In large part, they became affiliated with the United Packinghouse Workers of America, one of the more moderate unions on the left side of the CIO. Among the UCAPAWA locals that ended up in the UPWA was No. 78 in the Imperial Valley, which had a long history of organization, beginning in the late 1920's, when it was founded as the independent Wrap Packers Association. The shed workers in this local mounted a major strike in the Imperial Valley in 1935 after the CAWIU strike had been smashed.

One of the other unions that came into existence in the years preceding World War II was the Filipino Agricultural Laborers Association, an outgrowth of a walkout by 6,000 Filipino asparagus pickers to protest wage cuts in 1939.

This union, which later changed its name to the Federated Agricultural Laborers Association (FALA), got help from the CIO and from the AFL but initially remained unaffiliated. It worked closely with other independent unions made up mainly of Japanese and Mexican workers, and refused to cross picket lines set up by them. In late 1940, FALA was chartered by the American Federation of Labor.

Organized primarily among Filipino workers around the Sacramento, Stockton, and other California central valley communities, FALA won a number of important strikes, gained union recognition (including written contracts), wage increases and improved working conditions.

Like the UFWOC in later years, this union used many legal channels to prevent illegal exploitation of its members, such as farmers deducting workmen's compensation from the pay checks of Filipino farm workers. In order to help its members improve their economic position, FALA helped establish a food cooperative that sold groceries and Philippine Island foods. The National Advisory Committee on Farm Labor in its 1967 *Farm Labor Organizing, 1905-1967*, said "The unions' goals, like those of UFWOC at present, were not limited to wage increases and recognition by growers; their activities encompassed the farm workers' way of life."

6   The Bracero Era

". . . the class of labor we want is the kind we can send home when we get through with them."   G.W. Guiberson, grower, 1951

"The Mexican migrants of the period 1900-1942 drifted to California in fluctuating numbers and erratic ways. Wherever the Japanese, Filipinos or dustbowl refugees were in the ascendancy the Mexicians remained a source of field labor supplementary to them. In some areas they pushed ahead and became the dominant group. It was in this period that California farmers and the Mexican poor discovered one another, to mutual advantage. Enough Mexicans settled in the state to prove that they were a suitable replenisher of the agricultural labor pool." (Ernesto Galarza, *Merchants of Labor*—San Jose, Rosicrucian Press, Ltd., 1964)

This was the summary description of Mexican labor in California during the pre-bracero period, by Galarza.

With World War II came the expected tightening of the labor market, affecting the cities and fields alike. An adequate farm labor supply was deemed as necessary as was factory labor, to produce war material. The hit-and-miss system of labor recruitment that had so long characterized farm work no longer sufficed.

Mexican workers in the United States living in colonias (relatively isolated rural communities where they maintained their own culture and language) apparently were not able to meet the growers' needs at wages they were willing to pay. Even before Pearl Harbor,

Southwest growers had made known their demands for the massive importation of Mexican workers. They were joined by the Southern Pacific Railroad, which told federal authorities that it needed 5,000 Mexicans to work its maintenence-of-way operations.

As was often the case in matters affecting agribusiness, there was a paradoxical touch in the request to the federal government. The growers had long insisted that they were the epitome of rugged individualism, staunch opponents of government interference with their operations. This posture, of course, did not prevent them from requesting and getting massive government aid to support their often spurious land claims, as well as those of dubious validity. And then there was the whole irrigation system that turned deserts into productive fields—largely financed by government agencies upon the insistence of the growers.

Pressured by the growers, who in 1942 were faced by wholesale raids on the agricultural work force by higher-paying urban industries, the U.S. government worked out the first of a series of war emergency labor agreements with Mexico for the importation of braceros—the Spanish equivalent of a farm hand, one who works with his arms (brazos).

Almost overnight, the haphazard system of recruiting farm labor was replaced by a highly organized system of recruitment. By this method the growers insured themselves of a plentiful supply of cheap labor, and the Mexican government, on the other hand, sent its restless unemployed to work in the U.S. fields at rates of pay considerably above those prevailing on its own farmlands.

Galarza in his very complete and well-documented study on the bracero program said, "the experiment was a success. Logistically, farm labor contracting under government oversight was efficient. Farmers in northern California were supplied with braceros from contracting centers 800 miles away on 48 hours notice. Not a crop was lost. Wages were held in line. The bracero lived up to his reputation as a tractable, obedient, cheerful and eager worker." It was small wonder that the agricultural industry at that time opted in favor of the government-administered migration of Mexicans.

The increasingly tight labor market in agriculture was further aggravated by the sudden and brutal incarceration of Japanese on the West Coast. This removed a sizeable section of the farm-labor force available for picking the crops.

Months before the bombing of Pearl Harbor on December 7, 1941, and the formal entry of the United States into the war, growers were already pressuring Washington for the legalized migration of Mexican braceros. During the previous summer, cotton and beet growers in Arizona, New Mexico and Texas were pressuring the Roosevelt administration for imported Mexican labor. California beet growers called for 3,000 Mexican workers in their fields; orange and lemon growers called for 50,000 Mexican field workers at the rate of 10,000 a month.

On the surface, the agreement between the United States and Mexico appeared to be mutually beneficial. In the main, they provided that Mexican workers be imported only in cases of labor shortages in the United States, and that the Mexican workers be paid "prevailing wages" for the areas in which they worked, but no less than 30 cents an hour. In addition, they would be exempt from military service, and their living and traveling expenses would be paid by the growers. Other important aspects of these written agreements were provisions for employment for no less than three-fourths of the contract period, no discrimination in the United States against the workers, the right to purchase merchandise at places of their own choosing and the assurance of adequate living conditions.

To a greater or lesser degree, all of the above "guarantees" were violated, and some were the cause of major protests by the Mexican workers and their government.

Mexico had not entered into the agreement without some misgivings. All too well remembered was the deportation of more than 50,000 Mexican workers from the United States during the depression. Nor were other round-ups of Mexicans in the United States since the beginning of the 20th century forgotten. Each had taken place when growers no longer needed the imported labor force.

And, in Mexico, unemployment, poverty and disillusionment were prevalent. Mexicans had seen the second attempt in a hundred years to redistribute the land fail with the assassination in 1918 of Emiliano Zapata, who led the revolutionary forces in 1910. California and the United States were possible escapes from the virtually inhuman conditions in Mexico.

Garnished with patriotic rhetoric after Mexico joined in the war against the Axis, Mexican officials sought to place the bracero program in the most favorable light. Two years after the first agreements were consummated, Mexico's foreign secretary, Ezequiel Padilla, announced that they "provide an opportunity to earn high wages, a noble adventure for our youth and, above all, proof of our cooperation in the victory of our cause."

When the war ended, the railroads, whose bracero program was an adjunct to that reached with the growers, were understandably reluctant to terminate it. In 1944 they had contracted for 80,000 track maintenance braceros. When the railway bracero program ended in August, 1945, there were months of procrastination in repatriating the Mexicans.

The State Department on November 15, 1946, proposed the ending within 90 days of the bilateral bracero program in the fields. Not unexpectedly, the growers objected, and soon an extension of the program for agriculture to 1949 was in effect.

Any illusion that the bracero agreements were made between two equal partners was dispelled by events such as that in the Texas cotton fields in 1948. As was their custom, the growers arbitrarily decided that the prevailing price for first picking was $2.50 per hundred pounds, and the Department of Labor, which administered the bracero agreements, approved. In an unusual display of independence, the Mexican government insisted that the rate be set at $3. The U.S. government and the growers, acting to force Mexico into line, opened the borders to thousands of unemployed Mexicans, and soon thereafter the price per hundred pounds was down to $1.50.

Nonetheless, the agreements were again renewed in 1949. But a noticeable change had come about in the administration of the bracero program. Initially it was under the jurisdiction of the Farm Security Administration, a New Deal agency that was in great disfavor with the growers. Then the program was ceded to the War Manpower Commission, and at the end of World War II the Department of Labor took it over. In California, the Labor Department implemented its program through the state's Farm Placement Service, which over the years has virtually been an instrumentality of the growers.

There were Mexican workers who viewed the program, onerous and debasing as it was, as one of the few methods to excape from virtually certain lifelong peonage in Mexico, and there were occasions, as Galarza later related, when the braceros were not quite as tractable as the growers desired.

Years later, a young radical Mexican professor described the bracero program from the Mexican viewpoint. It was, he explained, preferable to a life of semi-starvation and hereditary poverty. "I was a bracero," he explained. He described the path he had taken, comparable to the underground railroad used by Black slaves before the Civil War. It included escaping from the growers to whom he had been contracted, attending U.S. schools and eventually, before returning home, earning a degree at a midwestern university.

While the California growers and those in other large farm states zealously fought for extension of the bracero programs, they simultaneously encouraged bringing across the border large numbers of so-called illegals—those who had not come through the designated bracero recruitment centers and had no documents.

In 1948, Galarza, who was then in the midst of a major organizing effort in the California fields, estimated that "the active wetback supply in California probably exceeded 40,000 men." That was almost 5,000 more than had passed through the bracero centers that year.

In many of the earlier works on farm labor there are many references to "wetbacks" and "illegals" in referring to Mexicans who crossed the border without U.S. documents. In recent years many Chicano movement activists, as well as scholars in Chicano studies, basing themselves on the rights guaranteed Mexicans under the Treaty of Guadalupe-Hidalgo in 1848, challenged the concept of the so-called illegals. They contended that under the treaty, free movement across the border had been guaranteed to Mexicans and that all legislation to the contrary was in violation of that international accord.

Inevitably this view conflicted with labor's traditional position, including that of Chicanos and their leaders like Galarza and Cesar Chavez, who viewed the bracero program and its successors as a direct threat to union organization.

In spite of the obvious difficulties created for unions by the bracero program and the migration of persons without documents, there were many attempts to organize farm workers in the post-

World War II era. In fact, it was the organizing drives of this period —especially the organization of the AFL-CIO Agricultural Workers Organizing Committee in 1959—which led to the 1965 Delano strike and the ultimate formation of the United Farm Workers of America.

When Public Law 78 was enacted in July, 1951, to succeed earlier bilateral pacts, the bracero program was well established, and codifying its regulations into law was relatively simple. By and large, the braceros had met the test that one of the growers, G. W. Guiberson, speaking for the Agricultural Labor Bureau of San Joaquin, described as follows: "We are asking for labor only at certain times of the year—at the peak of our harvest—and the class of labor we want is the kind we can send home when we get through with them."

For the growers the bracero system was ideally suited to combat unionism, even though this was technically in violation of international agreements and U.S. Department of Labor regulations. During the 1950's, strikes were smashed in the Imperial and San Joaquin Valleys through the use of braceros.

But the growers, not satisfied with a cheap labor supply arrangement, supplemented it with use of so-called illegals and then violated agreements, including those which pledged they would not use braceros as strikebreakers. So blatant were the excesses that by the early 1960's the protests mounted into a mass campaign to end the bracero system. The labor movement, Chicano political activists, farm labor unions, churchmen, liberals and other supporters of the farm workers combined to put sufficient pressure on Congress, which ultimately ordered termination of the braceros by December 31, 1964.

The major trade-union effort during much of this era was aimed at tightening or even closing the border to Mexican labor in order to facilitate organization of workers in the fields. It was always easier to organize during periods of a relatively tight labor market, and there were also instances when unionists and braceros joined together, at least temporarily, in common cause.

One such development took place during the 1947 strike against DiGiorgio Farms near Bakersfield. The chief official of the AFL-National Farm Labor Union on the scene was Galarza. He said:

"On the first day of the strike the braceros stopped work. This show of solidarity with the domestic farm hands was as unexpected as it was embarrassing. The sheriff, Mr. John Loustalot, and a representative of the U.S. Department of Agriculture were called in. What precisely they told the Mexicans is not known. The braceros went back to work. They continued on the ranch as its mainstay during the next six weeks, when the federal government yielded to the protests of the union and the men were withdrawn."

More typical have been different responses by Mexican workers. Over the years there have been many instances of persons without documents spirited into struck fields without being informed of the strike in progress, who would quietly leave the scene of the labor dispute as soon as they learned about the picketlines.

Despite the earlier characterization of braceros as subservient and submissive workers, they were not always so. Official government records of complaints by braceros are "worthless," according to Galarza. He reports that:

"The conversation in the camps, the work stoppages in the fields, the desertions, the violations which were obvious even to casual observers, the private legal actions by a few braceros, the quantity of mail addressed to their consuls, the pilgrimages of men from their camps to nearby towns in search of advice from anyone who would listen to them—all were symptoms of a distress which was not officially recorded."

In 1953, braceros harvesting lettuce in Salinas fields stopped work. Out of the 72 Mexican workers involved, nine made less than $20. weekly, 57 made less than $30. a week and 16 were paid more than that amount every week.

Work stoppages as a result of physical abuse evoked especially strong solidarity among the Mexican farm workers and on occasion resulted in work stoppages. There was one stoppage in which 200 men walked off the job and 26 walked to the police station in Delano to complain when an employer struck workers and insisted that his authority must not be challenged. On the Schrier ranch in southern San Joaquin valley, the employer pushed a bracero, manhandled another, threatened a third one and struck still another in the face.

More than 20 years later, in January, 1974, a Florida grower told the *Miami News* that, "We used to own our own slaves, now we rent them." The end of the bracero agreement did not terminate the practice of importing foreign labor. As late as 1974, Black workers from the British West Indies and from other Caribbean nations were brought to Florida to work at cutting cane sugar. It was in reference to these workers that the Florida grower made his comment. It was as applicable to California and Texas field workers in the bracero era as it was to Jamaicans and other Black workers in Florida in 1974.

Every farm-labor organizer expressed the view that unionizing the fields was virtually impossible as long as the growers were able to rely on the biggest pool of potential strikebreakers in the nation—the braceros. Two important developments took place between 1959 and 1962 which did much to set the stage for Congress voting to terminate the bracero program.

First, the lettuce strike in Imperial Valley in 1961, jointly conducted by the Agricultural Workers Organizing Committee and the United Packinghouse Workers Union, had as one of its major immediate goals the exposure of the use of braceros as strikebreakers and the ultimate goal of eliminating the bracero program. Clive Knowles, Packing Union representative who led that strike, believes that Public Law 78, the bracero law, was dealt a lethal blow as a result of this and other strikes in this period, which, in each instance, placed as a primary demand the immediate withdrawal of braceros from struck fields as soon as picket lines were set up.

Secondly, the Chicano political movement was spurred on by the "Viva Kennedy" upsurge prior to the 1960 presidential election. This new political thrust by Chicanos was destined to play an important role in the future organization of the farm workers. Even though President John F. Kennedy in one of his first presidential acts pulled the rug out from under the lettuce strikers, his administration and Congress were under continuous pressure to terminate the bracero program. In this campaign, officials of the Mexican American Political Association, including Bert Corona, who later became MAPA's president and who earlier had been one of the national leaders of the Association of Mexican Americans (ANMA), joined with many others in demanding termination of the bracero program.

A key congressional figure in the campaign to phase out the braceros program was a highly controversial Black member of the

House of Representatives, who, largely because of his ties to the labor movement, had long been a major target of the reactionaries. The late Congressman Adam Clayton Powell from Harlem headed the powerful House Education and Labor Committee, and it was in this committee that the proposed legislation to extend the bracero program was bottled up. Powell, deeply influenced by the militant Black movement and with strong sympathies for all other oppressed people, was the most important legislator in the fight against the bracero program, according to Corona, who was deeply involved in the campaign to end it.

Corona said Powell was the subject of much personal vilification, some of it as a result of his refusal to approve the extension of PL 78. Much of the attack on Powell, which ultimately led to his barring from the House, resulted from his opposition to PL 78's extension.

Difficult as it was to organize farm workers during the bracero era, efforts were made. Several unions attempted it, with varying degrees of success. As has so often been the case, jurisdictional battle over agriculture within the ranks of labor did much to impede the relatively small progress achieved.

Ignoring jurisdictional problems that might later arise with the AFL Amalgamated Meat Cutters and the CIO United Packinghouse Workers, the AFL, in 1946, chartered the National Farm Labor Union. This union, with jurisdiction over all farm workers, including small farmers, was an outgrowth of the Southern Tenant Farmers Union, which was still headed by H. L. Mitchell and which had remained independent since it left UCAPAWA.

In California, the union was led by Galarza, who had previously worked in the fields and was on occasion employed as a day laborer. Before assuming his union post, he had been a specialist on Latin-American affairs at the prestigious Foreign Policy Association; and between 1940 and 1947, he served as chief of the Pan American Union's division of labor and social reform.

By November, 1950, the NFLU organized 26 locals, including sugar cane and mill workers in Puerto Rico, cotton choppers in California, dairy farmers in Louisiana, fruit pickers in Florida and sharecroppers in Arkansas. Among the numerous strikes it conducted, the largest and best-known was against DiGiorgio in 1947, involving an estimated 15,000 workers.

The DiGiorgio family had been among the largest contributors to the fascistic Associated Farmers. After NFLU Local 218 set up its picket lines, the company recruited 200 Mexican-Americans from Texas as strikebreakers, and government officials openly escorted braceros across the picket lines.

This strike provides one of the memorable chapters in farm organizing. A court decision enjoined the union from picketing, because it was argued by the company that the picketing was in violation of the National Labor Relations Act provisions barring secondary boycotts. Even though farm workers were specifically excluded from the scope of this legislation, the court handed down the decision that the farm labor union was subject to its provisions in this instance. For 17 long months the union contested the decision and was ultimately vindicated by a National Labor Relations Board ruling But while the legal battle was in progress the strike was lost.

It was also in this strike that two antilabor figures, one of whom was to go on to the presidency and the other to the California governor's mansion, emerged. For unexplained reasons, Ronald Reagan, then president of the Screen Actor's Guild, was under consideration but had not been chosen to narrate the highly controversial 20-minute film about the strike, "Poverty in the Valley of Plenty." This was during Reagan's Democratic Party period. Harry F. Flannery, who ultimately did the narration, was one of the many involved in the two decades of litigation that followed it. One of a number of legislative probes of the strike—for its alleged Communist connections—was by the House Committee on UnAmerican Activities, which dispatched one of its members, Richard Nixon, to California for hearings. The details of the strike and the numerous hearings it engendered and its effect on future organizing are fully detailed in Galarza's *Spiders in the House and Workers in the Field*.

In one of the hearings before the California State Senate Committee on UnAmerican Activities, there was an airing of the charges made by the DiGiorgios but they failed to produce any evidence of communist tie-in with the union. The red-baiting and violence against the union once again showed that no union was immune from either form of attack. James Price, one of the strike leaders, was wounded when 17 gunmen riddled a cottage in Pixley, California, in which he was holding a union meeting.

The growers, and those who served them, whether in the media or in government, were unimpressed by the pious testimony of AFL officials who insisted that no AFL union could possibly be tainted by communism. Officials of the NFLU had long been known to be opponents of communism. As a matter of fact, at a later stage of the National Farm Labor Union's existence, Galarza, according to Clive Knowles who headed the Packinghouse drive in the fields, warned AFL president George Meany that the CIO Packinghouse Union was gaining adherents in the Imperial Valley and that a successful drive by this union would once again give the left a stronghold.

Before going on to some of the struggles led by the Agricultural Workers Organizing Committee and the Packinghouse Union which, together with the termination of the bracero program and other significant developments, set the stage for the relatively successful Delano strike and ultimate formation of the AFL-CIO United Farm Workers of America, it might be well to examine momentarily the aftermath of some of these organizing drives. After many of them, the organizers of the abortive campaigns reacted much as did Galarza when his National Farm Labor Union was superseded by the AFL-CIO Agricultural Workers Organizing Committee in 1959.

"In 1959, its time and money and stamina having run out, the National Farm Labor Union, now the National Agricultural Workers Union, died with its boots on. It had been broken by attrition from its enemies, while its friends in the high circles of organized labor, watching in disappointment mingled with relief, made other plans." (Ernesto Galarza, *Spiders in the House and Workers in the Fields*–University of Notre Dame Press, 1970)

After serving briefly as an organizer for the Agricultural Workers Organizing Committee (AWOC), Galarza returned to the academic world and to writing about much of the farm-labor history in which he had been involved. He also joined in the sucessful effort to win termination of the bracero program by congress.

While the anger and frustration reflected by Galarza's comments was typical of those who were forced by necessity to leave the fields in search of new endeavors, for most of the farm workers there were no such options. They had nowhere else to go. Among many, the bitterness grew as union after union struck the fields yet failed to win permanent gains for the workers, even though each struggle forced new concessions from the growers. Many who participated in them were blacklisted, and others were compelled to travel long distances in search of employment with growers who did not know of their militancy or union background.

Ultimately such experiences did much to create the atmosphere for the establishment of the most unique farm-labor organization in agricultural history—the National Farm Workers Association (NFWA). Organized by Cesar Chavez, this cooperative association of farm workers met in Fresno in 1962 with about 200 attending. The major emphasis was on building a credit union, cooperative and other "self-help" projects. Even though it was not organized as a trade union, the leaders of the NFWA set a significant five-year goal: to be able to bargain collectively with the growers by 1967.

It was led by farm workers from California's Central Valley, who from the outset made it clear that they would continue to live in the same style as others in the fields and that they would remain on the scene no matter how great the difficulties. The NFWA aimed to build a solid base by creating a dues-paying membership organization and structure which would make available to farm workers the kind of services readily available to much of the rest of the population. But even these modest goals of the new organization were not met within the time schedule outlined by the founders.

Historically, AWOC may well be recalled primarily as the forerunner of the later organization of the AFL-CIO United Farm Workers Union. If so, it was from all indications a necessary prelude to the formation of the militant union of agricultural workers, which by 1970 had made a greater breakthrough than any other in the history of farm-labor organizing.

With the formation of AWOC, there began a series of developments within a three-year period that in large measure set the stage for, and deeply affected, the grape strike which began in Delano on September 8, 1965. That strike was triggered by the rank-and-file decision of AWOC. After having initially won some concessions in the spring of 1965 in California's Coachella Valley, about 100 miles north of the Mexican boader, the Filipino grape pickers, who made up the largest part of the AWOC activists, demanded similar wages from Delano area ranchers. It was the refusal of these growers to meet the demands that brought on the strike that Chavez and his

NFWA voted to join, at a mass meeting on September 16, 1965.

From its inception, AWOC appeared to be foredoomed to failure. Its plans and financing were impressive enough, at least by standards set by previous farm labor unions, but in the selection of its leadership the AFL-CIO displayed a not-untypical lack of understanding of the special problems of farm organizing.

Norman Smith had shared in the glories of one of labor's finest movements—organization of the auto workers during the late 1930's. It was during that time, when the labor movement was desperately seeking trained or untrained organizers, that Smith found a likely union activist on a General Motors assembly line. He was Jack Livingstone, who by 1959 had risen to the post of AFL-CIO director of organization, and whose responsibility it was to choose the new AWOC director.

The 300-pound Smith was 62 when he left his supervisory position at the Kaiser steel mill in Fontana, California, to join once again in the work that most pleased him, organizing. Almost half a century had passed since Smith had come close to agriculture and then only on his parents' farm in Missouri. Smith, by all accounts, worked hard, but it was soon evident that the California valleys were far different from the pavements of Dearborn and Detroit.

According to the account of Joan London and Henry Anderson in *So Shall Ye Reap*, (New York, Appollo Editions, Inc., 1971), Franz Daniel, AFL-CIO assistant director of organization, told an AWOC staff meeting, "Don't kid yourself. Meany just got tired of going to international conventions and being needled by labor people from smaller, poorer foreign countries, who could point out that they at least had organized farm workers, while the American labor movement hadn't. He set up AWOC to get them off his back."

From all available accounts, this quote seems to sum up the situation accurately. Anderson was on the AWOC staff during its early days and apparently sat in at the meeting where Daniel spoke. But to place all of the blame on Meany and the top AFL-CIO officials for the developments during the AWOC era would seem to be too simplistic. Jurisdictional battles that involved the AFL Amalgamated Meat Cutters and Butcher Workmen and CIO Packinghouse Workers deeply affected the developments. The last named international had inherited locals that had been affiliated with the CIO Food, Tobacco and Agricultural Workers. These were shed workers, and it was mainly Anglos who held the higher-paid jobs. Earlier, some of these locals were among those in UCAPAWA.

Officials of the NFLU, by now the NAWU, embittered by Meany's chartering of AWOC and what they considered betrayal of the AFL-CIO obligation to the older union, entered the Amalgamated. Thus the jurisdiction over the farm workers became a pawn not only of the seemingly endless intrigue in the fields by generals, most of whom had no armies, but also of the over-all anti-Communist hysteria which was sweeping the labor movement. The Packinghouse Workers had retained its membership in the CIO, following the purge of the other left unions from the CIO in 1949. Even though it made a number of concessions to the witch-hunters as a price for continued CIO affiliation, it was nevertheless viewed by the CIO hierarchy as being to the left. In fact some of the union's most important bases were left-led. (In 1965 UPWA merged with the Amalgamated Meat Cutters.)

There were also accusations by Galarza and some AWOC staff members that AWOC was working too closely with the Packinghouse Union. While multinational in membership, and more particularly in the support it got from workers in the field, AWOC was predominantly Filipino-led by the time it began its series of strikes in 1965. In fact, one of the most significant accomplishments of AWOC was that it had become the center of activity for a large number of Filipino trade unionists, many of whom had been members of other farm unions.

C. Al Green succeeded Norman Smith as AWOC director in 1964. Green, a long-time organizer in the building trades, brought one highly dubious concept to field organizing—signing contracts with labor contractors. Instead of going after the prime exploiters —the growers—AWOC organizers went after this subsidiary force in the fields. It was true that the farm workers in many instances hated the contractors more then they did the growers, since the contractors extracted an additional fee that came out of the field worker's wage, but their resentment was no more effective than if city workers centered their main fire on employment agencies rather than on the corporations that employed and exploited them.

Nevertheless, according to the August, 1961, newsletter of the

National Advisory Committee on Farm Labor, "Farm wages in California rose about 25% from their mid-1958 levels. The number of Mexican nationals employed in the state dropped as higher wages attracted more domestic workers. Public pressure generated by the (AWOC) campaign helped to extend disability insurance to agriculture in California."

One of the most important battles in AWOC's brief existence took place in the Imperial Valley lettuce fields in 1961. At that time AWOC was in one of its perennial crises, and Smith responded to the urging of Clive Knowles that he move his staff from the dormant Stockton area to the Mexican border.

This provides us with an example of the difficulty in arriving at an unbiased view of the events of that period. To Anderson and London (Anderson having been on the AWOC staff) AWOC's participation in that strike was "an adventure with UPWA (Packinghouse) in Imperial Valley," and the same authors say that it proved again to Galarza that Smith was "very partial toward UPWA . . ."

One gets a completely different viewpoint from two of the union officials involved in that strike. Jerry Bresheares, executive secretary of UPWA Local 78B, who helped lead that strike, relates how it was a last-ditch fight to prevent bracero starvation wages being imposed on the entire work force.

To Knowles, the UPWA strategist in farm labor, the '61 lettuce strike presented a multifaceted challenge, which, if successful, would seriously weaken the impact of braceros. He, like Galarza and others, was convinced that successful union organization in the fields could not take place until the braceros were eliminated as as effective strike-breaking force. Knowles had been counting on several factors, one of which was the election in 1960 of Kennedy and the appointment of former CIO counsel Arthur Goldberg as the secretary of labor. This election might lead, Knowles figured, to the enforcement of the section in PL 78 that barred the use of braceros in strikes, a provision which had been largely ignored by growers and federal officials.

Local 78B, a state-wide local among shed workers, was in the main composed of Anglo workers, considered to be among the most skilled in the fields. It had a long and diversified history. Formed in the late 1920's, it struck in the Imperial Valley in 1935 and in the

Salinas Valley in 1936. Even though it did not join in the 1934 CAWIU strike, it was among the earliest affiliates of UCAPAWA.

When the local affiliated with UPWA in 1953, its members had undergone a traumatic experience. Shed workers, working in a man-and-wife team in the 1949-52 period, could earn more than $200 a week during the short season, according to Bresheares. "Then we were replaced by braceros at 70 cents and hour and the growers would cheat them out of half ot that and move them around like slaves."

With increased mechanization, including packing in the fields instead of in the sheds, the local decided to affiliate with UPWA. "We attempted to do one of two things," Bresheares explained, "either organize the field workers and bring the cost (of packing labor) up or prevent the importation of braceros by the government."

Knowles, who had been sent to California in 1957 by his union, said that the first idea of a strike in lettuce came in 1959 when he was approached by a delegation of union members led by "Machete" Francisco Olivares, whom he described as "a fantastic guy with a beautiful voice and a great presence."

But the idea of a strike was resisted on a local level and not even raised with the national union because Knowles believed that there was little, if any, support for the idea. In the years preceding 1960, the national UPWA campaigned incessantly for rigid enforcement of PL78.

In 1960, thousands of U.S. nationals residing in the Mexican border city of Mexicali, because the cost of living was considerably lower there, would cross the border daily and assemble in "the hole" in Calexico, adjoining the wire fence which separates the United States from Mexico. The growers would hire several hundred workers and the rest were told to go home. Then the growers brought in braceros to work the fields.

"PL78 was predicated on the fact that the braceros would not be used where it had an adverse effect on the domestic work force," Bresheares said. "That was a joke. The adverse effect was obvious and immediate but you had to prove it to the government and that was a difficult task."

Early in 1960 the Imperial Valley growers were paying Chicano and Filipino field workers piece rates, while braceros worked on an hourly basis. As a result, the pieceworkers, even those working in what Breasheares described as "the scrubby fields," made considerably more than the braceros. The union then tried to be cute, charging the growers with discrimination against the braceros. The growers responded first by setting the hourly wage at 83 cents an hour, while hiring domestic field workers exclusively through the labor contractors on piece-work rates. When the administration of Governor Edmund Brown gave signs of responding to the union complaints, the growers evened all wages out, 90 cents an hour for braceros and domestic workers alike.

More than 600 workers came to a union rally after the union put out a leaflet which demanded a $1.25 an hour rate plus piecework. Meanwhile, Knowles made contact with AWOC in Stockton and reported on the situation in the Imperial Valley. Knowles urged AWOC which had been ordered to concentrate its organizing in the Stockton area, to throw in its lot with UPWA in the Imperial Valley campaign, agreeing that all workers in the field would become AWOC members and all those on machines and in the sheds would be in UPWA jurisdiction.

The strike committee of 30 was all set to go on December 13, 1960—the deadline for the walkout. Knowles described the technique. It was typical of the kind of ingenuity which had to be used by a union seeking to overcome a combination of odds—from growers and government agencies.

"We had a decoy truck that would take off from El Centro and maybe head out for Brawley (to the north), Holtville (east) or some other damn place. And the sheriff's deputies and everybody else would take off, following the whole bunch of guys with picket signs. There was a law in that county that you couldn't use a loud speaker.

"Meanwhile, we'd have it all set up that in such and such a field there would be a walkout. And we would get out there with a couple of cars and a loudspeaker. Meanwhile, we had arranged for a truck to meet us there and pick up the people who we believed would come out of the field. Soon they (the field workers) heard the loudspeaker message and pretty soon a few backs would straighten up and pretty soon a slow walk would start and out they would come.

"At the same time we would have telephones in the staff cars

—that was a very key thing—and we would phone the Farm Placement Service that we had struck such and such location and that we would be by their office in five minutes to lead them out there." (Interview with Clive Knowles, June 1973)

Sixteen times this operation was repeated, and each time the state agency registered each and evey worker who had left the fields. The unions proved that they had the backing of an overwhelming majority of the more than 3,000 domestic workers, and the unions demanded that all braceros be removed from the fields, as was required by law.

Simultaneously, the demand for removing the braceros from the struck fields was relayed to union representatives in Mexico City and Washington, D.C. In Mexico City, union representatives made quite a point about the braceros being paid about a third of the wage domestic workers were getting.

While the striking unions had picket lines in Washington, D.C., and even reached into Mexico, the growers were making their own move to destroy the strike, and the jurisdictional fight within the AFL-CIO affected the UPWA's financial status. The so-called prolabor Kennedy administration was determined to ignore the demands of the unions.

Growers from throughout the state, obviously alarmed by the possibility of a successful strike in the Imperial Valley, organized a march down the state for an expected showdown. "These were all brass-knuckle boys and young foremen," Knowles said. It was obvious that a major fight was shaping up, probably north of Brawley, on a desert road.

On the morning of the scheduled battle, Imperial County sheriff's deputies were stationed near Brawley. But the expected battle never took place, because the unions, utilizing the element of surprise, had instead mobilized their members on the border at about 5 a.m. The union members drove to one of the major camps where braceros had assembled and, in a dramatic mass action, picketed with 1,500 workers. The gates were padlocked.

When the sheriff's deputies arrived at about 7 a.m., the pickets all sat down in the road. About 750 deputies and others stood there with shotguns. Meanwhile the fenced-in braceros were climbing

over the wire enclosure to join the striking workers. News and
union photographers were there, obviously influencing the conduct
of the deputies. Thirteen were arrested on a variety of charges that
morning and a few days later the deputies broke into the union hall
and made a mass arrest. A total of 52 were arrested and they were
held on a total of $450,000 bail.

This was the moment that AFL-CIO president George Meany
chose to announce that he was calling off the strike and that AFL-
CIO organizers were being recalled. Smith and his fellow organizers
left immediately thereafter.

"Later I found out that Kennedy had said to Goldberg, 'get rid of
that thing,' " Knowles said. So Meany was part of that operation that
Goldberg and Kennedy were putting on. In effect they were telling
Meany to 'get it (the Imperial Valley strike) out of our hair, we don't
have time for it'. "

Meanwhile, the promised financial support from the California
State Federation of Labor, which had been committed by
Secretary-Treasurer Thomas Pitts, was not forthcoming. The pledge
had been to donate $15,000 to the strike from the state organization
and to undertake to raise an additional $100,000 from its affiliates.
When asked about his promise, Pitts showed Knowles the telegram
he received from the Amalgamated Meat Cutters—which charged
that UPWA and AWOC were infringing on its jurisdiction. "It was
all part of the red threat business," Knowles later commented,
"That the Packinghouse Workers were the left coming in to take
over the farm workers."

The strike was broken, but it did have its impact. The determination of the farm workers to stick with the union was once again
displayed at the July, 1961, trial when farm workers from throughout the state returned to the scene of "the crime" to face the court.
Not a dime of the outrageous bail was forfeited.

As a result of the strike, "several of the growers did lose their
braceros that year," Knowles said. "The piece rate was put back on
and within a year or two workers were again making between two
and three dollars an hour at peak season.

"So the strike did succeed in getting the wages up and did begin
to break the back of the bracero system."

The Battle of the Bracero was fought not only on the picket

lines—although this by far was its most dramatic confrontation. But federal government officials found themselves plagued by this issue no matter where they went. At a Biltmore Hotel (Los Angeles) hearing on farm labor, Assistant Secretary of Labor W.Willard Wirtz was talking when 1,200 farm labor supporters marched into the hall. They had been picketing outside, and it was the militant Catholic priest, the Rev. Thomas McCullough of Stockton, who suggested they deliver their message personally to the assistant secretary. Among those leading that demonstration, organized by UPWA, was Ernesto Galarza.

During the lettuce strike Cesar Chavez had been in Brawley, where he was organizing for the Community Service Organization, a Chicano movement which had been started with the assistance of Saul Alinsky, Chicago organizer of community organization. In 1959 the UPWA, at Alinsky's urging, had funded a CSO program in Oxnard in Ventura County, and there Chavez organized an effective community organization while the UPWA concentrated its efforts on the field workers.

For a wide variety of reasons, many of the forces, related one way or another to the farm-labor movement, after the lettuce strike concentrated their main energies on ending the bracero program. It was a many-sided, unifying campaign that brought together people like Knowles and Galarza and that many in the Catholic clergy and the Chicano political movement joined.

In retrospect, Knowles said that "without the removal of the bracero system it never would have been possible to organize the farm workers in California. That was a pre-condition for organizing."

Interviews with Chicano political activists such as Bert Corona and veterans of farm labor organizing, including Galarza and Larry Itliong, reflected similar views. What the Viva Kennedy movement had not been able to influence during the Imperial Valley lettuce strike, immediately after President Kennedy's inauguration was accomplished in large measure through the activity of politically oriented Chicanos in helping to terminate Public Law 78.

7 Setting for Delano

"Let freedom ring from the curvaceous peaks of California."   Martin Luther King, Jr.

The single most important factor that triggered farm-labor developments in California in the mid-1960's was the termination of the bracero program. Not only was this recognized by veteran farm-labor organizers but also by churchmen and journalists who later studied the developments that led to the historic Delano strike. Rev. Wayne C. Hartmire, Jr., Director of the California Migrant Ministry (later renamed National Farm Workers Ministry), was one of the clergymen who had been associated with the National Farm Workers Association from its inception, having attended its founding convention in Fresno. On July 22, 1967, he published a relatively detailed study on *"The Church and the Emerging Farm Workers Movement."* In it he said:

"It must also be recognized that the Delano Strike began *after* the termination of the bracero program (PL 78). It is not possible to describe adequately the demoralizing effect this program had on domestic workers. Many strikes were crushed in advance by this demoralization; others were beaten by the use of braceros as strikebreakers or by the threatened use of 'braceros.' " (Emphasis by Rev. Hartmire.)

Another priest who for many years championed the cause of the farm workers was Father James L. Vizzard, S.J., of the National

115

Catholic Rural Life Conference. At a federal labor hearing in 1964, he said that growers "need to be made to understand in what century and in what kind of economy and society they are living and operating."

In his book *Delano*, (New York, Farrar, Strauss and Giroux, Inc. 1947) John Gregory Dunne observed that "the end of the bracero program stabilized California's labor force for the first time in years." He added that "no longer could growers drain off the south-of-the-border labor pool that kept domestic wages depressed and, because of the threat that Mexican nationals would take over the available jobs, discouraged agricultural unrest."

Bankers found it impossible to restrain their delight with the situation during the period when braceros flooded California's fields. "When a banker gets down on the farm, it's hard to hold back the superlatives," according to the January 1965 Southern California Report of the Security First National Bank. It was in this same report that the land in the fertile San Joaquin Valley was described as "among the richest in the world." and that "all that is required to produce bountiful crops in the Southland is water." And water was forthcoming, largely subsidized by U.S. taxpayers.

In 1963, farm production in the 14 southern California counties came to almost $2.4 billion. All but one of these counties were among the 100 top agricultural counties in the county. Fresno, Tulare and Kern Counties were the nation's top three counties in farm production. They were also the very counties that in 1965 became the prime targets for the Delano-based grape strike.

When the bracero program ended, some of the fear also left the fields. In describing the typical reaction of growers to workers' protests during the bracero era, Jerry Bresheares said, "In the old days the braceros were shipped back home and the domestics were fired outright and told they could walk home from the fields."

Bresheares, official of AFL-CIO United Packinghouse Local 78b, who had spent all of his adult life in Imperial Valley as a farm worker and as an elected union official, described the immediate aftereffect of the termination of the bracero program. "It was a kind of paradise as far as the lettuce workers were concerned." While in some instances wages overnight jumped sixfold, they soon "levelled off," he said. But the new level of wages for lettuce workers in Imperial

Valley remained at three times the earlier $1.25 an hour. In lettuce the season is short and intense, and relatively high hourly wages are not reflected in a high annual wage.

It was also during the bracero era that Cesar Chavez displayed the talent for utilizing press coverage that later became a major factor in calling national and international attention to the struggle he led in the Delano fields.

In the Oxnard, California, area Chavez headed the Community Service Organization (CSO), which was increasingly reacting to the plight of the farm workers. There braceros were being given work while other farm workers remained jobless. Every day, over a span of several months, Chavez led jobless farm laborers to the offices of the local growers' association and then later to the California Farm Placement Service. After filing 1,100 separate complaints, the workers, under Chavez's leadership, succeeded in getting an in- spector from the U.S. Labor Department to come to the fields. He ordered the hiring of unemployed domestic farm workers before permitting the use of braceros.

With typical grower arrogance, the domestic workers were fired and replaced by braceros once the inspector left the scene. This charade was repeated several times. Ultimately Chavez decided to try to bring this situation to the public's attention. One day, in the presence of television cameras and news reporters, he led a march of unemployed workers into the fields where braceros were work- ing. He came well prepared with documentary evidence that braceros were at work while local domestics were not.

The resulting publicity touched off a probe, after which the chief of the State Farm Placement Bureau and two other officials resigned under pressure, and another top official in this state agency was fired after it had been demonstrated that he had accepted bribes from the local growers. What was revealed was not unusual, in the opinion of many, but the fight-back and the exposure led by Chavez was out of the ordinary and a forerunner of things to come.

It was a difficult time for organizers in the fields. Trade unionists and community organizers in scores of small farm communities joined with a small but dedicated group of clergymen in trying to develop one or another form of collective organization. The frustra- tions were great but the cadre which was later to create the National

Farm Workers Association was learning well the hard and difficult lessons of organization.

Meanwhile, in much of the rest of the nation things were seething on the campuses and in the streets. The civil rights movement had gone through a rapid evolution from the "Freedom Rides" of 1961 to the massive August 28, 1963, "March on Washington," where the late Rev. Martin Luther King delivered his history-making "I Have A Dream" speech. The 1964 murder in Mississippi of Michael Schwerner, James E. Chaney and Andrew Goodman was followed the next year by the equally shocking assassination of Black nationalist Malcolm X in New York City.

It was a time of reassessment in the student and civil rights movements. The considerable effect of the Black nationalist movement and the new trends in the supportive white radical student movement was matched by the demand of Chicano activists for their own concept of equal time. Militant Catholic priests, no longer satisfied with pious phrases, seized upon the more progressive church encyclicals as a road to becoming socially involved. Some had done so in the civil rights movement, but others, long associated with the farm-labor struggle, began to become even more active. And an increasing number of younger priests openly cast their lot with the farm workers. These clergymen joined with Protestant ministers, who since 1957 had been working with the California Migrant Ministry in support of the movement among farm workers.

Communists, in keeping with their traditional working class position as well as with their Party's historic role in the fields, were among the very first to come to the support of the farm workers. Over the years the Communist Party had emphasized the special oppression of Chicanos and the urgency of backing all issues and organizations effectively fighting this oppression. In addition all organizations of the left appeared anxious to join in the support movement in behalf of the campesinos. The newly emerging farm labor movement provided the left with an opportunity to assist in the drive for unionization as well as the means to support the demands of the very poor and to join once again with the Chicanos and Mexicans, the single largest oppressed group on the West Coast.

Within the ranks of organized labor, organizations such as the

International Longshoremen's and Warehousemen's Union, the AFL-CIO United Packinghouse Workers Union and the independent Mine Mill and Smelter Workers with a large Chicano membership still were characterized by significant left influences. This was reflected in the support they gave to the emerging farm-labor movement.

Liberal Democrats in California, in search of a cause which would ally them with other than the largely white middle-class grouping that made up its own active core, was also waiting in the wings, so to speak.

In the view of the Rev. Hartmire, who was deeply involved in mobilizing strike support activity in the opening days of the Delano strike, the most important support came from "students, SNCC (Student Non-violent Coordinating Committee) and CORE (Congress of Racial Equality), the churches, the California Center for Community Development (CCCD) and some parts of the labor movement." (All quotes of Reverend Wayne C. Hartmire are from *The Church and the Emerging Farm Workers Movement. A Case Study*–National Farm Workers Ministry, 1967). SNCC and CORE later endorsed the union-initiated boycott of Schenley products.

Chavez has credited the Migrant Ministry with being the most important supportive group to the union during the early weeks of the strike. The CMM came to this stage as a result of unusual circumstances. Of the Migrant Ministry, Hartmire said, "In some ways this unit (CMM) is a stepchild of the denominations, weakly supported and out on the periphery doing a job that the mainstream of the (church) institution hasn't taken seriously. This is one of the important reasons why the CMM had the freedom to go as far as it did in relating to the NFWA and its revolutionary goals."

He added that "when the crisis over Delano came, it was not possible for church leadership to disown the CMM. The denominations were inevitably drawn into the farm labor conflict!"

An interesting account of the behind-the-scenes battle in the farm communities in the years preceding La Huelga was given by Hartmire:

"The bracero issue developed into a raging controversy in California from 1961 to 1964 because for the first time the forces that opposed the mass importation of foreign labor seemed to be gaining ground. In fact, in 1964, Congress refused to extend PL 78. The churches played an important role in that struggle and the CMM was at the center of it. The bracero fight prepared us psychologically for conflict (nobody—especially middle class preachers—likes going around calling them names); it also narrowed our base of support.

"Because of the bracero issue and some CO (Community Organizing) efforts by staff, the CMM began to lose financial support from growers and their business associates. J. G. Boswell (who had the fourth largest land holding in California at that time) cut off $6,147 of support over a two-year period. By the time Delano hit in 1965 we had already lost a substantial portion of the financial support that was tied to social amelioration and not at all to social change.

"Also, during the period of the bracero fight, denominational leaders and other churchmen were being exposed firsthand to the realities of social injustice in the southern part of the United States. When the Huelga (strike) conflict began to reach into the life of the churches these same leaders could not help but see the parallel."

In 1964 the CMM, in conjunction with other organizations, hired three staff representatives—the Rev. David Havens, Rev. James Drake and Gilberto Padilla—for a Tulare County project aimed at building "a coalition of people's organizations that would change the political shape of the county." As a result of this ambitious undertaking, which deeply involved three organizers who were to later play an important role in the Delano strike, the Tulare County churches withdrew their support from the Migrant Ministry.

Pleased as Chavez was over some early church support for his strike, he was also quite critical. In an interview with the Rev. Mark Day, a Franciscan priest who came to Delano as spiritual advisor to the strikers as well as an active picket, Chavez spelled out some of his criticism. The union leader said, "You know there are many changes in the church today. But many of these changes, like the new ritual of the Mass, are merely external. What I like to see is a priest get up and speak about things like racism and poverty. But, even when you hear about these things from the pulpit, you get the feeling that they aren't doing anything significant to alleviate these evils. They are just talking about them."

In Delano, "the church has been a stranger to us," said Chavez who had found the local Catholic Church doors closed to his union in the early days of the strike. (Cesar Chavez, interview with Mark Day, February, 1973)

Earlier in the strike Father James Vizzard had been told to leave the farm area and not to "interfere" with the local situations. Vizzard, whom Mark Day described as "a feisty and articulate Jesuit," had nevertheless come back to Delano on December 13, 1965 as the spokesman for the Catholic Church, following the California Farm Bureau Federation's scathing denunciation of church involvement in the strike. He was part of a delegation of eleven clergymen of all denominations who had come to Delano to declare, "We reject the heresy that churches and synagogues are to be concerned only with spiritual matters. The suffering of farm workers and their children cries to heaven and demands the attention of men of conscience."

They backed the strike since "no other procedures have been opened to the workers" and called on the Delano growers to negotiate with the striking unions—the NFWA and AWOC. They also publicly called for a congressional investigation into the situation in the Delano area.

The Catholic priests who had come to Delano followed in the tradition of earlier clergymen such as Father Thomas McCullough and Father Donald McDonnell, who had long been active in support of farm-labor organizing.

When the Kern County sheriff's deputies began arresting persons on the picket line for reading aloud Jack London's famous colorful description of a strikebreaker, the CMM organized a "Conference of Christian Concern" to challenge this latest attempt to strike the First Amendment of the Constitution from Kern County. Of the 44 persons arrested on the picketline on October 19, 1965, nine were ministers and there were twelve women.

Meanwhile, in Berkeley, Chavez was addressing a strike-support rally of hundreds of University of California students. He was one of the many union leaders who had quickly fanned out to the campuses in search of financial and other support. When Chavez told the students of the arrest of the 44 pickets and strike supporters, the students responded with more than $2,000 in donations. Many of them later came to Delano to join the picket lines established by the NFWA and AWOC.

The student support was not limited to such traditional centers of militant activity as Berkeley. Chicano students from throughout the state immediately became aware of the new development in the fields and some of them quickly made their way to Delano. One of them was Maria Flores, a young Chicana from Bakersfield, whose social consciousness was aroused by the civil rights movement and who later joined the strike movement as an active participant in the early activity of the NFWA.

Bert Corona was a long-time labor organizer and Chicano political activist who was involved in supporting the NFWA from its earliest days. He said, "It was only natural that in the 1960's the idea to organize the farm workers had come to its day. . . . It took the combination of the civil rights movement that was sweeping across the land involving Black people as well as new groups of people which later became the reservoir of support for the farm workers. Cesar Chavez recognized this." (Interview with Bert Corona, April 1973.)

In the Spring of 1965, six months before the beginning of the strike, Chavez invited some of the state's more active Chicano organizers to meet with him in Delano. "He made a very strong point," Corona said, "that the reason the farm workers organizing drive could win in the days ahead was because they could ally themselves with a new feature in American social and political activity—the movement for civil rights, the movement of the youth and the movement of the poor—to become involved in doing something about the farm workers' needs."

During the months preceding the Delano strike, the Chicano activists joined with many others in building support for the new movement of farm workers. Up and down the state a struggle was waged throughout the spring of 1965. The growers were demanding the return of the bracero program, or some form of it. In this they enlisted the aid of Governor Brown, who, despite some progressive acts, had long maintained a warm relationship with the growers, many of whom, like the governor, were Democrats.

So intense was the debate that Secretary of Labor W. Willard Wirtz came to California for an unprecedented four-day tour and arrived at the conclusion that there was no need to import braceros. But he did leave the door open for some recruiting of Mexican nationals under Public Law 414 of the McCarran Act.

It was at one of the public hearings conducted by Wirtz that the National Farm Workers Association testified flatly in opposition to the bracero program or any modification of it. Wirtz had set the "prevailing wage" for field workers at $1.40 an hour. This was the wage which had to be paid by the growers if they were to be eligible to recruit labor under PL 414. A number of growers decided that they no longer had a need for imported workers—not at those prices.

AWOC, which had hoped to spend a protracted period laying the groundwork for future strikes, suddenly found itself enmeshed in a series of them in the Imperial and Coachella Valleys. A strike had also broken out in Ventura County.

As a result of the Imperial Valley strike, wages rose to $1.40 an hour for the tomato harvest—in some cases this represented a 30-cents-an-hour raise. But no contracts were signed with the growers, only with some of the contractors.

The Coachella Valley grape strike in May, 1965, was the touchstone for the subsequent Delano area walkout. One of the more unusual strikes took place at the David Freedman Co. ranch, where the Filipinos sat in the camps for more than a week while Chicano AWOC members picketed the property. As in the Imperial Valley, AWOC succeeded in winning the $1.40 an hour rate but could not gain a contract.

This Coachella strike marked the precedent that directly affected the Delano walkout. In 1967, when it seemed as if the grape strike was stalemated following the big breakthroughs with Schenley and DiGiorgio, it was the Coachella growers who became the first local grape ranchers to settle and thereby set the stage for the Delano settlement that won the grape strike.

"My idea is that La Huelga is traced to the feelings about La Raza." This was Jerry Bresheares' comment about the interrelation between the Chicano movement and the farm strikes.

In the pre-strike period the sentiments about La Raza were reflected in another way. At the July 23-24, 1965 convention of the Mexican-American Political Association (MAPA) in Fresno, what was essentially a lovers' quarrel ended up in an amazing display of Raza unity.

MAPA had been one of the foremost organizations fighting to end the bracero program. The predominantly Democratic organization kept pressuring Governor Brown against further importation of braceros. In what some considered an ill advised action, MAPA agreed to help the governor with a labor-recruitment program, in part to answer the complaints of the growers about an alleged labor shortage.

One of the organizations that took exception to this was the National Farm Workers Association. Dolores Huerta, one of its top organizers and officers, led a small picket line in front of the MAPA convention in Fresno. But when she was invited into the hall to address the convention banquet, more than half the people there gave her a standing ovation. She spoke bluntly and told them to get out of the labor recruiting business.

In essence, the MAPA leaders told the NFWA that it was willing to comply with any wish that those who were organizing in the fields demanded. While MAPA over the years had played a significant and meaningful role in mobilizing support for the grape strikers, it has had its differences with Chavez and others on tactical questions. But, in the main, the differences have been kept at the family-quarrel level. Public displays such as the picket line in Fresno were rare.

Of all the support that the union drive got from La Raza—the Chicanos—there is little doubt that MAPA was not only among the first to come to its aid, but also probably the most consistent during the strike's early years.

Just as the civil rights movement moved millions of Black people, deeply affected the student movement, and developed consciousness of La Raza, so too did it have an impact on sections of the labor movement. Fortunately for the farm workers, one of the leaders of labor who reflected this new consciousness was Paul Schrade, then the United Auto Workers Union regional director on the West Coast.

Schrade was not an ordinary union official either in appearance or demeanor. He was a bearded young man, a former aerospace worker at the North American plant in Los Angeles, who responded with alacrity and enthusiasm to every call for assistance from the farm workers.

In 1962 he had taken a routine trip to Stockton to meet with the leaders of AWOC. This had been done at the request of UAW president Walter Reuther who, concerned over discussions in top AFL-CIO ranks abandoning AWOC, called on Schrade to check things out for him. In the opinion of the UAW national officers, it seemed that AFL-CIO President George Meany was preparing to scuttle this latest AFL-CIO campaign in the fields.

Trade-union politics being what it is, even those who try to emasculate programs are zealous of their jurisdiction. When the Washington D.C. office of the AFL-CIO got word that Schrade had been to Stockton, officials (AFL-CIO officers) made their first formal inquiry with AWOC to find out what Schrade was up to. Al Green later told UAW officials that this was the very first reaction to anything about AWOC that he had gotten from the national AFL-CIO.

Roy Reuther, Walter's brother and also a top UAW official, and Schrade met with Chavez around the time the strike began. They had also met with AWOC leaders but it was clear from the outset that their main allegiance was to the NFWA and to Chavez.

William Kircher, then the AFL-CIO national director of organization, who had come from the UAW ranks where he and Schrade were in opposing factions, was another union official who had a deep commitment to the farm workers. Time and again he, like Schrade, displayed his personal involvement in La Huelga.

Aside from such top union officials, there were many like Don Watson and James Herman from the ILWU Ship Clerks Local in the San Francisco Bay area who displayed a consistent commitment to the farm workers and Chavez. Whenever feasible they supported UFWOC's battles on the San Francisco docks and regularly collected funds and food from dock workers for the Huelgistas.

8 Delano

". . . she came back with groceries. She said,
'you take it because Cesar Chavez is a saint.'
And I told her no, he is a man."

Augustin Lira, farm worker, 1965

One night in 1962 in Delano a most unusual meeting took place. Filipino gamblers, apparently disturbed over a possibly successful AWOC organizing drive in the grape fields, met to discuss a course of action. Disturbance of the status quo, including their income, was of direct concern to the gambling fraternity. Thus they were talking about a strange subject—how to influence the growers to raise wages and thereby make it more difficult for the AFL-CIO union to organize.

Others, for more fundamentally concerned with wages and working conditions, were also among those present. Two persons in particular, who were destined to share the leadership in one of the most historic strikes in all of farm-labor history, were there. Larry Itliong, a small man who incessantly chomped away at a cigar, and who was a union organizer in the fields for many years, accompanied AWOC organizer Norman Smith. Also, there was Cesar Chavez, quietly taking it all in. Itliong and Chavez, who had never before worked jointly on any organizing campaign, exchanged no words, barely noting each other's presence. While no conclusions were arrived at that night, the meeting reflected the issue—union organization and some of the personalities involved.

In the early 1960's, there appeared to be several components in Delano, some of which were apparently not even conscious of the others. AWOC, organizing as the AFL-CIO union, had as its main base Filipino fieldworkers. Meanwhile, in 1962, Cesar Chavez had begun to organize the NFWA, overwhelmingly composed of Chicanos. And then there were the growers who, having successfully resisted unionism for decades, gave no sign that they felt their position threatened by the still relatively small organizations of union workers.

The fog that virtually engulfs Delano in the winter, even on occasion compelling the NFWA to cancel important meetings because of the dangerous travelling conditions, seemed similarly to envelop the movements in that small city. At that time, it seemed outlandish to presume that when Delano reached its hundreth anniversary in 1973, it would also signalize one of farm labor unionism's most impressive victories.

In most respects Delano is little different from scores of other communities in the rich Central Valley of California, and it shares much of what has gone to make up the valley's history.

On July 14, 1873, the Southern Pacific Railroad reached Delano, its southernmost point, and thereby gave that community a starting date for its history. If you wanted to travel farther south, you went by stagecoach. While traditional historians thus mark Delano's origin in terms of the Southern Pacific, those who view history as a reflection of social changes probably will designate September 8, 1965, as the date on which this community of less than 15,000 people truly emerged.

Just as the railroad empire finally made its way down the San Joaquin Valley toward the latter part of the 19th century, decades after much of the rest of the country had begun to fit into the burgeoning industrial complex of the United States, so too did the farm workers, almost a century later, make themselves belatedly felt as a viable part of the nation's labor movement.

Hardly any one in the so-called mainstream of the nation's life had heard of this small, out-of-the-way town before the start of the grape strike, which dragged Delano unwillingly into the center of an historic struggle. But among certain people the town was well known, if not admired or even liked. They were the farm workers who since the 1920's have for long or short periods called Delano home.

Black people were brought there from the South to pick cotton—but they found it difficult to compete with Mexican labor. Filipinos came from the Ilocos Islands, victims of a system of servitude under which banks and rich Filipinos financed their transportation at 50 percent interest. Oklahomans and other dust bowl refugees during the depression came desperately in search of work, some toiling for as little as 15 cents an hour, according to one oldtimer.

Of the Chinese railroad workers who sweated on the Southern Pacific, only a few settled permanently in Delano. At the beginning, the small railroad stop was settled by Midwesterners, who built wheat farms, and by European sheepherders. Originally, Delano was a shipping point for sheep, wool and wheat.

One of the frequent not-so-glamouous episodes that marked Delano's history deeply affected the local Japanese families during the early years of World War II. They had several businesses and many had farms there before the infamous 1942 concentration camp internment. While the Japanese were behind barbed wire, their Buddhist temple in Delano, which had been built in 1930, was razed.

During much of its history, Delano justifiably had the reputation of being a prostitution and gambling center, Some of the more prominent and "respectable" families were involved in these operations. In 1906 there reportedly were 14 liquor establishments and one grocery store. Delano's reputation as a wide-open town hung on for a long time. It was not until the Route 99 freeway was built through town in the mid-1950's that most of the honky-tonk district was demolished. The freeway resulted in the demolition of about 60 percent of these enterprises. Still surviving from that period are gambling houses in Delano that all too often are the source of outbreaks of violence.

Ernesto Galarza, in his *Spiders in the House and Workers in the Field,* (University of Notre Dame Press, 1970), provides glimpses of early Delano. "In the 1920's the Delano and Arvin countryside was anything but a produce farmer's paradise. Much of it was a wasteland of saline flats and Russian thistle with an annual rainfall, in favorable years, of five or six inches. . . . These parched flats were the areas of the dust storms that darkened the sun over Bakersfield. Joseph DiGiorgio bent down, fingered the soil, asked questions, and calculated the promise of the desolate land.

"He bought it in large tracts, altogether some 16,000 acres. But the land was only half of it. Without water it would remain useless. He discarded the traditional windmills and drilled hundreds of feet into the earth to tap the water table with powerful electric pumps. The blistered wilderness bloomed."

So enraptured did newspaper reporters become with DiGiorgio's irrigation system, an awesome operation for its time, that the *San Francisco Chronicle* reporter Gordon Pates wrote of the Arvin Ranch, "DiGiorgio is to farming what Tiffany's is to jewelry."

Twenty-five miles north of Delano was DiGiorgio's 5,000-acre Sierra Vista Ranch, which Galarza describes as "less spectacular, but equally prosperous." There was a self-contained community with a volunteer fire department, restaurant, recreational facilities and police.

By the late 1930's, many Yugoslavs from other West Coast areas and from the depression-ridden Pittsburgh steel region came to Delano. They became adept farmers, and the combination of cheap land and labor, plus individual hard work, paid off. Grape prices were high then.

Land which had been worth almost $3,000 an acre in 1922 plummeted to $150 an acre by 1929, according to Jack Zaninovich, grape-rancher and a member of the Delano Historical Society. Selling grapes for as high as $9 a box, despite government marketing regulations that held prices to $2 a box, growers rapidly amassed wealth. Generally, the gains were immediately put into acquiring new lands.

Nick Yap, one of the 1965 grape strikers, recalled how Andrew Zaninovich parlayed his 160-acre farm into a 2,000-acre ranch within five years. It was massive for its time. By 1965, the average grape farm in the Delano area was 2'000 acres, and by 1973 the conglomerates had moved in and there were ranches many times as large.

The extensive use of Mexican nationals in the grape fields in the

1930's gave further impetus to the development of the ranches. Grower sources showed that over 40 per cent of the Delano workers in those years were Mexican nationals who were resident aliens, subject to intimidation and deportation on the slightest pretext.

When the grape strike started in the fall of 1965, Delano seemed to be divided into three general categories. One was the grape growers and managers. Another was the townspeople, the local establishment that ran the city—the Chamber of Commerce types, and the businesses that serviced and profited from the residents as well as the farms. And then there were the farm workers, a necessary evil in the eyes of the growers, who, by and large, were segregated on the west side of town and in the camps in the fields. As in so many other communities, the farm workers were the dispensable majority, powerless and unorganized, to be tossed aside once they had done that for which they had been brought there—the production of wealth to sustain the ranchers and the business community.

It was during the grape strike that this traditional pattern substantially changed, not only for the farm workers but also for other sectors of Delano society. At first, the farm workers, who had been ignored except insofar as they were needed to toil in the fields, soon became the subjects of a paranoia that swept the grower and business communities. Later, this was replaced, by and large, by a studied hostility. But it was a hostility mixed with recognition of the newly found strength that had accrued to the laborers as a result of their successful union campaign.

Growers and townspeople who had been distant over the years were brought closer together as a result of their common cause —opposition to the strike. Even their social life began to merge. One might have thought from the reaction of the growers and the businessmen that there had never before been a strike in the local fields. It was as if some alien-spawned holocaust had overtaken them.

During the 1930's, there were seven grape strikes in Kern County. (Delano in on the Kern-Tulare county line.) Involved in those strikes were 8,403 workers. One strike involved more than 1,000 workers.

One of the union locals in the memorable cotton strike in 1933 was in Delano. The strike centered in Kern, Tulare and Kings

Counties and was led by the Cannery and Agricultural Workers Industrial Union. The list of communities in which the CAWIU established 19 new locals in 1933 was almost a duplicate of those in which the Farm Workers Union was centered in the grape strike 32 years later.

Again, in January 1938, it was a small strike of 68 grape pickers in Kern County which touched off a series of labor disputes that ended with another massive cotton strike. At that time, CIO organizers came in to help the workers fight against wage cuts and succeeded in restoring the original wages.

In August of that year, 150 peach pickers walked off the job, demanding a raise. They were assisted by organizers of the United Cannery, Agricultural, Packing and Allied Workers, CIO. This led to still another strike of 3,000 in the Shafter area, near Delano.

Two things happened during that strike which previewed developments of the grape strike of the 1960s.

Firstly, the growers had reduced the piecework rate of a hundredweight from 90 cents to 75 cents. Some of the growers indicated they were prepared to pay either 85 or 90 cents a hundredweight rather than take a strike. But it was the pressure of the big growers and their association that maintained a firm hold on the situation. It was class solidarity among employers.

Similarly, during the early days of the 1965 grape strike, a number of ranchers indicated to the union and mediating parties that they were ready to come to agreement with the striking unions. However, they reportedly said, in effect, "We don't dare do it because the other growers and the banks would make it impossible for us to live in this community if we dared break ranks."

Secondly, during the 1938 cotton strike, District Attorney Roger Welch said he would enforce Kern County's anti-picketing ordinance and would order the police "to stop strikes before they got started."

More than three decades later, it became clear that little had changed on the part of state machinery in Kern County insofar as farm strikes were concerned. When the AWOC members initiated the strike in grapes on September 8, 1965, they stayed in the only homes they had—the camps inside the grape fields. When the growers ordered them out, they refused to leave. Not only because

there was nowhere to go but also because leaving the camps meant
providing havens for strikebreakers. Gas and electricity were cut
off, and finally they were ousted. In one instance, a family was
cooking a meal in their improvised kitchen along the country road
and a sheriff's deputy kicked over the pot and food.

In all probability the events that day were, for many, reminiscent
of a strike 13 years earlier—in 1952—in the same fields. That walkout, led by the AFL National Farm Labor Union, involved 600
Filipino workers whose wages had been cut from a dollar an hour to
ninety cents. Bracero crews had been moved into the areas and
additional braceros were scheduled to arrive. After a short walkout,
the growers retreated and reinstated the doller an hour wage for
pruning (the grape vines).

A Catholic priest who had agreed to permit the NFWA to hold its
historic mass meeting on his church grounds on September 16,
1965, told the independent union that he was pressured by the
growers to revoke his agreement, and no future meetings were held
at that church.

By 1972, some things in Delano had obviously changed from the
rough days of the 1930's. But others hadn't. Police Chief Al Es-
pinosa told a reporter that "peace just settled on the town." That
was in January, 1972. If anything, it was an uneasy peace and it
turned out to be just a truce before the next confrontation between
the growers and workers, which came in 1973. When the grape
strike started, Delano and Kern County officials pulled out all the
stops in their frantic attempts to prevent its development.

Months before the strike, the NFWA had applied for a grant
under the federal "war on poverty" program. The $268,000 grant
was approved by Washington shortly before the strike began; it
provided for a program that included citizenship education, consumer education and research and administration.

Then came a move by NFWA that appeared confusing to outsiders. But it made sense to those on the inside. The union asked the
government to hold back the "war on poverty" money for the
strike's duration. NFWA had discovered that in its ambivalent position it could not do two things at once—run a strike and administer a
sizeable federally funded program. There simply wasn't the leadership available for both. In fact, it was difficult enough to conduct

either project alone. Obviously, the strike had to come first. So the hold-off application was made and Washington approved.

Nevertheless, the attack on the funding was escalated by the Delano City Council. It passed a resolution declaring that Cesar Chavez "does not merit the trust of the council with regard to the administration of the grant." Congressman Harlan Hagen, whose constituency included the strike areas of Kern and Tulare Counties, and who has earlier given his strong support to the grant, now questioned whether the NFWA could "objectively administer a federally sponsored education program." Then California's allegedly liberal Republican Senator Thomas Kuchel got into the act and also questioned "the experience and competence of the sponsors" of the project.

While the local and statewide echoes of the growers were resounding, the union reminded its supporters that Sargeant Shriver, when head of the Peace Corps, had offered Chavez a $21,000-a-year-post with that agency.

The reign of terror unleashed against the strikers during the early days of La Huelga, was not as blatant as were the attacks in earlier struggles. But it was as pervasive.

On the fifth day of the strike, Cesar Chavez described the setting in an interview in *The Movement,* a periodical which supported the Student Non-Violent Coordinating Committee.

"Yesterday we saw two buses of strikebreakers come in from Fresno, and one from Los Angeles. One grower had a crew of 40 scabs, some less than 13 years old. Some of the scabs are union members from other industries; they will come out of the fields when you tell them there is a strike. We also have spies (better known in union circles as 'submarines') working inside the field gangs to convince them they should leave the job. But without three years of growing (NFWA) membership it would have been impossible. Basically it's guerrilla warfare. The growers even have airplanes and helicopters."

The growers and the police resorted to legal and illegal tactics to frustrate the strike. Injunctions drastically limiting the number of pickets were obtained by the growers; pickets were prevented from being "noisy" on their lines at the edges of the fields. Even the shouting of "Huelga"—strike—was ruled illegal by the police.

The union dramatically responded by mobilizing a picket line of 44 one day, and the Rev. David Havens, of the California Migrant Ministry, who had been assisting the NFWA organizing effort for more than a year, read aloud Jack London's definition of a strike-breaker. The union had deliberately challenged the growers and police to arrest the large number of pickets. All were arrested but they were released when the court threw out the arrest as violating constitutional rights.

A copy of London's word picture of a strikebreaker had an honored place at the September 16 NFWA meeting. It was one of three adornments in the front of the hall. The other two were Emiliano Zapata, Mexican revolutionary, and a flag emblazoned with the union's thunder bird insignia.

Eugene Nelson, son of a grape rancher, who had come to Delano to assist and then was assigned by the union to write the first account of the early days of the strike, in part dedicated his book *Huelga*, (Farm Workers Press, 1966) "to the memory of Jack London, who, fifty years after his death, played a magnificent role in this strike." This is the definition that London gave of a strike-breaker, which was so highly appreciated by the farm workers and so infuriating to the police and growers.

"After God had finished the rattlesnake, the toad and the vampire, he had some awful substance left with which he made a Strikebreaker. A Strikebreaker is a two-legged animal with a cork-screw soul, a water-logged brain, and a combination backbone made of jelly and glue. Where others have hearts, he carried a tumor of rotten principles.

"When a Strikebreaker comes down the street men turn their backs and angels weep in Heaven, and the devil shuts the gates of hell to keep him out. No man has the right to be a Strikebreaker, so long as there is a pool of water deep enough to drown his body in, or a rope long enough to hang his carcass with. Judas Iscariot was a gentleman. . .compared to a Strikebreaker. For betraying his Master, he had the character to hang himself. . .a Strikebreaker hasn't.

"Esau sold his birthright for a mess of pottage. Judas Iscariot sold his Savior for thirty pieces of silver. Benedict Arnold sold his country for the promise of a commision in the British Army. The modern Strikebreaker sells his birthright, his country, his wife, his children, and his fellow men for an unfulfilled promise from his employer, trust or corporation.

"Esau was a traitor to himself. Judas Iscariot was a traitor to his God. Benedict Arnold was a traitor to his country. A Strikebreaker is a traitor to himself, a traitor to his God, a traitor to his country, a traitor to his family and a traitor to his class.

There is nothing lower than a Strikebreaker."

Desperately trying to get the voice of the strikers heard in the fields, Chavez one day spoke to them from an airplane driven by a Catholic priest. He was arrested for illegally using a public address system.

But the gowers' excesses in the fields, and that of their agents in and out of uniform, did not go unnoticed or unchallenged. They had obviously underestimated the strength of the strikers' allies. From almost the first day of the stike, civil rights activists from the Congress of Racial Equality (CORE), the Student Non-violent Coordinating Committee (SNCC), the California Migrant Ministry, and militant trade unionists and activists in the Chicano movement began streaming into Delano.

Food caravans poured in from throughout the state. Among those early supporters were members of the DuBois Clubs, the Emma Lazarus Clubs and other left-wing organizations. It was as if a tremendous force was pulling these diverse elements together to fill the vacuum in Delano.

It might have been expected that the greater focus in the strike would have been on the AWOC walkout which, after all, precipitated the grape strike. Had it not been for the sitdown in the fields by the Filipino workers the evening of September 7, against the advice of the AWOC leadership, the strike in Delano would not have begun. Even before the NFWA on September 16 voted to join the AWOC strike in grapes, many Mexican workers, who had been working side by side with the Filipinos at the time of the initial work stoppage, also stopped work.

Of the small group of radical farm workers who went on strike almost all were Filipinos who had participated in earlier walkouts, some of them under Communist leadership. But many of the young radicals who came to support the grape strike were victims of their own prejudices, and the AFL-CIO label, it seemed, was enough to scare them off from AWOC. Paradoxically, the Communist newspaper, the *People's World*, was openly displayed on the shelves at Filipino Hall, where AWOC was headquartered, but was kept under the top shelf in the NFWA office on Albany Avenue. And this was at a time when the workers were very anxious to read about their struggle and were more than happy to read any newspaper which accurately and fully reflected the struggle they were waging.

Nevertheless, virtually all of the new volunteer recruits to the farm-labor strike in Delano were concentrated on the NFWA, a largely unstructurd organzation with a life style which attracted radicals and civil rights activists. In contrast, AWOC was conducting its strike along traditional trade union lines, which was alien to the young activists and was of little interest to them.

But it was more than the contrast between the NFWA and AWOC that appealed to the left and activist forces, many of whom had done yeoman work in the civil rights movement. It was in large measure the realization that the time had come, at long last, for focusing attention on, and giving support to, the growing movement among Mexican-Americans. Not necessarily related to the strike, but no doubt influenced by it, the movement of Mexican-Americans became known as the Chicano movement in the course of the strike. The change in identification was quite similar to the development among Negroes who sought a new name—Black people—to reflect their more militant stance.

Militant Catholic priests, some of whom had been fighting for decades in the attempt to arouse their church and other people to the plight of the farm workers, arrived on the scene, much to the consternation of many in the church hierarchy and to the great irritation of the growers, most of whom were Catholics. And the energetic and talented George Ballis, photographer and editor of the AFL-CIO *Valley Labor Citizen*, was there lending his support in countless ways.

From among the Mexican-American political activists came Hector Abeytia, who was assaulted by a grower during one of the numerous attacks on the strike supporters. And frequent visitors to the strike scene were Paul Schrade, then Western Regional director of the United Auto Workers, and Bert Corona, one of the leading officials of MAPA and chairman of the Mexican-American Unity Council Farm Labor Committee.

All of these volunteers, and many more, witnessed the repression in Delano and joined in the fight-back campaign.

The *People's World*, the *Movement* and the embryonic Chicano press had reporters on the scene much of the time in the first days of the strike, and George Ballis pinch-hit for some of the labor press. The commercial press and television also became aware of the battle at a relatively early date, although its coverage was sparse and all too infrequent.

One of the long-time liberally oriented farm-labor support groups, the Emergency Committee to Aid Farm Workers, described the situation at the time in a newsletter. It reported:

"No one was really surprised when growers turned to more violent acts to discourage strikers, but what shocked and what really hurt is the assist growers are getting from local law enforcement authorities. Again and again striking workers are being run down and threatened, while local sheriff's deputies stand by or disappear.

"On September 25, Jack Radovich, the 18-year-old son of a struck grower, imitated a tactic attempted several days earlier by another ranch owner. He drove a spray rig down a public road and covered sixteen pickets with deadly sulfur spray. As he passed the last picket, he turned around and laid a second dose over half the group before the sheriff's deputies, who watched the entire episode, finally intervened. (All of the pickets were temporarily blinded, some for several days.) While this sort of thing has continued, strikers' complaints have been either ignored by the local DAs or actually denied by on-the-scene deputies."

By October 13, 1965, the situation had so deteriorated that Bert Corona, acting in his capacity as chairman of the farm-labor committee of the California-Mexican-American Unity Council, called on Governor Brown and the state attorney general to take measures "to protect the lives and persons of Mexican-American leaders active in Delano on behalf of the strike of grape pickers."

He cited specifically the grower attack on Hector Abeytia, a former organizer for the Agricultural Workers Organizing Committee, and the arrest of Dolores Huerta, one of the leading officers of

NFWA. He said they "and others are being harassed constantly by Delano police and the growers' personal violence."

On October 11, 1965, Hector Abeytia was assaulted on a Delano Street by the brother of one of the growers. Abeytia was beaten as a Kern County sheriff's car drove by without stopping. Abeytia is lame as a result of a physical disability. Before beating him up, the grower had stopped Abeytia and said, "You're the son of a bitch I'm going to get one of these days." Minutes later Abeytia was slugged, and only the intervention of another unionist prevented serious injury.

Eugene Nelson was grabbed by the throat by a grower on one of the picket lines. Nelson filed a complaint with the police. At the union hall, strikers cheered when they got the news. In those days complaints by unionists against growers were so rarely recognized by local authorities that the mere announcement that one had been successfully filed was an occasion for cheers.

While a large part of the Delano Filipino and Mexican-American communities sympathized with the strike, so great was the intimidation that many feared to associate themselves publicly with the struggle. There were about 1,500 Filipinos and 1,800 Mexican-Americans living permanently in the city.

Every person on the picket lines was photographed by the police. Many were questioned. All auto licenses of strike supporters were recorded and, in many instances, citations were issued. That is why on many occasions a major part of the picket lines was composed of "outsiders."

This was used by growers who kept insisting, "There is no strike." But what the growers and the commercial press were not conscious of was the solidarity that was growing in and around Delano. Every night, strikers would visit persons working in the fields and prepare for the next day's pull-outs. More often than not, the dramatic response of people in the fields to the "huelga" shout was the result of hard, painstaking organization, not a spur-of-the-moment decision.

The method of organization was similar to that which Chavez and his co-workers employed during the formative years of NFWA, long before there was any prospect of a strike. They went from house to house, patiently explaining the purpose of the organization, and laying the basis of a solid organization, which was to withstand the barrage of intimidation and red-baiting that was hurled at it during the strike.

It was touch-and-go at the end of the second week of the strike. The question was whether the two striking unions could pull workers out of the fields (who were imported from considerable distances) faster than growers could replace them. The number of people working in the fields was decreasing and Chavez, in a thank-you note to a strike supporter, said, "Maybe the strike is starting all over."

In a further report to a supporter, Chavez, in the third week, said, "Our cooperation with AWOC and the Filipino strikers continues. About 200 pickets work daily from 5 a.m. until 3 p.m. and many work evenings visiting esquiroles (strikebreakers) in their homes. The strike is holding and shows no sign of failing."

Sharing in the trials and tribulations of the early strike days were young men and women who had come from disparate backgrounds and whose paths finally led them to Delano. Young farm workers such as Eliseo Medina found themselves addressing student audiences at the universities and, much to their surprise, getting a big response. Cesar Chavez went to the steps of Sproul Hall in Berkeley in search of financial and volunteer support.

Almost overnight Delano was transformed. Augustin Lira, a farm worker who was performing weekends in night clubs, came to Delano from Stockton to see of it was "for real." He was convinced that it was. And from San Jose came Luis Valdez, who was born in Delano and left at an early age. He had gone to Cuba for a visit, a fact which was to be made much of by the growers and the John Birch Society. By the time the strike had begun, Valdez was a radical. Once he saw what was happening in his hometown, he decided to return and join in the struggle.

In response to frantic appeals from long-time activists such as Wendy Goepel, Bob Fisher and Bob Solodow came from Los Angeles. Marshall Ganz was a Harvard graduated SNCC organizer who made Delano his home. Bill Esher came to edit the *El Malcriado*, the union newspaper. Eugene Nelson came as a picket-line activist, was among those beaten on the line, and wrote his book, *Huelga*, in between other union assignments.

Augie Lira, who was later to be one of the main organizers of the Teatro Campesino—the farm workers' theatre—was one of those who came to stay. He was but a child when his mother, grandmother and two uncles swam the Rio Grande River in the late 1940's. Escaping the bullets shot at them by the border patrol, they desperately tried to find a way out of the perpetual poverty which was their lot in Mexico.

He was one of the 12 children, only eight of whom survived infancy. With understandable bitterness, he recalled the fate of his two uncles who had come to the United States in search of well-being, and instead ended up as winos. Both were decorated in the armed services of the United States during World Was II; one was among those who raised the flag at Iwo Jima. "They were destroyed by the war. They came home and became winos," Lira said.

When the strike started, Augie was picking grapes near Stockton for less than a dollar an hour and "on my off nights," he said, "I was playing music in night clubs and learning how to survive in the jungle. Stockton is quite a jungle."

Having read about the strike in Delano, he decided to go down and see for himself. An Army lieutenant gave him a lift to Delano. He said, "I was going there to see if it was only bullshit or if there was a real struggle going on. There were many people of all races and creeds and I got very interested. It was true that there were very few farm workers on the picket lines in the very beginning (of the strike). Berkeley hippies and cats out of Oakland who were searching for a new revolution. I suppose you could include me in that except that I was a Mexican, and knew it, and was damned proud of it." Lire was very much impressed with the participation of the Filipinos in the strike. (Interview with Augie Lira, January 1973)

One of the wild-eyed radicals Lira met in Delano was Bob Fisher, a 1964 graduate of the University of California at Los Angeles, who had all of the appearance of a hippie of that period. Fisher's claim to fame at that time was that he had been the only person in Los Angeles County in 1964 whose voting registration was "anarchist."

In the summer before the grape strike, the Rev. Jim Drake of the California Migrant Ministry, who had been working with the NFWA, called on Fisher to come to the valley and help organize the housing march from Linell to Visalia, which was mainly a NFWA project. Fisher, who came from a middle-class Jewish home on the Los Angeles West Side, was active in CORE. At that time he was employed in the California Department of Highways. After returning from Visalia, Fisher served a one-week jail sentence in Orange County because of his activities in the civil rights movement.

Fisher had been impressed by a number of things during his first visit to the Delano area. In the union office where he met Cesar Chavez, there were pictures of Emiliano Zapata, Benito Juarez and Pancho Villa. "Two days after NFWA went out on strike we (in CORE) got a frantic call from Wendy Goepel that people were being beaten up and there was a danger that the farm workers in response would start killing and attacking those who were hitting them. I came to Delano officially as a teacher of nonviolence. I don't think I taught a single class in nonviolence in all the time I was in Delano. . . . On the picket line on my first day in Delano I was attacked by (grower) Charley Dispoto."

"What's a nice Jewish boy like you doing picketing on Saturday?" Jack Pandol, a grower, asked Fisher in one of his anti-Semitic barbs. Fisher replied, "What's a nice Yugoslav boy like you doing not granting a union wage?" (Interview with Bob Fisher, January 1973)

To protest the attacks against the farm workers on the picket lines, the NFWA organized at least two marches in the predominantly Mexican West Side of Delano, and hundreds marched in response to the union's call. Included among those who marched in support of the farm workers were persons who had responded to the union's initial strike call but who had since returned to work in the fields because of economic pressure.

For the first time, volunteers such as Fisher realized the special character of this strike. It was on these marches that they first met NFWA members from Parlier, West Fresno and Earlimart who had been members of the NFWA for a considerable period of time. The participation of persons who worked in the fields during the strike in union activity revealed the deep national aspect of the struggle. Jerry Bresheares in *El Centro* later said, "They were striking for La Raza."

In the second month of the strike, Lira was going house to house in Parlier seeking food donations for the strike. "When you need something you go to the poor unless you know the rich," he explained. A crippled old lady came to the door at one of the houses he visited.

"I told her we were collecting food for the families on strike. And she said, 'They (the growers) deserve it.' She walked away with the aid of her crutch and came back and put five dollars in my hand. And I started to cry. I said no, I thought she needed it more than we did. But she said, 'No, we have got to get those ranchers—take the money.' Then she came back with groceries. She said, 'You take it because Cesar Chavez is a saint.' And I told her no, he is a man."

Another poignant episode of that period was related by Fisher, who told of an incident in McFarland while he was canvassing house to house in search of persons who might be scabbing.

"I knocked on one man's door and he told me he was for the union but that he had to work. I told him about the police attacks on the pickets, and he took off his shirt and undershirt and showed me old welts on his back. He said, 'The damned L.A. police did that to me in the 1940s. That's why I haven't set foot in L.A. for 20 years.' I hung my head in shame. At that point I understood the nature of the strike. It was a movement of people who had scars on their backs, and crutches and scars on their mind."

Early in the strike I hitched a ride to Delano with a delegation of liberals from the California Democratic Council. Ross Clark, then a southern California CDC official, got a taste of local police hostility. His failure to display his auto registration resulted in a traffic citation. That was but a small sample of the kind of reception in store for "outsiders" coming in to assist the strikers.

The CDCers with whom I had travelled had parked near the railroad freight depot, where pickets were attempting to prevent the shipment of scab grapes. A policeman approached the car, quickly checked out lights, registration card and other sundry matter that might result in a traffic ticket. All was in order. Then we got the usual treatment to which just about all out-of-towners, including rabbis and priests, were subjected. We were questioned as to our identities and our business in town.

After being told that we were there to assist the farm workers, each of the occupants were closely scrutinized, with two of the occupants seemingly singled out for special attention. One was a

Black woman and the other was the writer, a reporter for the Communist *People's World*, and already quite well known to the local police.

We were pointedly told that it would be in the best interest of all concerned for us to get out of town. This bit of advice, which sounded more like a threat despite the polite manner in which it was phrased, was ignored by the CDCers. Fortunately, this was also the reaction of others who had come to do what they could to help the farm workers.

There were other visitors in Delano, among them a writer for the John Birch Society magazine, *American Opinion*. He had come there to report on the latest "revolution" in the United States. And what he saw alarmed him. He was as alarmed as the growers. The *American Opinion* report was straight out of the Delano police files.

This was pinpointed at a subsequent legislative hearing on the strike where much was made of the allegation that Mickey Lima, chairman of the Northern California District of the Communist Party, had been one of the many radical visitors to Delano soon after the strike started. It was true that Lima's car was in Delano. He had lent it to his daughter, Margie, to deliver food collected by Communists and others to help feed the strikers. But the Delano police had not bothered to do anything but dutifully list all of the out-of-town license numbers and then turn them over to the John Birch Society writer.

When Lima later appeared at a legislative hearing and swore under oath that he had never been in Delano, he was hurriedly dismissed from the stand by the abashed inquisitors.

But this was all too typical of the official police line during the strike, which came from the growers and was transmitted to the ultra-rightists who had come to Delano. When the strike started, local police agencies, ranchers and businessmen scoffed at every mention of the union and the strike.

A little over six years later, Chamber of Commerce types and policemen had to concede a most obvious fact—that there was a union in existence. After all, by that time there were over 40 growers with union contracts in the Delano area, and also the physical evidence—the cluster of union buildings just west of the city.

Still, they could not quite get themselves to admit that it was real

Even at that late date, virtually every mention of the union or the strike was preceded by "so-called."

Like so many other small towns, Delano tries to brief every new-comer on the local points of pride. One cannot find a single mention of the union, the strike or the union headquarters in the Chamber of Commerce brochure distributed in early 1972. Mentioned are such edifices as the American Slavonic Clubhouse, the town library, and "a 35-bed acute hospital." But not a word about the Filipino Hall, where for more than five years the strikers met, nor of the United Farm Workers Union nor of their impressive headquartes, one of the most modern buildings in all of Delano.

However, prime attention is given the Delano Relay Station, operated by the United States Information Agency to relay the Voice of America and Armed Forces Radio to the Orient and South America. It is hailed as "a federal agency of much importance to the Delano District." And jobs being what they are in Delano, mention is made of the 25 men employed there.

Yet the outfit directly across the street from the relay station, which employed 97 people full time and which was used by more than 10,000 persons annually, was ignored. It was a non-place. It was and is Delano headquarters for the Farm Workers Union. It is the "Forty Acres" on which there is a modern, well-equipped clinic, a gas station, a hiring hall, a credit union, a service center, a retirement village for old farm workers and several other departments of the union.

9   Labor Faces a Challenge and a Dilemma

"We have to find some cross between being a movement and being a union."

Cesar Chavez, 1965

"**A**rrest us arrest us." This was the challenge of Cesar Chavez to the Delano police who were walking alongside leaders of the "illegal" street parade in that city on December 16, 1965.

The strike in the fields was barely three monthe old, and the City Council had already reacted in typical knee-jerk fashion; passing an ordinance outlawing parades without permits. Traditionally, striking farm workers have paraded and demonstrated in the cities and fields to publicize their walkouts and to make known their demands. Virtually all other means of communications were closed to them in the communities that were owned lock, stock and barrel by the growers. The Delano grape strikers had begun to employ this tactic when the Council tried to clamp down on them.

Chavez, a usually mild-mannered man with deep roots in the land, has a keen sense of the dramatic. His experience had taught him to avoid confrontations and nonessential entanglement with the Delano police. (Unless otherwise noted, the biographical material of Cesar Chavez is from an interview with Cesar Chavez in the *Farm Worker Press*, 1966 ed.)

Twenty-two years earlier—in 1943—he had come home for a visit with his family in Delano. The teen-age Cesar Chavez went to the local movie during that visit and noticed that all the Anglos sat on one side of the theater and the Mexican-Americans on the other. This was also the year in which President Franklin D. Roosevelt, in his message to Congress, said, "We shall not be able to claim that we have gained total victory in this war if any vestige of fascism in any of its malignant forms is permitted to survive anywhere in this world." The same president, in a radio address on May 2, 1943, told the nation, "I believe now, as I have all my life, in the right of workers to join unions and to protect their unions."

But Chavez, it appeared, was living in an altogether different world; one in which a fascist-like regime was imposed on Mexican-Americans. In the Delano theater where Chavez had sat down in the "Anglo section," he was told by a theater employee that "Mexican people have to sit on the other side of the aisle." After Chavez ignored a similar command from the movie's manager, he found two husky policemen standing over him. One of them told him, Chavez later recalled, "You broke the law of this theater, now let's get moving." When Chavez still refused to comply, he was told by one of the policemen, "Look, are you coming with us, or do I have to use a little persuasion?" Pulled out of his seat by the police, Chavez was pushed in the direction of the theater entrance and taken to the local police station.

For Chavez this was but one of the many indignities heaped on him, as it was on all others of Mexican descent. Born in Yuma, Arizona, in 1927, Cesar Estrada Chavez was one of five children who, together with their parents, barely eked out a living on a small farm near the Colorado River. The great depression of the '30s took its toll of small farmers, and the Chavez family, like so many others, became migrant farm workers. Their small farm had gone bankrupt.

When he was ten years old, the family began working the fields of Arizona and California, following the crops. When he was in the eighth grade Chavez was compelled to drop out so that he could help his family in the fields. He later recalled, "Those early days when we first came to California were rough. We were really green, and whenever a labor contractor told us something, we fell for it, hook, line and sinker. We didn't know the ropes yet and we got hooked every time. I remember the first year we ended up in the fall picking wine grapes for a contractor near Fresno. They were bad grapes; there were very few bunches on the vines, and we were the only family working in the field. But we were too green to wonder why we were the only ones, you see. After the first week of work my father asked the contractor for his pay. 'I can't pay you because I haven't been paid by the winery,' the contractor told my father. But we were broke, absolutely broke with nothing at all to eat, so the contractor finally gave us twenty dollars, and said we'd get a big check later when the winery paid him. We worked for seven weeks like that, and each pay day the contractor said he couldn't pay us because the winery hadn't paid him yet. At the end of the seventh week we went to the contractor's house and it was empty—he owed us for seven weeks pay, and we haven't seen him to this day."

He recalled also that in the winter of 1938, "I had to walk to school barefoot through the mud, we were so poor." After attending the segregated school, Cesar Chavez said he "fished the canal and cut wild mustard greens, otherwise we would have starved."

He vividly remembered many other hardships from his early youth, such as the time his mother sold crocheting in the streets of Los Angeles so that the family could have gas money for the old Studebaker, and of living three days in the family car in Brawley, California, before the Chavez family could locate a house it could afford.

The winter of 1939 was a particularly memorable one for Chavez. Stranded in Oxnard, California, his family lived in a tent. His parents arose every morning to go to the fields at 5:30 a.m. to pick peas. Transportation costs from the tent to the fields were 70 cents a round-trip "and some days they did not even make enough for their transportation," he said.

In the ensuing years Chavez followed the crops, settled for a while in Delano, during which time he married Helen Favila, joined unions and walked picket lines. It was during this period that Eugene Nelson in his book *Huelga* says Chavez "mingled with whites and learned that they had problems, too, and that prejudice was not an inborn human quality but something that could be overcome; he gained a new devotion to working people of all races and beliefs."

While living in San Jose in 1950, Chavez met Father Donald

McDonnell. Years later Chavez recollected that the priest "sat with me past midnight telling me about social justice and the Church's stand on farm labor and reading from the encyclicals of Pope Leo XIII in which he upheld labor unions." So anxious was Chavez to learn more about labor history from the "bracero priest" that he went with him to bracero camps to assist in the mass and to the city jails where the priest talked with the prisoners. At every possible opportunity, Chavez said he accompanied Father McDonnell "so that he could tell me more about the farm-labor movement."

Two years later Cesar Chavez and his brother Richard, who lived across the street from him in San Jose's barrio called Sal Si Puedes (get out if you can), worked in the nearby apricot groves. It was at this time that Father McDonnell introduced Cesar to Fred Ross, who was then organizing the CSO (Community Service Organization) chapters and who perceived that Chavez had the potential for becoming an effective community organizer. Chavez viewed the CSO as one route to unionizing farm workers.

"I always believed that the union had to come in order to bring some changes about," said Chavez in recalling his approach to his early CSO days. "In fact when I joined CSO back in 1952, the first thing I asked Fred Ross was, 'what about the farm workers? I want to do something that will give the workers a union.' Fred told me, 'if CSO gets big enough, CSO will become a union.' So I said, 'Fine,' and I joined. But, of course, it never did."

The CSO, a project initiated by Saul Alinsky's Industrial Areas Foundation, had often been described as a "Mexican NAACP." Alinsky, who described himself as a "social activist," was based in Chicago, and for many years concentrated on assisting in the development of local organizations in minority communities throughout the nation.

Ross and Chavez became good friends as well as fellow organizers for the CSO. Within months Alinsky approved the hiring of Chavez as an organizer who would work with voter registration and citizenship projects. Small, thin and scarcely able to read, the 27-year-old Chavez went about the business of organizing CSO chapters. At first the experience terrified him; nevertheless he became a proficient organizer and was soon placed in charge of CSO for the entire San Joaquin Valley.

Chavez got a taste of the red-baiting of the cold war era in the early 1950's, when members of his own Madera Chapter, heavily influenced by local "patriots" who believed that anyone organizing Mexican Americans to vote must be some kind of subversive, began an investigation into Chavez's possible connections with communism. When he found out about this investigation, he demanded a face-to-face confrontation so that the allegations could be made in his presence. At that point his accusers retreated.

Soon Chavez was organizing CSO chapters throughout California and Arizona, including many in rural areas. It was while he headed the CSO organization that Chavez started pressuring it to concentrate on building a union of farm workers. He also began to protest dramatically against the life-style of many CSO officials by appearing at meetings tieless and often unshaven. To this day Cahvez refuses to wear ties, although he is clean-shaven.

Having failed to win over the CSO to a program of organizing farm workers, Chavez, in 1962, resigned his steady-paying job as its director, and at about the same time turned down an offer of $21,000 a year as Peace Corps director for four Latin-American countries. He took a $1.25-an-hour job pruning grape vines in Delano. It was then that he started traveling up and down the San Joaquin valley contacting farm workers and laying the basis of the National Farm Workers Association.

By December 16, 1965, Chavez, his members on the picketlines having joined with the members of the AFL-CIO Agricultural Workers Organizing Committee in the most publicized grape strike in history, had already put into practice many of the lessons he had learned during his days as CSO organizer. During the first week of the Delano strike, he said, "We have to find some cross between being a movement and being a union."

His successful appeals to students, civil rights activists and clergymen demonstrated his ability to enlist "movement" forces behind the strikers. Early in the strike he wrote to "movement" supporters that "in the third week of the strike in grapes, we remain active and united. Workers who have never spoken out before are becoming self-confident pickets and neighborhood leaders. They have maintained the atmosphere of non-violence which we believe is morally essential in our work. Our cooperation with AWOC and their

Filipino strikers continues. About 200 pickets work daily from 5 a.m. to 3 p.m. and many work evenings visiting esquiroles (strikebreakers) in their homes. the strike is holding and shows no sign of failing. . . . We have dedicated workers, but we must have food and gas in order to maintain our effort."

During the opening days of the Delano strike, the growers attacked along several fronts. By the end of the first week of the strike Chavez estimated that only10 percent of the normal work force was in the fields. Soon strikebreakers were en route from Bakersfield, Fresno and Los Angeles as well as from Texas. There were numerous instances of these workers being recruited without being told that a strike was in progress. False statements by growers that the strike was over were broadcast on the Bakersfield radio.

Growers also insisted to the press that the strike was not of any significance. At any event, they argued that it was no more than a giant civil rights demonstration involving SNCC, CORE and clergymen. There were repeated charges by grower representatives that NFWA and AWOC were little more than "Communist fronts."

To counter this barrage the strikers were in need of demonstrative labor support. While some local unions and central labor councils came to the aid of the agricultural workers early in the strike, the obvious need was for "respectable" labor backing. It was to this end that some of the labor supporters of the strike, especially those in the West Coast region of the United Auto Workers, centered their efforts.

Less than two months after the beginning of the Delano strike, a national AFL-CIO convention was held in San Francisco, and one of the United Auto Worker's union delegates was Paul Schrade, who by that time had already become deeply involved in the Delano events. The fact that the resolution to support the strike was passed was itself a tribute to the momentum the strike had already achieved. The AFL-CIO is not given to precipitate action. In spite of this, the pressure from California unions, from the UAW was sufficient to overcome the reluctance of AFL-CIO President George Meany to back the strike.

Schrade and Thomas Pitts, secretary-treasurer of the California state AFL-CIO, spoke unequivocally for all-out strike support, while Mort Brandenburg, president of the state AFL-CIO Distillery

Workers Union, backed the strile but criticized the NFWA, which had already launched its boycott of Schenley products as part of its strike strategy. Brandenburg's union had a contract with Schenley's and did not take kindly to the boycott tactic.

For Schrade and other pro-farm workers delegates at the San Francisco convention, this was not considered sufficient. They wanted a more dramatic demonstration of labor's support for the strike in the fields. Schrade urged Meany to go to Delano and to personally pledge the labor movement's support. Meany, who had earlier boasted that he had never walked a picket line, rejected the idea of his picketing in the San Joaquin Valley.

Ultimately, Meany signed a letter written by Schrade that the AFL-CIO president agreed should be delivered to the strikers by UAW President Walter Reuther, who headed the AFL-CIO Industrial Union Department. A few days after the NFWA announced the boycott of Schenley products, Walter Reuther, on December 16, 1965 came to Delano, accompanied by many labor reporters and television crews many of whom covered the AFL-CIO convention. The $5,000-a-month donation pledged by organized labor, half of it from the UAW, was enthusiastically welcomed. But also heartily greeted was the march that day through the streets of Delano, deliberately flouting a newly passed city ordinance barring such parades without a permit.

"Our strategy," said Schrade, "was to put the strike on the national scene." According to the West Coast UAW leader, it was Reuther who devised this strategy although Schrade was very cognizant of its extreme importance to AWOC and the NFWA. It was Reuther who started the parade by telling Chavez and Itliong, "Let's march, let them arrest us if they want to." As the cameras rolled, the farm workers marched and cheered and took over the streets of Delano.

It was in the course of that march, led by Chavez, Itliong and Reuther, that Chavez hurled his challenge at the local police. As expected, it was ignored, since about the last thing in the world the local officials desired was a series of arrests in front of the newsmen and cameras.

The strike of the grape pickers assumed meaningful proportions for the labor movement, as it had for the other movements which had carried on a major part of the strike support activity in the opening weeks and months of the walkout. For the growers and local authorities it was still an unbelievable nightmare and they continued to insist there really was no strike and that it was all little more than a huge publicity buildup by Chavez and Itliong and their "outside" supporters.

The jurisdiction issue raised by the Distillery Workers was not the only one that bugged Meany and others in the AFL-CIO. They were also upset over the strike's support from militants and activists in the radical, communist, church and student movements.

Itliong, who was present on occasions when Meany and others discussed the grape strike, said that the AFL-CIO president "disapproved of many things" in the Delano-based strike, and, "I got the impression he disapproved the very active church involvement and the participation of many from the left in it."

Al Green, while still formally heading up the AWOC organization, wanted all AFL-CIO contributions routed through his organization and not jointly with equal contributions going to both striking organizations.

While just about all new AFL-CIO affiliates go through an initial period in which differences of approach and policy within the parent organization are often resolved by compromise, it was obvious from the very outset that the new farm-labor union would present extraordinary challenges to officials in the labor movement. Differences over political issues between the AFL-CIO officials and the newly organized farm workers appeared in the earliest days and kept recurring.

On April 6, 1966, just a few short months after the AFL-CIO put its seal of approval on the grape strike, the first political fracas took place. The California state AFL-CIO Committee on Political Education (COPE) endorsed Congressman Harlan Hagen (Democrat from Kern, King and Tulare Counties) for re-election despite a major dabate in its ranks and a sharp condemnation of the incumbent congressman by the NFWA. At the COPE meeting strong pleas by UAW and the Packing Union spokesmen to deny labor's endorsement to the antilabor incumbent congressman went unheeded.

The NFWA had declared, "Congressman Hagen is playing the role of a professional strikebreaker, using the oldest tricks of the growers in an attempt to break the strike." Ironically, the COPE action was taken on the same day and in the same hotel where Cesar Chavez was announcing to a crowded press conference the culmination of the union's first successful drive, the signing of a contract with Schenley Industries, the second largest grape company involved in the strike. And, in large measure, this victory was achieved as a result of the strong support the strikers received from the labor movement.

In the earliest days of the strike, two of the unions that played an important role in rallying support to it were independents, not affiliated with the AFL-CIO. They were the Teamsters Union, which sanctioned the strike and whose members refused to cross picket lines set up by fieldworkers, and the International Longshoremen's and Warehousemen's Union, which labelled scab grapes as "hot cargo" and refused to load them on ships.

Each of these unions apparently had some hope of getting the striking independent Farm Workers Union to affiliate with it. In the past the Teamsters and the ILWU had been among the unions that had tried to organize fieldworkers. But they had no more success than did others in the field.

Among those who addressed the huge 1966 Easter Sunday rally on the steps of the state capitol in Sacramento, at the conclusion of a historic Delano-to-Sacramento pilgrimage, were Louis Goldblatt, ILWU secretary-treasurer, and Jack Goldberger, Teamster Union international organizer who, on that occasion, was also the special representative of Teamster Union President James R. Hoffa. William Kircher, national director of organization of the AFL-CIO, also spoke at the rally.

It was at this capital mall assemblage that Chavez paid special tribute to all of the unions that had backed the strike. He singled out the ILWU for special attention. "I want to thank the ILWU for the unfailing help they gave us every time we picketed the docks. We pledge that we will not sign any contract with any grower until the lawsuits against the ILWU are dropped." The ILWU was then faced with more than $300,000 in lawsuits because its members refused to load scab grapes.

Bert Corona said later that the Teamster shutdown of the Schenley warehouse in San Francisco was the catalyst which precipitated the series of events that led to the signing of the NFWA contract with that major corporation. The San Francisco shutdown took place while the strikers and their supporters, including many non-union farm workers, were on the 25-day, 300-mile pilgrimage from Delano to Sacramento.

In short order, "Blackie" Leavitt, head of the Los Angeles Culinary Workers Union Joint Council, who had contact with Sidney Korshak, Schenley's attorney, was involved and so was Kircher. Just on the eve of the pilgrimage's arrival in Sacramento, the grape strikers' first victory had been won. The solidarity of the strikers—Schenley's was the NFWA's main base—was primary. Support groups in many parts of the nation promoted the boycott of Schenley products, and this company, which advertised widely in the labor press as part of its campaign to promote its image as a pro-union company, was hurting. The economic pain was especially felt by the management in the sale of its alcoholic beverages. With the necessary assistance of organized labor, the farmworkers put it all together and won their initial contract in grapes.

It was also in the Schenley drive that the NFWA began to develop a tactic which seemed to reverse the traditional trade-union approach. It went after the large companies first, not the smaller ones. In the conglomerate age an effective boycott had suddenly taken on a new significance. Schenley's, a large company with only a small part of its investment in grapes, was the first to throw in the towel—the cost of the boycott was too high for its other products.

While the Teamsters and the ILWU support at the beginning of the strike was probably decisive, these unions provided an interesting footnote in the longer-range history of the grape strike. When the Teamsters Union became an active protagonist opposing the AFL-CIO farm union in the DiGiorgio, Perelli-Minetti and Salinas lettuce situation, it encountered active opposition from its own rank and file, especially in the lettuce situation, during which many Los Angeles teamsters called on their union leaders to stop interfering with the farm workers union organization. And when some ILWU leaders cooled in their support of the grape strike, especially after the farm workers union were chartered as a single AFL-CIO organization, important locals in that union kept up their support of the Delano strikers and continued shipping food and sending delegations in demonstrative solidarity.

It was evident from almost the outset of the grape strike that William Kircher, the AFL-CIO's top official on the strike scene, was courting the NFWA—seeking a merger with AWOC and bringing both organizations into the AFL-CIO as a viable organization. Kircher had played an important role in the Schenley settlement even though it was reached with the NFWA, an independent labor organization. He was one of the signatories to that agreement.

In commenting on Kircher's role in the early strike period, Itliong, who logically should have been Kircher's closest union associate, said, "Kircher came in with a very heavy hand. In the negotiations with Schenley, in which Kircher was involved, I was not consulted and did not participate in any manner. I believe he felt that our role in AWOC was just secondary so he didn't have to worry about us. Everything he did from that time on indicated that. I just let it go." (Interview with Larry Itliong, June 1973)

In a formal sense Itliong remained second in command to Chavez for more than six years. Virtually all observers on the scene at that time were convinced that next to Chavez, Dolores Huerta, not Itliong, was the top leader of the union. Itliong's contention that he was "frozen out" out of the union leadership by persons who surrounded Chavez is challenged by many union leaders as too simplistic a view of the actual events. One of the union's officials argued that Itliong had never broken with his AFL-CIO habits. The movement type union, with its long hours was alien to Itliong, he said. Also Itliong's financial demands on the union, it was contended, were far in excess of those made by any of the other leaders of the agricultural workers union.

Nevertheless, Itliong insists that it was during the Schenley talks, and shortly thereafter, that Kircher relegated him to a subordinate role. In effect, the AWOC-NFWA merger which was announced by Meany on August 22, 1966 was, according to Itliong, engineered by Kircher. He said:

"We were in several meetings in Bakersfield, talking about the structure, the benefits from merger, especially money, and organizational assistance. He was selling it to the NFWA. He promised them free movement—autonomy—freedom to do what they had been doing. He promised that a million dollars would be available in a revolving fund, to be replenished at the end of the year. It was a big inducement because the NFWA had almost nothing on hand. I wasn't aware of it. At that time AWOC had almost $12,000 left in its treasury and we figured we had about 12,000 members."

One of the things that disturbed the new United Farm Workers Organizing Committee, AFL-CIO, was the bureaucracy within the AFL-CIO. This was a subject of much discussion among grape-strike supporters, many frankly doubting Chavez's statement that the farm labor union would maintain its autonomy and life style within the AFL-CIO. But Chavez insisted that the NFWA must make the moves that were necessary in the best interest of its members rather than bow to the wishes of those who supported the strike.

It was ironic, Itliong later commented, that the farm union, which was so concerned about AFL-CIO bureaucracy, would in the ensuing years develop its own form of bureaucratic structure.

Even after the AFL-CIO consummated the merger of the two cooperating farm labor organizations, jurisdiction and political differences continued to plague the parent labor organization and its new affiliate. In part, this was reflected in the almost routine AFL-CIO announcement by Meany in the spring of 1972 that an international union charter had been issued to the newly named United Farm Workers National Union.

The AFL-CIO, which had cheered Chavez and Itliong at an earlier convention, procrasinated for months in the spring of 1972 before deciding, without any fanfare, to grant the charter to the farm union. The decision as to whether to issue the charter had been left to Meany, as were so many of the other decisions of the AFL-CIO, and he finally gave his approval.

Before the formal AWOC-NFWA merger took place, there were a series of developments which minimized the role of the AFL-CIO union that had so dramatically, on September 8, 1965, initiated the Delano grape strike. The walkouts and sitdowns were led and carried on in the main by Filipino farm workers, but also included a large number of Chicanos.

Manuel Vasquez, a truck driver, and Eliseo Medina, a field worker, who later became leading organizers for the united farm labor union, were among the Chicanos who left the fields when the AWOC leadership, bowing to the insistent demands of its rank and file, struck the fields.

The Filipinos, who constituted a major part of the membership and the overwhelming proportion of the AWOC leadership, included many migrant workers whose only permanent residence was in the work camps on the ranches. At the time the grape strike started, a large part of the work force was composed of Filipinos; Itliong believes they made up its majority.

Physically ousted from the camps following their short-lived sit-ins, many of the Filipino strikers left the strike zone. Mindful of their relatively small treasury, the AWOC leaders, in fact, encouraged the exodus. Maintaining a strike kitchen and meeting minimal strike expenses, such as gasoline, auto repairs and emergency expenses of strikers, represented a considerable drain on the meager available resources.

In recruiting a work force to replace the thousands who had walked out of the fields, the growers turned to the largest available major labor supply, Mexicanos from south of the Mexican border and Chicanos who were residents of the United States. Strikebreakers were recruited from as far away as Texas, where many, like Juan Flores, signed up for work without knowing that a strike was in progress. But the very extensive and highly expensive recruitment program only resulted in more diligent and imaginative efforts by the striking unions, which succeeded in bringing these workers out of the fields. In this process, the ethnic composition of the strike drastically changed. It became overwhelmingly Chicano and Mexicano.

Meanwhile the AWOC leadership was in disarray. Involved in a strike considerably larger and far different from those in which it was previously engaged, 19 out of the 24 AWOC organizers left its staff. Only three Filipinos and two Chicanos remained. Others——Filipinos, Chicanos and Anglos——were apparently convinced that the Delano effort, mainly led by Chavez and the NFWA, was principally concerned with community organizing and was not along classic trade-union lines.

Itliong, southern regional director of AWOC, was the acknowledged leader among the Filipino farm workers. With joint picket lines, a common strike kitchen and a united strike strategy, the two organizations brought Chavez and Itliong into a close working relationship. This created some friction between Green, who habitually referred to the Filipinos as "my boys," and Itliong. The cooperation between Chavez and Itliong was too close, he complained.

Meanwhile, unknown to Itliong, Green was conducting his own meetings with Chavez to arrange the necessary coordination between the two organizations. Itliong saw the NFWA-AWOC operation as one that was interlinked. The support groups that had been attracted to Delano mainly by the NFWA campaign did not turn him off. On the contrary, he welcomed them. Green, on the other hand, a former building-trades union official, looked askance at the church, student and civil rights support to the strike in Delano.

Until AWOC and the NFWA merged, Green was the titular head of the AFL-CIO affiliate. But by December 1965, he had, to all intents and purposes, lost control of the situation. When the Filipino workers ignored Green's directives and joined with the Chavez-led pilgrimage to Sacramento, carrying their union banner alongside the red-and-black NFWA flag at the head of the line of march during the entire 25-day, 300-mile walk, it dramatically illustrated the oneness of the strike and rejection of all advice and leaders who preached division.

Itliong was among those who ignored Green's instructions. He joined the march, which attracted thousands of farm workers and strike supporters and which, in many respects, became the catalyst that expanded the influence of the grape strikers and their unions to other crops and other areas. Lettuce pickers from Salinas and row-crop field workers from Arizona were among those who came to join in the burgeoning farm labor movement.

Old-line trade unionists were taken aback by the religious mass which was a daily part of the pilgrimage. The presence of bearded youths from the campuses and civil rights movements was even less understandable. And the growing number of Chicano activists from the barrios and the campuses who participated in the pilgrimage also represented something new in the strike. Along with them were the ILWU warehousemen from southern California, the California auto workers from South Gate and Fremont and shed workers from Imperial Valley, members of the Packinghouse Workers Union.

Thus, to many it was truly a "movement strike," with volunteers sleeping on cement floors en route, as they had earlier in the

Filipino Hall and at the NFWA headquarters. They marched as they had worked, long hours, for the chance to be part of what appeared destined to become a historic breakthrough in the fields.

They wrote leaflets; many translated them into Spanish; they operated mimeograph machines but, above all, picketed and recruited more volunteers as word spread throughout the state of California and the southwestern part of the United States that a new movement was being born. The atmosphere was electric with excitement, while the Delano growers, the police and the grower-controlled press inveighed against "the outsiders."

True, there were indeed outsiders among the ranks of the strikers. But as Bob Fisher, one of the CORE volunteers who had come from Los Angeles to Delano in response to frantic appeals for help, emphasized, it was the farm workers who called the decisive turn on strike strategy—Cesar Chavez, Dolores Huerta, Gilberto Padilla, Julio Hernandez and many others.

Meanwhile, within the AFL-CIO family there was a degree of confusion. Irwin DeShetler, southern California AFL-CIO regional director during the early strike period, recalled that while the state AFL-CIO was attempting to channel financial contributions from organized labor to AWOC, many of the unions were responding directly to the NFWA appeals for funds because Cesar Chavez was in the public limelight. This resulted in the NFWA getting a share of labor's donations. "In the beginning everyone wanted to help the farm strike," DeShetler said. "But the financial response depended on who was talking to the union—and this was at a time that the state federation was subsidizing AWOC."

But AWOC's machinery, which included San Joaquin Valley AFL-CIO unions that looked upon the Delano events with varying degrees of disfavor, could not match Cesar Chavez's army of volunteers since they not only covered every available union but also student, Chicano, political and fraternal organizations.

Probably more than any other union officer, Paul Schrade assisted the Delano strikers in a variety of ways. He was among those who made it clear from the outset which side he was on. As an anti-war activist and as one who spoke often on the campuses, he was very much at home in Delano. While some of the auto locals with large number of Chicanos were pleasantly surprised to find their union's regional officials so deeply involved in the strike, others in the UAW used it as a factional weapon with which to attack Schrade. He was accused of neglecting his own union affairs as a result of his involvement in the grape strike.

Despite this, Schrade points with some pride to the fact that it was during the period of the grape strike that a Chicano caucus was established in his union and that TELECU (The East Los Angeles Community Union) was transformed from the drawing-board stage to a reality in the Los Angeles barrio.

As word of La Huelga—as the strike in the grape fields was commonly known—spread across the nation and into Canada, trade unionists in New York, Cleveland, Toronto, Chicago, Houston and in other cities met field workers first-hand. They learned about Chicano and Filipino oppression from farm workers who had come to promote the union-sponsored boycott of scab products. A new consciousness of the Chicano in the United States was born as a result of the Huelga—especially in the trade-union movement.

Schrade recalled some of the initial steps taken by grape strike supporters in the labor movement that within a brief span of time led to the AWOC-NFWA merger. When Reuther came to Delano, the AFL-CIO and the UAW had already come to the agreement that funds would be contributed equally to both striking unions. However, this was not known to Chavez, so when the UAW president arrived the NFWA director assigned some of his supporters to stick closely to Schrade and Jack Conway, AFL-CIO Industrial Union Department executive, who were Reuther's two top aides on the scene.

The visit of the UAW leaders to Delano also reflected the division within organized labor in relation to the grape strike. Meany had been invited to come to Delano but chose to personally remain aloof from this struggle, leaving the field wide open for Reuther and the UAW to assume the dynamic role that it pursued on that occasion and thereafter.

Probably the most significant aspect of the December 1965 visit of the labor officials to Delano was that it helped place the strike in national spotlight. Not insignificant by any means was the financial commitment made on that occasion—a pledge of $5,000 a month until the end of the strike, half coming from the UAW and the remainder from the AFL-CIO Industrial Union Department. Also on that occasion Delano Mayor Dr. Clifford Loader could not ignore the visit to his city of distinguished national personalities. He came to the union hall to extend a welcome to Reuther and also arranged an informal session with the local growers—the first contact between strike supporters and the owners of the struck grape ranches.

That visit also set the stage for another occasion that would again spotlight the strike in the grape fields. Jack Conway, former official in the administration of the late President John F. Kennedy, in which he held several high-level posts, had close ties with the president's family. It was he who helped arrange a significant event.

Senator Robert F. Kennedy, who was destined to play an important role in the grape strike, and in whose life the farm workers were to play a very special role, was at that time a member of the U.S. Senate Farm Labor sub-committee. This committee conducted three days of hearings in California the following March (1966). Sacramento, Visalia and Delano were the cities in which the well-publicized hearings took place, and it was during these sessions that Kennedy reminded the local sherrif to brush up on the rights of all people, including farm workers, as guaranteed by the U.S. Constitution. These hearings did much to expose the role of the local police, the growers and the labor contractors.

Not since the 1930's when Eleanor Roosevelt became deeply and personally involved in some of the more progressive causes during her husband's administration, has a politically powerful family like the Kennedys become so deeply involved in a labor struggle. Robert Kennedy, according to Schrade who knew him well, "was trying to find himself" during the time of the grape strike. It was a time when he carried on long conversations with Black militants and with students.

It was in this mood, and in the atmosphere generated by the Delano strike, that he made his first visit to the fields. Kennedy, in his brief visit with the farm workers, became their friend. Because of his outspoken role at the hearings, in full view of the farm workers, he endeared himself to them. Schrade accurately described the response to Kennedy when he said "the reaction from union members [to Kennedy] was just tremendous. The intimate friendship with the farm workers was immediate." (Interview with Paul Schrade, March 1973)

"One of the best moments I have had in my whole life," Schrade said, "was marching in front of the DiGiorgio Ranch where there was this half-mile picketline of farm workers under the blue skies and in the wide open spaces of the San Joaquin Valley and Bob (Kennedy) came marching down the line shaking hands with all of the pickets. And you could hear coming from a distance these great voices shouting 'Viva Kennedy' and 'Kennedy por presidente' and it was a great time when you knew that friendship had been cemented and Bob wouldn't forget; that the farmworkers wouldn't forget. It really was very important towards building the movement."

During that initial trip Kennedy made to Delano, he engaged in an exchange with a small grower and his wife. In the presence of the press and many farm workers, Kennedy explained to the grower that it was not the union that he had to fear but the big growers, who constituted the major problem both for the farm workers and the small growers.

Throughout the following years, Kennedy reportedly did much to support the strike, including backing the boycott. And his wife Ethel became involved in fund-raisers for the farm workers and in other activity to support their cause. Whenever Chavez wanted to consult with Kennedy by phone, he was always available, according to Schrade. On one occassion, on March 10, 1968, when Chavez ended his 25-day fast to protest the increasing signs of violence in the strike, he was joined by Robert Kennedy who had flown to Delano especially for this occassion. At least once during the fast, Schrade reported, when there were signs that it would seriously impair the health of the Chicano labor leader, Kennedy phoned Chavez and asked him to end it in the best interest of all concerned.

Violence and political assassination was in the air. On the occasion that Chavez, in the presence of more than 5,000 farm workers and strike supporters in Delano Memorial Park, broke his fast, the outstanding civil rights leader, Rev. Martin Luther King, Jr. telegraphed, "My colleagues and I commend you for your bravery, salute you for your indefatigable work against poverty and injustice, and pray for your health and continuing service as one of the outstanding men of America. The plight of your people and ours is so grave that we all desperately need the inspiring example and effective leadership you have given."

Weeks later King came to Los Angeles to address a California

Democratic Council dinner. At that time he said his schedule did not then permit a trip to Delano to see Chavez, but that he planned to do so in the very near future. Plans were announced for a national unity meeting in Washington on April 22, where Blacks, Chicanos and the poor whites from Appalachia would assemble. All these future plans were cut down by a racist assassin's bullet on April 4, 1968, in Memphis, where King had gone to lend his assistance to striking sanitary workers.

Sixty-three days later Kennedy too was assassinated. The place was Los Angeles' Ambassador Hotel where, moments before, in the presence of a large contingent of farm workers who had worked diligently for his successful presidenial primary campaign in California, he had paid tribute to the farm workers of California.

Despite Chavez's limited formal education, he was an avid reader, who had literally devoured all that had been previously written about farm-labor strikes. Violence was no stranger to those struggles. Even in the grape strike, violence stayed barely beneath the surface many times during the early days. I saw a grower on the picket line, his rifle slung across the back window of his pick-up truck, in full view. In every struggle it was the farm workers who were the victims—after almost every major strike they counted their dead and wounded.

Chavez knew that the farm workers could not begin to match the growers in either economic or other kinds of power. His weapon was nonviolence, a powerful moral weapon with which the growers found it very difficult to cope. His Ghandian stance, which won the admiration of King and Kennedy, also frustrated the growers, who were prepared for the usual show of physical strength in which they would outnumber and outgun the field workers. But it was also frustrating to many of the strikers who were fed up with a lifetime of "turning the other cheek." Many were anxious to use their newly discovered union strength to reply in kind to the growers. It was because this feeling among the strikers was growing that Chavez put his personal prestige on the line in the Spring of 1968 and began the 25-day fast—to make his point dramatically.

But the fast also served another purpose—it put the national spotlight on the strike at a time when it was badly needed. It also tapped the deeply religious sentiments of the predominantly

Catholic Mexican workers, many of whom came to the room where Chavez stayed as if they were paying tribute to a saint. This was not particularly pleasing to non-Catholic strikers and to many of the volunteer organizers. But, as usual, Chavez insisted that if the large majority of the field workers approved, it would be done. And that they obviously did.

Chavez operated on the principle that he would accept help from almost any and all sources—with no strings attached. The one exception Chavez made, and this probably was more on the advice of some of his "liberal" advisors than because of his own feelings, was in accepting open support from the Communist Party, despite its long history of leadership and support in past farm workers struggles. Of course Communists were among those who joined in the many movements supporting the strike—and, in Chicago during the boycott, Eliseo Medina, the UFWOC representative, was among those who endorsed a Communist running for office. But the top union leadership, obviously fearful of red-baiting, drew its line.

Accepting help from all, with the exception noted, went along with support for those who had been loyal to the strike. It was this precept that brought about the first major political confrontation with the AFL-CIO.

In the 1968 Democratic Party presidential primaries, many of the left-of-center volunteer organizers among the farm workers looked with considerable favor on U.S. Senator Eugene McCarthy, primarily because of his strong challenge to President Johnson's hawkish position on the Vietnam war. But his failure to relate to the problems of the ghettoes and the barrios as well as to those of the Anglo working people tempered their enthusiasm.

The AFL-CIO choice for the presidency, Vice President Hubert Humphrey, did little to inspire either the farm workers or the union activists. And while there were some who had misgivings about Kennedy, mindful of his non-too-liberal record during his brother's presidency and deeply concerned about the Kennedy millionaire image, there was little doubt that he was the popular choice of the Chicanos and other farm workers. He had come to their aid at times when they most needed it. The fact that he was Catholic, while perhaps not decisive, was also of importance to some.

Irwin DeShetler, who had moved to Delano at Kircher's request, was the AFL-CIO coordinator for farm work, and he pleaded the case for the AFL-CIO position. "I spoke my heart out against it," DeShetler said, in referring to the union's endorsement of Kennedy. "I did it because the AFL-CIO was for Humphrey. They listened politely to me and when I got through they moved to endorse Kennedy. The vote was unanimous. I was like a voice crying in the wilderness. Not because they didn't like or respect me. But this is what they were going to do, and they didn't give a damn for anybody else. At that time it was Kennedy or nothing." (Interview with Irwin DeShelter, May 1973.)

However, according to Itliong, a private agreement had been reached between the farm union leaders and the top AFL-CIO officials. Under it, UFWOC, as it was then known, would maintain its principle of autonomy and give its political backing to the candidate of its choice, regardless of the position taken by the top AFL-CIO. But after the Democratic Party convention, the farm workers, like all other AFL-CIO unions, would support the nominee of the convention, who was Humphrey. And, as it turned out, the farm workers worked for Humphrey's election perhaps not as diligently as they had for Kennedy in the California Democratic primary, but at least as dutifully.

The Kennedy campaign was an all-out effort by the farm workers. In Los Angeles and in other cities, they called on all of their supporters to join them in the historic primary campaign. Day after day they knocked on doors in the barrios, registered voters in the Democratic Party ranks and campaigned for Kennedy. They worked as no other political activists. Hours meant nothing to them and they accepted hardships such as sleeping on floors in churches and meeting halls as a necessary part of their struggle.

Bruce Page, Godfrey Hodgson and Lewis Chester, reporters for the *London Sunday Times,* in their authoritative book on the 1968 election, *An American Melodrama,* reported, "No other American politician could have drawn the response that the grape pickers gave Kennedy—chiefly because no other had done so much to deserve it."

The decision to support Kennedy was a difficult one for all in the labor movement and most especially Chavez. He had to count heavily on the AFL-CIO unions for support, and these were the unions which backed Humphrey. Paul Schrade was alone in the UAW executive board in his backing of Kennedy and it was he who, at Kennedy's request, asked Chavez to be a Kennedy delegate to the Democratic Party convention. The third labor figure on the California Kennedy slate, Thomas Consiglio of the Steelworkers' Union, was later forced to withdraw as a result of pressures within the labor movement.,

After the hard campaign, the Kennedy slate won out by a very slim margin. The British authors reflected the viewpoint of many political commentators when they wrote, "In the end, the votes of Chavez's Mexican-Americans contributed most of the slender margin by which Kennedy beat (Eugene) McCarthy in California."

Primary day started out as a most joyous one for the farm workers and all others who had supported Kennedy. While other unionists were beating the bushes for Hubert Humphrey and anti-war activists were campaigning hard for McCarthy, the farm workers had just put in their hardest day in behalf of Kennedy.

And wearing their finest—yet shabby compared to that worn by many of Kennedy's other supporters—they came to the hotel party to enjoy the fruits of the victory to which they had contributed so much. Chavez was there, tieless as usual, in the unfamiliar surroundings of the Ambassador Hotel, and so were other leaders of the union. The results were all but final, and it was clear that Kennedy had eked out a hard-fought victory.

"The farm workers had made the difference," Schrade said, in commenting on Kennedy's vote margin. In 1968, Kennedy had converted California into a political miracle (having entered the primary race late after McCarthy's surprisingly strong showing in New Hampshire) and it was the farm workers who made it possible."

The crowd was large, and Chavez was among those who left the hotel early. When Kennedy appeared on the platform to receive the plaudits of the crowd and to accept the victory that was his in California that night, one of those on the platform with him was Dolores Huerta, UFWOC official. She was among those who had been invited to join Kennedy and his family in their suite for the private victory celebration.

In the course of the evening, Schrade and Kennedy talked of the contribution that the farm workers made to the election results that night and how they had made it possible.

The story of that night was at the Ambassador Hotel, and those of us who were stationed at the Los Angeles County Registrar of Voters office, getting the latest on local contests, were hurrying in order to get to the Ambassador and the Kennedy celebration. I was most anxious to join my friends among the farm workers who were there. Suddenly, and unbelievably, one of the newsmen who had been talking to his office raised his hand and shouted, "Kennedy has been shot." Within minutes I was left among the handful at the county building. All others had, at the instructions of their offices, rushed to the Ambassador. They were there to report on the final episode in Kennedy's life.

Among those who were shot in that rear passageway of the Ambassador, where the assassin awaited Kennedy, was Schrade. A bullet had pierced his upper brow. Kennedy was fatally shot. And just 15 feet behind him was his wife Ethel, walking alongside Dolores Huerta in what had been a triumphant and joyous victory caravan.

Before many hours passed Robert Kennedy's life ended and so did the first major political confrontation between UFWOC and the AFL-CIO.

For Dolores Huerta the events that day were especially depressing. For almost a decade she had been campaigning among politicians and other public figures seeking to enlist support for the campesinos. She was equally at home at a barrio rally as well as at a Massachusetts cocktail party at which funds were being raised for the farm workers' union. Among many on the left she had been called "La Pasionaria". This was not necessarily because she had the same politics as did Dolores Iburrari, Communist Party leader in Spain who became world famous as "La Pasionaria" during the fight against fascism in her country. Dolores Huerta, to many in this country is a woman of great stature and inspires thousands to support the cause she so eloquently represents.

One of the first organizers on the staff of the AFL-CIO Agricultural Workers Organizing Committee in 1959 she soon joined with the Community Service Organization where she worked with Chavez and others. One of her jobs at that time was to influence legislators in Sacramento in behalf of farm labor legislation. Today several laws are a tribute to her skill and persuasiveness in the halls of the California capitol.

Unlike so many others who succumbed to the lure of the middle class type of existence in the legislative halls, Huerta was more at home among the campesinos than anywhere else. Imaginative, outspoken, hard-working and a person of many talents, she had been a picket cap`iin, fund raiser and legislative representative. Later she was to be the union's top contract negotiator.

In the first National Farm Workers Association strike in April 1965, among the McFarland (California) rose workers, she blocked the driveway of a house with a truck where workers were getting ready to drive to work. Later that morning she went to the company offices representing the union. There she was called a "Communist" and evicted from the premises. The rose workers won their raise but did not get a union contract.

Early, in the movement against the Vietnam war, Huerta and Gilberto Padilla were among those who spoke out against U.S. imperialist aggression, to the consternation of Chavez who also opposed the U.S. military action but believed that many of the campesinos felt that only "Communists" opposed the military intervention. Later the union came out in opposition to U.S. troops in Southeast Asia.

Among farm union activists Huerta's outspokenness is legendary. Her differences on tactics with Chavez were well known. Still she was his most able lieutenant and was always available for assignment, large or small. If legislators had to be convinced about one or another matter she was dispatched to Sacramento or Washington D.C. If food and housing had to be arranged for marchers on the first night of the Delano to Sacramento pilgrimage she would go to Ducor, (with this author as her chauffeur), to arrange housing and dinner for the pilgrims, while at the same time raising funds for strikers.

In New York City, in the dead of winter, she led boycott picketlines of farm workers and others and rallied union men and women to the farm workers' cause. Union officials, including some of the most conservative, gasped as she spoke out at meetings in a most forthright manner while rank and filers cheered her words as representative of the deep desires of all of the poor, not just those who toiled in the fields.

10   El Triunfo

*"Respect for the rights of others
is peace."*   Benito Juarez, 1858

Never in the history of farm labor organizing had workers in
the fields triumphed as they did on July 29, 1970. It was a day that
climaxed what was then presumed to be the first stage in the forthcoming series of victories by the AFL-CIO United Farm Workers
Organizing Committee.

No matter what lay ahead, that day was destined to remain a
landmark in the annals of labor, in the Chicano movement and in
the lives of the untold number of social activists who for decades had
worked to bring about just such an event. Cesar Chavez's army of
farm workers, supported by much of the labor movement and
others, had toiled for almost five long years, and the fruits of their
labors, having fallen slowly over the span of several years, were now
beginning to come down in bunches. Yet there was a fear that
others, for example the Teamsters Union, were waiting on the
sidelines, preparing to gather the harvest that had been sown and
cultivated by the Delano strikers. Word had already reached Delano that Teamsters Union organizers, at the invitation of the Salinas
lettuce growers, were busily trying to derail the UFWOC victory
march.

The large UFWOC hiring hall just outside of Delano that day was
jammed to capacity by farm workers and their supporters. Teatro

171

Campesino's Augie Lira had led them in the singing of strike songs
and in repeated "Vivas" for the strike, the union and for Chavez. It
was a festive occasion; the heady wine of victory seemed to intoxi-
cate all present.

Newspaper, radio and television reporters, many of whom had
trudged the fields with the strikers at times when it appeared that
this struggle, like so many others, would just be a footnote in farm
labor history, another abortive effort to organize the fields, crowded
up around the head tables where the union leaders and the 26
Delano employers of more than 7,000 workers were to sign the
historic table-grape agreement.

The entrance of the union leaders, the growers and the clergymen who mediated much of the bargaining evoked a huge demonstration, including repeated chants of "Huelga," a none too pleasant
reminder to the growers that it was the strike that had brought them
to the table. To further emphasize the point, the strikers had their
hands raised in the "V"sign. It was a victory rally, and none of the
strikers wanted any of those present to miss the point.

It was paradoxical that the growers had come to the union building, specifically to its hiring hall to surrender. Among those who
were present was grower Martin Zaninovich, who, on September
18, 1966, told a U.S. Senate sub-committee on farm labor: "The
simple truth is, gentlemen, there is no strike in Delano."

Among the other growers were many who had who had vowed
never to sign up with Chavez's union, and especially that they
would not agree to the hiring hall provision.

On June 30, 1970, John Giumarra, Jr., general counsel for
Giumarra Vineyards and spokesman for the Delano grape growers,
foreshadowed the day of settlement, when he conceded that the
union-sponsored boycott had become especially effective, consider-
ing the agreements reached with Coachella and other grape growers. Giumarra said, "It (the boycott) is having a major effect now
that there are union grapes in the market. We have to have unifor-
mity and we don't have it." The solid front of the grape growers had
been broken. Less than two weeks prior to the signing, farm-labor
contractor Cornelio Macias told a state Senate sub-committee,
composed of two right-wing Republicans, "The growers just want
that bird on that box." The unionized grape ranches had the black

Aztec thunderbird—the UFWOC insignia—stamped on each box. They were selling in the market at a price higher than those of the non-union firms.

Henry Reider, vice-president of the Coachella Valley CID (Coachella-Imperial Distributors), had conceded earlier that year when his company was among those that signed up with UFWOC that the symbol was "an asset instead of a detriment with this boycott business."

Chavez, wearing a formal white linen shirt jacket that had been presented to him by Filipino workers, tried to tone down the gloating of many in the crowd at the contract-signing ceremony. While warning of the struggle ahead in Salinas, he optimistically predicted that the battle in the grape fields had come to an end and this day marked the beginning of a new era.

He also emphasized the high cost of the victory for the farm workers. During the five-year battle, 95 per cent of the farm workers involved lost their homes and their cars. He also pointed out, however, that in these five years wages had risen from $1.10 an hour, which many field workers were getting in 1965, to $1.80 an hour, provided for in the union contract. In addition, the first agreement provided for a 20-cent bonus for each box of grapes picked (usually between three and four each hour), with an additional 10 cents per hour contribution to the union-sponsored health and welfare plan. The growers also agreed to pay two cents for each box into the union's economic development fund, designed to cope with the effect of automation in the fields.

Giumarra, speaking for the growers, said, "In the future I only want to hear applause, not huelga." And instead of "boycott grapes", he said he was anxious to hear "compre los uvas"—buy the grapes. A number of the growers could not pass up the opportunity to call for "more production" with which to meet the increased labor cost of the new contract.

It was also a time for remembering—the fasts by Chavez and others as well as the long marches from Delano to Sacramento, from Rio Grande City to Austin, Texas, from Coachella to the Mexican border.

The very hall where the contracts were being signed had come into existence because of an unusual confluence of forces and movements that supported the strike. On March 11, 1968, Chavez completed a controversial 25-day fast on the same Forty Acres. It started out as his own personal religious fast in response to the increasing number of violent incidents in the fields and out of his fear that these might escalate and drown in blood the efforts to win the strike. His devotion to the concept of nonviolence never blinded Chavez to the violent potential that was always near the surface.

Chavez stayed within the service-station building on the union's property, and his fast evoked a great emotional response from many farm workers, while others from the fields as well as some strike supporters openly voiced their opposition to Chavez's dramatic fast—some on religious grounds, others for tactical considerations. Finally, having lost 35 pounds and having seriously jeopardized his health, he agreed to end the fast. The late Senator Robert Kennedy came to Delano to join in the dramatic fast-ending ceremony in that city's Memorial Park.

It was at that time that Chavez approached the UAW leaders on the scene, with the aim of negotiating a $50,000 loan to construct a union administration building. UFWOC offices were then spread out in many buildings throughout the city, and their rentals were considerable. The time had come to put all of the union services under a single roof—the hiring hall, credit union, membership office, boycott department, etc. Instead of agreeing to a loan, the UAW donated $50,000 for the construction of this project.

The erection of the Roy Reuther Memorial Hall, as it was called upon completion, was a cooperative project involving union labor from many parts of the state of California. In commenting on the cooperative effort that went into the building of the large office and union-service complex, Schrade said that "it proved that it was possible to get people together for a truly constructive purpose rather than getting people to support [the late President] Johnson's war in Vietnam as [AFL-CIO President George] Meany has been trying [to do]."

Probably no construction job has ever been more deserving of the union label than the building on Forty Acres. With great care and at very little expense to UFWOC, it was constructed as a labor of love and of devotion to the concept of building a home for a successful union of field workers.

Members of the Operating Engineers Union in San Francisco came to Delano to set the stage for the construction. Carrying their own supply of conduits, wires, lights and fixtures, 45 members of the International Brotherhood of Electrical Workers came up weekends and installed all of the necessary electrical facilities in the administration building as well as in the already constructed service station cooperative.

Electricians, carpenters and tile setters came from nearby Bakersfield. Members of the Cement Masons Union poured the concrete; union members from the Carpet and Linoleum Workers organization who came to install the flooring found it impossible to finish their labors because so much of the work was being done simultaneously. They had to leave it for the farm workers to finish. At one point, Chavez had to "escape" from the building through a window, because workers were busily engaged in construction on all sides of him, and there was no other way to get out.

For many rank-and-file union member who came to help build the union structures, it was their first contact with the grape strikers. Some of their unions had made financial donations, but that was a relatively easy thing to do. Giving one's labor free, sharing the food in the strike kitchen and having a beer or two with these Chicano and Filipino workers was something else again. DeShetler said "these workers were real sellers (of the grape strike) later on. They went around and told others about it."

While projects such as the building of the union halls met with universal approval in labor's ranks, other activities, such as the boycott of scab products, did not. Public disapproval of the Schenley boycott by the NFWA was voiced at the 1965 AFL-CIO convention by the Distillery Workers Union. During the Perelli-Minetti boycott, some of the smaller AFL-CIO union that had contracts with this firm complained to Meany but he ignored these beefs. However, when it came to the Heublein boycott it was a different matter. This company was a conglomerate with agreements with some powerful unions. Meany told Chavez that the AFL-CIO could not sanction this boycott.

Despite this disapproval from on high, Chavez and UFWOC said that the Heublein boycott was an essential part of its organizing strategy and could not be abandoned. The language of the rejection was soft and the words temperate; they were nevertheless firm. And there were some red faces in the AFL-CIO hierarchy when UFWOC succeeded in winning a contract with Heublein, largely as a result of its successful boycott. When the AFL-CIO said no to the boycott, UFWOC turned to its other allies for support—the Chicano movement, students, activists in the church movements and trade unionists who rejected the top AFL-CIO strictures.

Organized labor has long looked upon the boycott as one of its most valuable weapons, at least in a formal way. The AFL-CIO has a Union Label Department which was created to encourage union members and others to purchase only goods with the union insignia. Union publications throughout the nation are replete with lists of products and services which are on the unfair list. In Los Angeles, this includes the open shop *Los Angeles Times* which, ironically, can be found on the desk of virtually every union official every morning.

And printed appeals for support in political and other campaigns made to AFL-CIO members will more than likely be relegated to the wastepaper basket if they do not have the printing trades "bug" on them. Nevertheless, over the years the labor boycott has largely become a formality in the union movement. It has remained more a matter of tradition than an effective weapon.

That is perhaps why DeShetler said "when they (UFWOC) announced they were going to boycott I thought they were crazy." Suddenly the boycott became the farm-workers' most important weapon, to the amazement of old-timers in the labor movement.

Having viewed many of labor's boycotts, on which DeShetler estimated the unions have spent "billions," he watched the successful farm-union operation with astonishment. And he was by no means the only one. Usually the boycott in the labor movement is resorted to when the picket lines have ceased to be effective. It has usually been viewed as a last-ditch effort to salvage a losing strike. There never was a boycott as successful as the one initiated by the farm union. Other unions have since tried to emulate it.

Taking a leaf from UFWOC tactics, the Amalgamated Clothing Workers of America in 1971 began a nation-wide boycott of Farah Manufacturing Company. The union had organized this company and was compelled to strike. Eighty-five per cent of the work force in the Texas and New Mexico plants of Farah was made up of Chicanos. After a 21-month strike and boycott, supported by UFWOC and other sections of the organized labor movement as well as by the Chicano movement and other people's organizations, many of which had their baptism of fire in the boycott struggle in the grape boycott, these workers were victorious and won a contract with the long-time anti-union southwest firm in March 1974.

With a smile, DeShetler described the boycott as run "by these new guys who weren't supposed to know anything." He ascribed the success of the boycott to "these people who were so dedicated, they didn't worry how much they were going to get paid—they wanted to do this because they wanted a union." The activity of the farm workers and their supporters in the boycott was compared to that of the union struggles in the 1930's, when untold thousands joined in the movement to build the industrial unions.

In city after city farm workers arrived on boycott assignment with just a few dollars in their pockets. Their first job was to make contact with strike supporters—in the labor movement, the Chicano organizations, the churches or among local radicals—in order to set up a boycott structure. In Delano no questions were asked about the support groups; there was just the insistence that a boycott apparatus be established.

One of the most successful of all the boycott operations in the United States took place in New York City, where the trade-union movement was spurred on by the AFL-CIO Central Labor Council. It was there that taxi drivers, who had probably never before met a farm worker, marched on picket lines with campesinos who never before had encountered the cold winter in New York, let alone ride in a taxi.

It was also in New York that one of the most incongruous relations developed—between the farm workers and the Seaman's Union, headed by Paul Hall. This union, one of the most conservative in the AFL-CIO and, beyond doubt, one of the least democratic in the nation, provided living quarters for farm workers from Delano, furnished them with transportation and made available offices out of which the strikers operated. Nonetheless, in 1972, Hall endorsed the re-election of President Richard Nixon—an acknowledged opponent of the farm union—while UFWOC backed the losing Democrat, Senator George McGovern.

Hall, who is often mentioned as a possible successor to Meany, also contributed large sums to the strike. DeShetler estimated that this union did more than any other single organization to help finance the farm-union organizing drive and strike.

"I have been in the trade-union movement all my life and I have seen support for all kinds of strikes but I have never seen the kind of support that developed for the farm workers," DeShetler said. "Every union in the AFL-CIO made some kind of contribution to this strike. It was the first time I saw such an opening of the pocketbooks to help another union. They sent in millions."

For many, the farm strike evoked militant sentiments —reminders of earlier days in their unions. Others gave to prove that "the labor movement had a heart," as Itliong put it. And still others, like Hall of the Seafarers Union, probably gave support to the farm workers in order to gild an otherwise tarnished image.

The boycott was international in scope, and some of its great achievements were outside the borders of the United States. In Toronto, Canada, the trade-union movement, in concert with the church movements, effectively made that city off-limits for scab grapes. One of the leaders of that movement was Dennis MacDermott, Canadian director of the UAW, who was the leader of the delegation to Delano and the Coachella Valley in 1969 to meet with the striking farm workers. In the Canadian contingent, aside from trade unionists, there were churchmen, lawyers, teachers and students. They returned home even more dedicated in their support of the boycott and the California strike.

Meanwhile, a bitter battle was being waged on the European continent. In February, 1969, London dockers refused to unload 70,000 pounds of grapes, and the Transport and General Workers Union endorsed the boycott. This was also true in the Scandanavian countries. Ironically, the European unions with Communist leadership were among the staunchest supporters of the boycott, while in many countries the AFL-CIO representatives, more concerned with bludgeoning the European labor movement into support of the U.S. foreign policy than with the economic well-being of the workers in this country, either ignored the boycott grapes compaign or, in some instances, sought to counter it.

In the 1968 presidential campaign, scab grapes became an issue. Three U.S. Senators and Vice President Humphrey were among those vying for the Democratic Party presidental nomination endorsed the boycott. They were Kennedy, Eugene McCarthy and George McGovern. On the Republican side, Richard Nixon and California Governor Ronald Reagan ostentatiously had grapes on their campaign banquet tables at the height of the boycott.

Despite multimillion dollar lawsuits by the growers and high-powered professional public relations campaigns against the boycott, it continued to affect grape sales adversely. Attempts by the U.S. Department of Defense to bolster the lagging sales by making grapes one of its prized culinary delicacies on armed services tables in Vietnam and in Europe resulted in picket lines at military bases, where farm workers and anti-war activists joined in common cause.

All antilabor forces joined in denouncing the boycott. Jack Pandol, a Delano grower, who was one of the leaders of the anti-union California Right-to-Work Committee, called the boycott "unmoral, illegal, un-Christian and un-American."

Because the farm workers were not covered by federal labor laws such as the Landrum-Griffin Act, they remained unaffected by sections of this legislation that made the use of the secondary boycott illegal. The farm workers contended that the entire boycott campaign was an exercise in free speech and one that was in no manner barred or limited by federal labor legislation.

When ten growers in the Coachella Valley announced on June 13, 1969, that they were prepared to enter into negotiations with the farm labor union, it marked a dramatic turn in the strike. Once again it was Coachella Valley that was to shape the destiny of the farm-labor organizing drive. Four years earlier it was the AWOC strike in the Coachella Valley that set the stage for the Delano strike. Now once again this oasis in the desert was destined to chart the future of the union drive.

Two days before the growers announced their readiness to negotiate, Coachella growers were reeling from the effect of May 10, 1969, International Grape Boycott Day, which saw demonstrations in more than 100 cities against the sale of scab grapes. And on May 18 the eight-day, 100-mile march through the Coachella and Imperial Valleys reached a dramatic climax on the Mexican border, where more than a thousand farm workers rallied in support of their union's demands.

Suddenly the whole campaign took on a different outlook. After more than a year-and-a-half of stalemate, during which much of the farm union's financial resources were drained, according to Itliong, there was a new ray of hope and a change in tactics. Up to that point the union had sought to be included in coverage under the Federal Labor law. This would have assured them the right to have representation elections under the jurisdiction of the National Labor Relations Board. Also it would have deprived the union of what had become its most publicized tactic, the boycott.

At one stage of the game, virtually the entire union leadership had gone to Washington to appear at a hearing where they asked for inclusion under the regulatory federal labor law. But with the Coachella breakthrough there also came a change in position. The union demanded that it be given the rights that labor had under the original Wagner Act. Under these provisions it could continue to wage its boycott campaign.

With considerable logic, Chavez contended that since farm workers had been unjustly deprived of rights granted all other workers during the New Deal period when the Wagner Act was enacted, it was only fair that similar rights now be accorded to them. Under such legislation, the farm workers would be able to utilize federal machinery for representation elections; they would be in a positon to insist that the growers refrain from unfair labor practices, while also having the right to institute secondary boycotts whenever the farm workers believed that was necessary.

However, logic has a way of being defied by employers once they have succeeded in weakening labor legislation. That is what happened during the domestic cold war against labor, following World War II, when the Congress, in 1947, passed the Taft-Hartley Labor Relations Act, over President Truman's veto. Under its provisions, some of the more liberal sections of the Wagner Act were weakened. Others were completely eliminated. The right of the secondary boycott was prohibited. Also, anti-Communist provisions were written into the law, which were used to weaken and destroy many of the more progressive unions. (Later, even this law was made more restrictive in the Landrum-Griffin Act.)

The AFL-CIO top leadership, having learned how to accommodate itself to this new law, took the position that the farm workers be given "justice" by subjecting them to the same terms as all other unions under the Taft-Hartley law. Having tasted the fruits of victory as the result of its use of the boycott, UFWOC no longer wanted coverage under the Taft-Hartley law, since it would be deprived of its most potent weapon, the secondary boycott.

In an amazing reversal of form, growers and other anti-union organizations, who campaigned vigorously and successfully for many years to deprive the farm workers of even minimal protection under federal labor laws, now seek to include them in such legislation with special onerous conditions.

Among the legislative proposals introduced in a variety of states, there were provisions that would have included outlawing of strikes during harvest-time as well as making the secondary boycott illegal. Frustrated by the limited, but nevertheless discernible, success of the farm labor organizing drive, the growers and those who supported their position sought a new approach with which to stalemate the unionization of farm workers.

In turn, this thrust the farm labor union into a political-action drive aimed at defeating the legislative campaigns that sought to achieve in the state capitols what the growers had been unable to accomplish in the fields and in the boycott centers throughout the nation. This gave rise to a unique development in the farm labor union. It negotiated some of its contracts to include a special "paid holiday," the terms of which provided payment of the annual day's pay into the union's political-action fund. No other union had yet achieved such an agreement.

Once again the farm workers union had displayed a unique talent for quickly shifting gears—moving from one major campaign to another—within a very short period of time.

As a result of these developments, the new union found itself traveling a different path from that being pursued by the AFL-CIO. The farm workers persisted in opposing all legislation that inhibited their right to carry on full-scale boycotts, while the AFL-CIO lobbied for legislation that included farm workers on the same basis as other unions, regardless of whether proposed laws included prohibitions of the secondary boycott. The differences were real but were kept on a low key.

While other unions may have donated more money to the farm-labor strike and organizing drive than the United Auto Workers, probably none were more effective in supporting it. And almost invariably the UAW was the center of controversy, as a result of which many other labor organizations were pressured into substantial commitment to the cause of the farm workers.

The late Ann Draper drove Roy Reuther and Schrade to Delano in their first visit with AWOC and NFWA leaders, on which occasion they first met Chavez. Of all the urban supporters of the farm labor movement, Ann Draper of the Amalgamated Clothing Workers Union's union label department, was among the most persistent. All through the grape strike she organized support caravans of food and helped guide trade unionists from many unions to the farm-labor strike. At union conventions, including the 1965 AFL-CIO meeting in San Francisco, she allied herself with other farm-labor movement supporters to win backing for the grape strike.

"We found it easier than anyone expected" to get support in the UAW for the farm workers," Schrade said. "In the UAW rank and file, many of the Chicanos, Blacks and Anglos came from farm backgrounds—especially those on the West Coast."

Despite its stong commitment to UFWOC, the Auto Workers Union was unable to convince its ALA (Alliance for Labor Action) partner, the Teamsters Union, to join in a combined effort in behalf of the farm workers. After the UAW left the AFL-CIO there was an agreement in the ALA to develop a series of projects in behalf of the working poor, but this did not include any projects to aid the farm-labor union. The closest the UAW and the Teamsters came to that was on the West Coast where, at Schrade's suggestion, a council on jurisdiction was established which included the UAW, the UFWOC, the Packinghouse and the Teamsters Unions. Nevertheless, the leaders of the huge Teamsters Union continued, from time to time, to interject themselves into the farm-labor situation.

Probably the greatest impetus the farm workers got within the UAW was at the 1966 Long Beach convention of the auto workers, the first ever held by that union on the West Coast. Tears streamed from the eyes of many of the battle-wise and seasoned delegates, participants in the historic auto sit-ins in the militant upsurge of the 1930's, as the farmworkers marched into the convention hall singing their songs and waving their union banners. "We really did something for the soul of the union," Schrade commented. "It was one of the things that really helped the boycott succeed."

When the delegates recessed their meeting to join in a mass picketline of a nearby Safeway store because the management was selling scab grapes, I. W. Abel, president of the AFL-CIO Steelworkers Union, who had come to address the convention, was among those who joined the demonstration.

In 1967, when the UAW fracas with the AFL-CIO top leadership was coming to a head, one of the points of difference was support to the farm workers. At the West Coast regional meeting meeting in Fresno in March, the delegates to Region 6, UAW, called on their international union to withhold all dues per capita to the AFL-CIO and to allocate it instead to help the farm-workers union.

It was during these days that the two most influential trade unionists who were most often in Delano as well as at other points where the farm labor campaign was at its height, were the AFL-CIO's Kircher and UAW's Schrade. Ironically, both of them were products of ths UAW, where they had been on opposite sides during the bitter factional days when the Reuther leadership won out over the more progressive members of the UAW international executive board. Schrade with strong ties with the youth and civil rights movements, was in those days Reuther's young and relatively conservative protegee. Kircher, the representative of the AFL-CIO bureaucracy, had then been aligned with the more progressive grouping in the UAW.

The hangover from this bitter inner UAW fight was reflected in the farm-labor campaign. Schrade did not believe that the competition between the UAW and the AFL-CIO was necessarily harmful to the farm workers' effort. This competition, in fact, in his opinion, resulted in even greater support for the new farm workers union.

Schrade, working closely with Chavez, viewed him as "a great leader" and one who had "charisma." Furthermore, he said, Chavez "communicates a great deal of sincerity; he's one of the most intelligent people I know, self-educated, reads widely and deeply and is very interested in people. He has a very easy relationship with farm worker families and also with some of the most important leaders—he gets across to people more than anyone else in the trade union movement. In addition he has a keen interest in the long term development of the union as well as the immediate."

Doleres Huerta has many of the same qualities as Chavez, in Schrade's opinion ". . . an activist, a firebrand in such a good way.". The auto union official noticed other traits in Dolores Huerta about which many other observers have also commented. She is a tougher fighter than Cesar; she's tough, hard, fast on her feet and really brilliant. She likes confrontation with growers . . ."

To Schrade, Itliong was "more the practitioner who has been around the labor movement a long time—very practical and serious as an organizer and negotiator."

Probably no traditional trade unionist had as good an opportunity to view Delano first-hand as did Irwin DeShetler, who began his trade-union experience in the late 1920's, was president of the Flat Glass Workers Union and had been involved in all of the inner fights in the labor movement until he retired, at age 65, in June, 1971. For the last three years of his trade-union activity he lived in Delano, mainly assisting in the negotiation of union contracts but also participating in many other union activities.

Since September 1966, he had been spending much of his time in Delano. There he met with Chavez, Rev. Jim Drake, then his administrative assistant, and Fred Ross, long-time associate of the union leader and probably his closest confidant since they were together in the Community Service Organization (CSO). He was made welcome by all of them.

DeShetler was a man of considerable loyalty—to the trade-union movement and to Cesar Chavez. When these loyalties appeared to conflict, he invariably resolved them by siding with Chavez. The Delano strike was like starting a new life for this veteran union organizer. "When I went to Delano it was like beginning all over again in the labor movement," he said. He recalled "the police brutality and the viciousness of the employers," which to him were comparable "to the 1930's in the labor movement."

Delano did for DeShetler what it did for many others—it rejuvenated them. "It made me young again," he said. "I was doing things again that I didn't believe possible such as getting up at two or three in the morning to go out on the picketlines. Freezing your butt off and in the summer time, the mosquitoes eating the hell out of you. It was a wonderful way of ending up in the trade union movement."

He recalled one day the mobilization to stop a train loaded with grapes. Inside of 45 minutes there were 500 people on the tracks. It reminded him of ants, who seem to be scurrying aimlessly but each of whom has a mission. "That was what it was like in Delano and Cesar planned all of these missions." And in his eyes Chavez "was truly a great leader, but unorthodox as far as the trade-union movement was concerned. They did so many things that were foreign to the trade-union movement, as I knew it before I went up there, but they were things other people couldn't have done because they didn't know how to do them that way. And that's why they were such a great success."

As for those who became UFWOC's negotiators, DeShetler worked with them all in the bargaining sessions, beginning with Schenley's, until he retired from the farm-labor scene. He had nothing but praise for Dolores Huerta, the union's top bargainer. Even her digressions from normal collective bargaining intrigued him. So did the talents of Mack Lyons, a Black farm worker from the DiGiorgio Ranch in Arvin who became a union organizer, and Marshall Ganz, a volunteer who came from the ranks of the Student Nonviolent Coordinating Committee to join the strike in its earliest days.

About the same time another long-time trade unionist came to Delano to offer his services. Clive Knowles, having left the Packinghouse Union, and having worked with Chavez in projects in Oxnard and Brawley when the Chicano organizer was a CSO official, came to Delano to offer his services as a volunteer organizer. He did some research for UFWOC, helped organize DeGiorgio workers in Marysville and then looked around for a place where he could be useful to the organizing effort. He finally left, convinced that Chavez was too busy to work out a program with him and that some of Chavez's closest co-workers were not anxious to have him around.

Knowles had many years of experience as a union organizer in the factories and in the fields. The farm workers union was in need of experienced organizers. "I knew Cesar Chavez very well, we knew each other for a long time and respected each other. Our relationship was a good one and Cesar welcomed my involvement." But within the first week he sensed a hostility to him from two of Chavez's top advisors. He believed that hostility was due to "my being pegged as someone from the AFL-CIO."

When he was asked by Chavez to assist in organizing the DiGiorgio workers in Marysville, he welcomed the change. And he had nothing but praise for UFWOC organizer Gilberto Padilla, with whom he worked in Marysville for about a month. "He's a dedicated guy and a damned good organizer," Knowles said in describing Padilla.

But when he returned to Delano, Knowles felt "the clerical guys took over." This was a reference to the representatives of the California Migrant Ministry who had been assisting Chavez since the earliest days of the NFWA. "On the surface I found the relationship pleasant enough, but underneath I felt I was pegged as a red by some of them who had long been associated with the professional red-baiters in the labor movement. I was eased out of operation at that point I would have been a left influence and that's why they put the skids to me."

A different view of some of these events was given by Jim Drake. "The influence on the union of persons who Knowles apparently believed to be associated with so-called professional red-baiters was, at best, miniscule. Knowles did not fit into the team for other, personal, reasons. It had nothing to do with his political past or his outlook, about which we knew very little at that time". (Interview with Jim Drake, associate of Cesar Chavez, June 1974)

Despite this experience, Knowles, in 1967, was called upon to check out the organizing potential among 30,000 Black farm workers in the Florida delta. He went there at the request of Conway and Ralph Helstein, president of the Packing Union. After three months, working with an all-white staff, he advised his union to pull out of the situation and instead to donate its money to Cesar Chavez and UFWOC. In 1972 UFWOC made its first break in Florida and negotiated a contract with a subsidiary of Coca Cola for 1,200 field workers.

Differences of approach continued, tactically and policy-wise, among supporters of the grape strike during much of its turbulent five-year strike-boycott history. But so great was the historic impact of this struggle that the momentary and relatively minor differences, which at some moments appeared to assume major dimensions, faded into the background, overwhelmed by the surge of support from the rank and file of movements backing the latest drive to organize the workers in the fields.

Even while unionists in Canada and Europe were joining with large sections of the U.S. labor movement in supporting the strike-boycott, the members of the farm-labor union were not meeting with similar success much closer to home—in the San Joaquin Valley. This valley is traditionally conservative, a factor that affected the viewpoint of the union members living there. Many of them were from the South and, like so many below the Mason and Dixon line, were Democrats with conservative viewpoints.

This was close to home and developments in this valley were more often reflected in the local press in which there were rarely reported strike and boycott activities in the rest of the state, nation and even overseas. However the local events were but a small part of the over-all picture. The impact of the strike was far reaching and had its effect on the labor movement, in politics, among religious leaders and many others. The next few pages will deal briefly with some examples that illustrate the scope of the influence of the farm labor movement.

The *Valley Labor Citizen*, official AFL-CIO organ for unions in the Fresno area, was edited by George Ballis, a perceptive and talented photo-journalist. His viewpoint was considerably to the left of that of the leaders of organized labor in the southern half of the San Joaquin Valley. And his enthusiastic support of the striking farm workers soon became a bone of contention with those who controlled the paper. His articles and photos of the early days of the strike were among the most sympathetic written in any journal. In addition, he assisted the struggling new union of campesinos in many other ways, especially as a photographer.

His loyalty to the farm workers soon led him into irreconcilable clashes with the local labor leaders, and he finally decided to leave the *Valley Labor Citizen* to devote his full-time energies to helping the farm workers in their strike and boycott.

In the fourth month of the strike and shortly after the boycott of scab grapes was initiated, the key role of organized labor was dramatically illustrated on the Oakland, California docks, where ILWU Local 10 and 34 members stopped work and decided for the second time in six weeks not to load scab grapes destined for Europe. Among the six pickets arrested on December 27, 1966, in front of the Johnson Line's S.S. Bataan, were five farm workers and one longshoreman, Bart Abbot, an ILWU member.

So pervasive was the impact of the strike in the fields that the Teamsters Union announced its support of the grape strike and joined with AWOC in a jurisdictional agreement for Tulare County —the field workers were to be enrolled in AWOC and the drivers in the Teamsters.

On January 24, 1966 the consumer boycott of Schenley products was announced in San Francisco, and three days later they mourned the first casualty of the strike. Roger Terronez, 32, was fatally injured while trying to start one of the union's aged cars so that he could get back to his boycott assignment in the San Francisco-Bay area. The Delano medical clinic was later named The Roger Terronez Memorial Clinic.

While the headlines for the California Democratic Council convention in Bakersfield in mid-February were centered on the antiwar position of that organization and the drive to oust its president Simon Casady, it was also the occasion for a massive demonstration in support of the grape strikers. The liberal Democrats brought enough food to the convention to feed the strikers for about two weeks and donated $4,177, following a speech by Chavez and a collection appeal by Black Assemblyman Willie Brown. In addition, delegates pledged another $1,410 to the strikers.

Chavez told the delegates, "We feel that the CDC (California Democratic Council) is our only hope within the Democratic Party to fight for justice for the underdog."

The leaders of the grape strike were not merely relying on strong arguments to win support. They brought over 50 pickets with them to the convention, led by Dolores Huerta. It was they who surrounded Governor Edmund G. Brown and forced him to promise to intervene in the Delano dispute, his first public commitment on the issue.

No sooner had the three days of U.S. Senate sub-committee hearings in Sacramento, Visalia and Delano ended, in the middle of March, than the farm workers began their historic 300-mile, 25-day pilgrimage to Sacramento. It was such diversity of activity, some of it accompanied by headlines in the state's major newspapers, that forced into the open the issue of the strike in the fields. Traditional trade unionists shook their heads in disbelief as they sceptically viewed the almost frenetic series of events. Chavez and his co-workers were not about to let the people of California ignore the strike. Meanwhile, it became a catalyst for farm workers throughout the state, many of whom had participated in earlier strikes and who now saw the new drive as the answer to their long-awaited desire for organization. Robert Powell, a Black farm worker from Salinas, came to the march with a delegation. He said, "Sometimes it takes a jolt to get you to move the way you should." That march was a jolt for many farm workers as well as for many others.

On April 6, ten days before the pilgrims were scheduled to come to Sacramento on Easter Sunday, the farm workers won their first strike when Schenley signed up. Six days later the Christian Brothers' Mont LaSalle Vineyards in Napa Valley signed up with the union. Huerta greeted the first two contracts with the statement that "the development of the past seven months are only a slight indication of what is to come."

Each succeeding month brought its own highlights and increased public recognition that this struggle in the fields was different from all previous ones. At the Long Beach UAW convention, Chavez and Itliong spoke, and $11,000 was collected in behalf of the strikers. In addition, there was the previously mentioned $5000 a month commitment.

June, 1966 was one of the more eventful times for the organized farm workers. In the early part of the month, melon-pickers struck the Texas fields, and the NFWA, having reached a jurisdictional agreement with the Teamsters Union (which turned out to be very short-lived), credited the ILWU with being instrumental in bringing it about.

It was also the month in which the agreement with Schenley was worked out in contract form, providing for a hiring hall and 35-cents-an-hour wage increase. On the same day (June 21) that the contract was made public, the DiGiorgio Farms announced unilaterally that it was scheduling a representation election among its workers on June 29. Chavez called on the workers to boycott these elections and more than half of the workers refused to cast ballots. The Teamsters Union was declared the winner of the balloting but, on the insistence of Chavez and the Mexican American Political Association, Governor Brown appointed Ronald Houghton, co-director of the Institute of Labor and Industrial Relations at Wayne State University (Michigan) to investigate the situation. A new DiGiorgio election was recommended by Houghton for August 30.

On the Sunday preceding the new election date, 3,500 gathered in the Kern County National Guard Armory to mobilize the farm workers union for the expected victory. It was called to witness the charter presentation from the AFL-CIO to the new United Farm Workers Organizing Committee, which included the former NFWA and AWOC organizations. Among those present at the rally were DiGiorgio workers, who had come from Mexico, Texas, Arizona and many other distant places. They had come to campaign and to cast their votes for the union. Some workers who had never even worked for DiGiorgio but who had heard about an election in the fields came nevertheless to share in the moment of triumph.

Meanwhile, the company was telling the workers that it wanted them to vote for the Teamsters. At the same time, Teamsters Union officials unleashed a bitter red-baiting attack against the new AFL-CIO organization.

At the California AFL-CIO convention, shortly before the DiGiorgio election, the delegates responded to the plea for help for the farm strikers with donations totalling $1,500. But on the convention floor attempts to criticise the Teamsters were ruled out of order. Too many of the delegates, it appeared, had close working relations with this powerful union in their home cities. The misgivings among some AFL-CIO unions over the merger were also reflected in Kircher's talk to the convention. He said there was some division in union ranks on this question, but among the farm workers the sentiment for merger into a united farm labor organization was unanimous.

In the days before the balloting, Eliseo Medina, UFWOC organizer, was beaten so severely that he needed four stitches in his lip. Richard Edmonds, another UFWOC representative, was also beaten over the head and had both his eyes blackened.

When the ballots were counted in the first major ballot test in the fields, UFWOC came out the big winner, getting 528 votes to 328 for the Teamsters. Only seven workers voted for no union. This was the vote among the field workers. Another, the same day, took place among shed workers and miscellaneous workers. The Teamsters won this one by getting 97 votes, while 43 voted for UFWOC.

The national impact of the new union was reflected in Texas where, in September, 1966, 1,500 rallied to support the striking campesinos. U.S. Senator Ralph Yarborough and Archbishop Robert E. Lucey addressed the San Antonio gathering.

The largest Labor Day rally in Texas history took place that year, following the 400-mile march by farm workers from Rio Grande City on the Mexixan border to Austin. As in California, the Texas governor, John Connally, was not present when the marchers arrived in Austin. He met them in New Braunfels, a short distance away, after they had been marching in protest since July 4. A reported 25,000 farm workers and union supporters thronged the capitol grounds on Labor Day.

On October 31, in Roma, Texas, Mexican union members and UFWOC strikers stood on the international bridge with the red-and-black strike flag. Mexican workers who had been recruited as strikebreakers turned back and refused to come to the U.S. fields. It was a remarkable display of international solidarity.

In November, the UFWOC members at the DiGiorgio ranch had an opportunity to join with those at the company's Borrego Springs and Sierra Vista Ranches who had earlier voted for the new AFL-CIO Union. The Arvin campaign, which was led by Mack Lyons, a Black field worker from the company's Arvin Ranch, resulted in a 283-to-199 win for UFWOC. And, at about the same time, in mid-November, the grape pickers from the Mosesian, Hourigan and Goldberg property near Delano voted 285 to 38 to be represented by UFWOC.

While 1966 was the year of the breakthrough for UFWOC, it was also the first full year of struggle to win the battle of Delano. That was not to come until four years later in 1970.

Stemming the recruitment of strike breakers from Mexico still remained one of UFWOC's major challenges in 1970. The table-grape strike in Delano had not yet been won, although many of the wine-grape ranches had been brought under contract with UFWOC. It had nevertheless become increasingly clear that the union's strength in the fields and in the cities was mounting.

In Los Angeles, during the first week of the new year, 130 farm workers, who had come from the fields to Los Angeles to assist the labor movement, were able to report that 300 stores in that city had cleared non-union grapes from their shelves over the Christmas holidays.

Cesar Chavez, on January 17, addressed a membership-drive meeting of 1,200 farm workers in Calexico on the Mexican border, which has a population of 8,000. He said "the growers are using the poor in Mexico against us, the poor in California. To the ranchers and others who oppose us we tell them as Benito Juarez one said, 'The respect for the rights of others is peace.' "

The Union's boycott was in force in over 100 U.S. and Canadian cities, and it was evident that the years of struggle had toughened the new union. The growers were getting less peace than ever before. At a government hearing in Bakersfield on January 31 on "decertification of strikes," Chavez bluntly accused the growers of racism. He testified in Spanish so as to protest the fact that none of those conducting the hearing spoke the language. (The only Spanish-speaking person on the government side of the table was a Cuban translator.) At the hearing, Chavez said, "We're farm workers; Black brothers, Mexican brothers, white brothers and Filipino brothers." This was translated as "there is no difference between niggers etc. . . . ." It was only after Mack Lyons, Black UFWOC organizer, stated that the use of the word "nigger" was personally offensive to him that the translator apologized.

On the Perelli-Minetti & Sons Ranch in the Delano area, UFWOC demonstrated that it was fighting for the rights of all workers, including Black workers, in a concrete manner. In March 1970, this old-time company for the first time in its history had Black workers in its fields. Out of the 55 workers sent to the firm from the Union hiring hall, 17 were Black.

The loyalty to UFWOC of those under contract was reflected in the fact that the Schenley workers, who were already paying

$3.50-a-month dues and a voluntary one-dollar-a-week assessment to assist the strikers, raised their contribution to the strike by an additional two dollars a month in early 1970. Meanwhile, another dimension of the strike was emerging. It was a firm anti-war position. Douglas Rippey, a volunteer organizer, told a membership meeting, "It is impossible for me to go to Vietnam and make war on farmers there and to spray poison on their fields while we are striving for life and health here." The Rev. Mark Day, the Franciscan priest who had been acting as the Catholic chaplain for the strikers, Pablo Espinoza and Gilberto Padilla were selected as an official union delegation to be present in court when Rippey challenged his induction.

Yet regardless of other activities, UFWOC centered its main effort on prosecuting the boycott of table grapes. Despite the grower's multimillion-dollar publicity campaign mapped out by the high-powered San Francisco firm of Whittaker and Baxter, the boycott was having its desired effect. Galvanizing the boycott effort were more than 100 strikers, who had fanned out to 36 major table-grape selling cities throughout the continent. In the 1966 to 1969 period, the union claimed it had cut the sale of the forbidden fruit by almost one-third in these cities.

The suit brought by the growers early in 1970 confirmed this claim. It charged that the boycott had resulted in $75 million damages. The growers sought an injunction against the boycott, and Chavez and others said if necessary they would violate any such injunction and would carry on their activities from behind jail bars.

By March 23, the strikers had already had their second face-to-face meeting with the growers. It was held in Fresno and had been arranged by the Bishop's Committee on Farm Labor.

To UFWOC, the Coachella Valley appeared to be the soft underbelly of the growers' resistance movement. The previous year, this area, a sometimes marginal profit market for table grapes, had, as a result of the 1969 boycott, seen its sales cut by ten percent. On April 4, ten days before the scheduled restriking of the Coachella fields, a contract was reached for the table-grape-field workers on three Coachella Valley ranches. It covered about 750 workers at peak season employed on 7,800 acres—one-seventh of all Coachella table grapes.

It was a landmark agreement for UFWOC, with increases of 22 cents an hour in wages and benefits. The new minimum rate was $1.75 an hour, plus 25 cents for each box picked, ten cents an hour to be contributed to the union's health and welfare program, the hiring hall and the ban on deadly pesticides in the field, while two cents was contributed into the economic development program for each box of grapes picked.

Shortly thereafter, over 300 AFL-CIO representatives of 22 of California's 31 central labor councils came to Delano, where John Henning, executive secretary of the state AFL-CIO, promised that union labor would be "stepping up its boycott activity." Anticipating the coming events, Chavez told the assembled unionists, "We're always ready to talk with the growers. We're prepared for a settlement this year, but we can go another year or as many years as it will take to win the strike."

Shortly thereafter, UFWOC intensified its picketing activity in the fields. A rally of 2,500 took place in Coachella. The day after this rally took place, Chavez met with three large growers, including one from Delano. The dam was beginning to crack. Meanwhile on April 18, 1970, UFWOC was demonstrating that it could also renew old contracts with wine-grape growers by negotiating a $2.20-an-hour minimum for field workers on the Gallo Brothers ranch. In 1967 Gallo had signed a three-year agreement with UFWOC, and the renewal of this contract as the Delano crisis was coming to a head further strengthened UFWOC's position.

On May 20, two Delano-based companies, Bruno Disposo Co. and Bianco Fruit Co. became the first Delano area growers to sign with UFWOC. These contracts brought the number of separate agreements with the racalcitrant growers to sixteen. The Delano contracts were also significant because they allowed the union to expand its representation to workers in crops other than grapes. If the union could show that it had as members a majority of the workers in any crop, the companies agreed that UFWOC could bargain for them.

At the strike fever spread, including a school boycott by Delano children to protest alleged discrimination and demanding the hiring of Spanish-speaking teachers, as well as a spontaneous walkout by peach-and plum-orchard workers in King and Fresno Counties,

Chavez pressed harder for settlements. He warned of a possible "general farm labor strike (that) will shut down agriculture in California this summer or next" and talked of the "impatient farm workers in other crops [who] see striking workers winning contracts."

On June 6, after a three-day strike, UFWOC won a contract with Abatti Bros. Produce Co. in Imperial Valley; on June 10, Roberts Farms in McFarland, less than 10 miles south of Delano, signed up for its 2,000 workers on 46,000 acres in Kern, Fresno, Tulare and King Counties. It covered workers in table and wine grapes, almonds, citrus and peaches.

It was reported that on June 22 Teamsters Union members in Oakland had refused to handle non-UFWOC grapes, after 60 farm workers and their supporters marched around the offices of Grant J. Hunt, largest handler of scab grapes in the East Bay area. By June 27, the number of contracts had increased to 18

Even while UFWOC was closing in on its goal, shots were being fired into its auto-service station on Forty Acres, and Larry Itliong's garage was destroyed by fire. Also at that time Tenneco, one of the conglomerates that had bought into grapes, was accused of pressuring some of the smaller grape ranches to resist signing up with UFWOC. Nevertheless, six more Arvin area growers fell into line and Tenneco (Tennessee Oil Co.), the 34th largest company in the United States, signed up with the union, as did S. A. Camp, successor to the huge DiGiorgio holdings, who two years previously had refused to honor the agreements that the union had reached earlier with DiGiorgio.

A last-ditch stalling attempt by California Governor Ronald Reagan to hold elections in the fields was rejected out of hand by UFWOC. "Too little, too late," was UFWOC's response to Reagan's public suggestion. By mid-July the circle around Delano was tightening. More than one-third of all table-grape firms were under contract.

11 Diversions and Deaths

> *"This is a war, this a real war—all of the growers and right-wing elements . . . are trying to crush the farm workers . . . we have to act like it's a real war."*
>
> Dolores Huerta, 1973

Having scored the single largest victory in farm-labor organizing history, UFWOC faced new challenges similar to those encountered by other rank-and-file oriented unions. The aura of success was pervasive and the demands for organization by many others, who had patiently waited until the grape pickers had won their battle, were persistent. None were more insistent in their demands for organization into the new union than were the lettuce-pickers, traditionally among the most militant of farm workers.

As far back as 1966, a delegation of Salinas area farm workers joined the pilgrimage from Delano to Sacramento with the request that they too be included in the massive strike in the fields. They, like others, heeded the advice of UFWOC officials to stay in the fields and continue organizing until such time as the grapepickers were victorious. In the summer of 1970, the time had come for the redemption of these promises.

Growers, looking at the outcome of the grape strike and boycott, became restive, fearing that they too would be placed in the same

position as were the grape-ranch owners. The Salinas lettuce growers were prepared to combat UFWOC. They had at their disposal a
long-time precedent, one that succeeded against an earlier unionization effort in the Salinas fields during the 1961-1962 lettuce strikes
by the United Packinghouse Workers of America and AWOC. At
that time, Bud Antle publicly complained in the June, 1961,
California Farmer about restrictions against the use of the braceros
in the struck fields. He also claimed that he alone among the
lettuce-growers fought off the organizing efforts of Packing Union's
Local 78 among the shed workers. At about the same time, Antle
signed a contract with the Teamsters Union, which specifically excluded "foreign workers" and in which the Teamsters promised that
they would "assist Bud Antle, Inc. in obtaining foreign supplemen-
tal workers . . . in its harvesting operation."

The contract between the Teamsters Union and this lettuce
grower, which the Teamsters now cite as its "precedent" for the
organizing field workers, reportedly covered only 50 workers out of
approximately 1,000 working for the Antle Company. The contract
also gave the company a free hand to hire and fire workers at will.
The management, it said, "shall have the right to direct the work
force, to determine the means and accomplishment of any work, to
determine the number of workers required for any job, and shall
have the right to hire and fire workers."

In 1962 and 1963, while other labor organizations, Chicano leaders, liberals and church activists were calling for an end to the bracero program, Bud Kenyon, secretary-treasurer of Teamster Local
890, came out for the extension of the foreign-labor program for
another five years. And in 1963 the troubled Antle Company was
loaned one million by the Central and Southern States Pension
funds of the Teamsters Union. In effect, the Teamsters Union was
on both sides of the bargaining table during negotiations with this
company.

On July 23, 1970, while Chavez and the other UFWOC officials
were preparing for the Delano settlement, the lettuce-growers met
in a local motel and decided to call in the Teamsters Union. Four
days later, on July 27, the Teamsters and the shipper-growers in the
Salinas-Watsonville region announced that they had signed a
collective-bargaining agreement. The next day Chavez challenged

the validity of this contract and announced that it would be challenged in the courts.

Virtually the entire UFWOC staff was brought to the Salinas Valley, leaving unguarded for the time being the contracts just reached with the Delano area grape growers. Instead of devoting its energies to consolidating its victory in grapes and retraining many of its organizers so that UFWOC could better service the workers under contract, the union once again was in crisis.

The pressure from the workers and from UFWOC supporters was relentless and, on August 12, a jurisdictional agreement was again reached with the Teamsters Union under which field workers would be under the jurisdiction of Chavez's union. Three years later, in the midst of still another battle between the Teamsters and Chavez's union, William Grami, chief farm-labor organizer for the Teamsters, said that "political and church pressure forced the Teamsters into a (1970) jurisdictional agreement."

The Catholic Bishops Farm Labor Committee mediated the UFWOC-Teamsters agreement, as they did many other disputes in agriculture. Herb Fleming, president of the Vegetable Growers and Shippers Association, promptly rejected the agreement, contending that, "We have the proper and legal contracts with the Teamsters Union." In addition, he declared that the Teamsters "have assured us they will honor these contracts, and we intend to do the same."

A mass meeting of 5,000 workers in the lettuce fields instructed UFWOC to strike the fields if the growers failed to reach an agreement with the union. On August 24, the strike began and so did the violence. Despite the agreement, Teamsters were involved in violence from the outset. On the third day of the strike UFWOC attorney Jerry Cohen was hospitalized, following an attack by a 290-pound Teamsters Union organizer.

The first company to agree to a UFWOC contract was Interharvest, a United Fruit Company subsidiary. The threat of a boycott of Chiquita bananas, the big money crop of United Fruit, was believed to be instrumental in bringing this company to the bargaining table. Other companies which signed up with UFWOC were Freshpict, a subsidiary of Purex, and D'Arrigo Brothers.

In the course of this strike, the red-baiting of the union was intense. One of the bumper stickers of the growers was "Reds,

Lettuce Alone!" The red-and-black UFWOC Aztec eagle banners were countered by opponents of the union with flags of the United States. The clergy which had negotiated the tenuous armistice between the Teamsters and UFWOC were also targeted for public criticism by a newly formed committee called Citizens for Local Justice. Their bumper stickers said, "Boycott the Church, Pray Direct!"

Court injunctions issued by local judges were handed down against UFWOC with regularity. One of them ordered the union to end its boycott, and another ordered the union to post a $2.75-million bond to be set aside for the growers if it could later be shown that the boycott had been effective. Chavez was jailed for violating one of the court orders on December 4. On December 6, Ethel Kennedy, the widow of the late Senator Robert F. Kennedy, came to visit him in jail and to participate in a candlelight parade through Salinas. Chavez was later freed from jail when a higher court ordered his release.

More than two years later, on December 29, 1972, the California State Supreme Court ruled that the UFWOC picketing in Salinas was legal and declared that the Teamsters had signed contracts with 45 growers without showing any evidence that it represented the workers or was acting in their behalf.

If Delano demonstrated the new union's ability to win a long-range battle, the campaigns in Salinas and Santa Maria showed that it could also wage a shorter-term campaign with effectiveness and some considerable success.

Meanwhile the farm workers union was going about the business of setting its house in order. Even while the lettuce boycott was in progress against non—UFW lettuce, new departments were being established in Delano to organize systematic servicing of the membership. Growers were not yet accustomed to living with union contracts and workers did not take too kindly to some of the foremen who were formerly labor contractors. The social revolution that was UFWOC still had some rough edges to overcome, some from angry workers, others from stubborn bosses.

The union's showplace in Delano was its hiring hall. Chris Sanchez, hiring hall dispatcher, who was better known as the union's photographer, noted that the hiring hall in the 1971-1972 winter season had two rather special features. For the first time, women workers were being used in the pruning of grape vines and many more Blacks and Anglo workers were coming to the union hiring hall in search of work.

Traditionally, pruning operations had been limited to men. But that year the union sent out all workers, regardless of sex, to available jobs. During the previous season, many of the men, in anticipation of the new era, had taught their wives the intricacies of pruning. When the 1971-1972 winter season came around, whole families were prepared to work in the fields.

Aside from the fact that this ended anti-women bias in the fields, it also helped tide families over during the no-work period. Picking begins in April and may run as late as early November in Delano.

Urban unemployment, especially among Black, Chicano and Anglo workers at the bottom of the economic ladder, appeared to increase hiring-hall activity for persons working on a union job for the first time. About two-thirds of those seeking jobs at the hall were either Mexicans or Chicanos. The remainder included Filipino, Arab, Black, Japanese and Anglo workers.

Alice Tapia, another hiring hall dispatcher, has long, blond tresses and is deceptively young in appearance. She worked as a packer and picker at the Delano Di Giorgio Ranch before the strike, and cheerfully admitted to being a grandmother. A considerable percentage of those who came to the hiring hall, she said, were Mexicans who worked in the United States and who returned home at the end of each season. Others came to the hall from as far away as Oregon in search of a job.

There was a small sign in the hiring hall announcing that 25 men were wanted for strawberries at the Jack Pandol Ranch. She explained, "Some jobs, like strawberries are considered too hard for women. It includes working with a knife. But women can go out on these jobs if they want to."

Most impressive of all the buildings at the Forty Acres was the new Roger Terronez Memorial Clinic, adjacent to the administration headquarters in which the hiring hall was located. Opened on October 21, 1971, the clinic was dedicated to the memory of the young striker who died in a 1966 accident just a few hundred yards from the present clinic.

On a single day, the clinic had 17 men, women and children in the waiting room—an immaculate spacious area, furnished in excellent taste, far exceeding what could be found in either private or public clinics in urban areas where the poor live.

More than 400 campesinos and their families signed in each week as patients. And there were thousands working around the Delano perimeter on ranches with union contracts, all of which included coverage under the Robert F. Kennedy Farm Workers Medical Plan.

One of the many union benefits won in the contract negotiations with the growers was a ten-cent-an-hour payment into the fund for every hour worked by each worker. It was this fund that financed the plan, which was in operation throughout the union.

At the Terronez Clinic, there were four full-time doctors, three registered nurses, three aides, a full-time X-Ray technician and clerical and maintenance workers. The doctors, under contract for a two-year period, were then getting paid $6,000 annually. They had just completed their internship, and Margaret Murphy, one of the registered nurses who also directed the entire medical operation in Delano, proudly described them as "tops."

Supervising the union's contract enforcement department in Delano was Frank Ortiz, uniquely equipped to supervise his staff of seven organizers, three of whom were Chicanos, two Filipinos and two Anglos. One of the Anglo organizers was a woman. All but one of the organizers had been field workers.

"I have worked in just about every ranch around here in the last 25 years," said the burly chief of one of the union's most important arms. When asked about what his previous experience was in handling union contracts, he commented in a matter-of-fact manner, "There is not much to it as long as you work with people."

He got his primary education in the fields. Formal schooling was limited to completing grammar school at night. A long-time friend of Cesar and Richard Chavez, he initially came from Imperial Valley, and when La Huelga started he had already been living in the Delano area for over a decade.

His only prior union experience had been limited to a strike against a Delano concrete-pipe firm in 1952. "We did not win a contract then. The strikers all drifted away after a while. In a way we won, we got the wages raised."

Ortiz, who was responsible for seeing to it that wages and conditions of field workers were protected, was working a fifteen-hour day, from 5 a.m. to 8 p.m. Before working full-time for the union, he was averaging between six and eight thousand dollars a year. He was a man of many skills, including being a truck driver.

But he left all that behind him for the usual union organizer's wage of five dollars a week plus subsistence. "Maybe it's because I just like to do it and I want to do it." That was his simple explanation for the drastic change he had made in his life style.

Gloria Soto had been picking grapes all morning at her job on the Caratan and Sons ranch. In the afternoon, she came to the union building to make a payment in the credit union, another department in the seemingly all-purpose union headquarters. Then this is what happened to her.

"Susan Drake asked me if I knew anybody who wanted to work in the Service Center and I said, 'yes, I do.' So she said, 'talk to Richard Chavez, Cesar's brother' (then in charge of the Service Center). I talked to Richard and told him 'I don't know how to type, I don't know anything about immigration, I don't know welfare—I don't know anything but I'm willing to try.' "

She was put on probation for a two-week period to see if see could handle the department, which is older than the union. It was one of Chavez's initial concepts during the formative days of the National Farm Workers Association. The Service Center was one of these concepts, and the Credit Union was another.

An important aspect of the credit union's service was its consumer education literature in English and Spanish which warned persons to bypass commercial loan agencies in Delano and elsewhere who charged 30% interest annually on an unpaid balance, compared to the credit union's 12%. Workers were cautioned about "pots and pans" salesmen who charged $500 for a $40 set or $500 for a vacuum cleaner.

Sal Santos, 32, came from a farm worker family in Hanford and spent most of his life in the San Joaquin Valley. He was one of the Chicanos who allegedly had it made. He was a senior investigator for the California Rural Legal Assistance program, a federally funded project. His assignment was in MacFarland, due south of Delano.

In 1970, when UFWOC got into a dispute with the CRLA over its services and set up picketlines in front of the poverty program office, he walked out and joined the picket line. Shortly thereafter he found himself working for the union and was by January 1972 one of the three-member staff for the credit union.

Four days before Christmas, in 1971, the farm workers' union took still another step towards fulfilling an important part of the dream of many agricultural workers, especially among the Filipinos. It was ground-breaking day for the Paulo Agbayani Retirement Village, projected as "the first housing project undertaken by the National Farm Workers Service Center, a non-profit organization."

Located on a corner of the Forty Acres, directly east of Terronez Memorial Clinic, the retirement village was planned to accommodate 60 single workers in a motel-like complex, a huge improvement over the facilities one finds in the grower-owned and operated camps in the fields. Quite fittingly the first shovelful of dirt for the new retirement village was dug by the oldest of all the grape strikers, 85 year old Martin Galaport. Philip Vera Cruz, then 67 years old and the oldest among the officers of UFWOC. was responsible for the plans for its erection.

In 1966, Vera Cruz said, Agbayani was picketing the Perelli-Minetti ranch when he fell down, laid low by a stroke. He never did get up. One of the original strikers, Agbayani was in his mid-fifties when he died.

It seemed ironic indeed that the Delano City Council, the city manager, the planning director and others of that city's governmental structure tried to stop the construction of this retirement village at its Forty Acres site. They unsuccessfully argued before the Kern County Board of Zoning Adjustment that the retirement village should be located at a site they preferred, which was within the city limits of Delano.

It was indeed an odd position on the part of staunch upholders of so-called free enterprise to insist that the union construct its facility at a location in their city. Furthermore, they urged forcing the "so-called union" to do it with its own money to please a city government, by which it had been opposed tooth and nail.

The union's position nonetheless prevailed with the Kern County governmental body. It successfully argued that the plans for the retirement village was an integral part of the already approved master plan for the Forty Acres.

The development of these and other departments by the fledging union, however, did not continue at an even pace. The still embattled union, fighting to mount a lettuce boycott that proved to be more difficult to carry out than the grape boycott, was compelled to call on all of its reserves, including those in the service units. AFL-CIO George Meany, when informed of the lettuce boycott plans, reportedly said, "No, not again!" He had never been enthusiastic about the grape boycott and was less so about the one in lettuce.

Beset by legal, legislative and other problems, the union was constantly on a war footing. The highly centralized top operation of the union was further inhibited by the dramatic revelation at the end of 1971 that a "contract" had been issued on the life of Cesar Chavez. Security was tightened to protect his life. It was also during this period that Larry Itliong, the assistant director of UFWOC, publicly resigned from his post following a protracted disagreement with some of the other union officers.

Meanwhile, the American Farm Bureau opened up a state-by-state campaign to outlaw secondary boycotts by agricultural workers unions, aimed at crippling the most effective weapon of the new farm workers union. In July, 1971, the union and labor movement in California mobilized 4,500 persons for a Sacramento rally in front of the capitol in a successful campaign to defeat a projected law that would have made them ineffective. In Arizona, such a law was passed, as it was in several other western and midwest states, and the union organized a broad-based recall campaign against the Republican Governor Jack Williams. Sufficient signatures were collected to force the recall, but by the time the courts acted on all of the appeals, time had run out and this issue was to be placed before the state's electorate in the 1974 regular election.

Having failed in their attempt to get the California state legislature to enact legislation to inhibit UFWOC, the growers and their supporters sought to accomplish the same thing in a state-wide initiative vote in November, 1972. All of the anti-union forces in the state, including the far right-wing American Nazi Party were involved, one way or another, in the plans to get this initiative on the ballot. In some cases fraud was proven in the collection of signatures.

The issue came to a vote in the November elections. The farm workers, who had endorsed Senator McGovern for president, waged one of the most intensive political campaigns in California history. Throughout much of the state they posted "living billboards" with farm workers carrying them. They called on the electorate to support them. Nixon carried the state big in the 1972 elections. But the margin of defeat against Proposition 22 was even greater than was Nixon's margin of victory.

The farm workers had demonstrated that with the support of the labor movement and their other allies they could beat down the growers at the ballot box. However, it was a campaign that strained every resource of the new union, with hundreds coming to Los Angeles and San Francisco for weeks to campaign successfully against Proposition 22, the anti-farm-labor initiative.

The main architects of the campaign to defeat Proposition 22 was Leroy Chatfield, who several years earlier was the vice-principal of Garces High School, a Christian Brothers (Catholic) institution in Bakersfield, California. He left his post in the Catholic institution as well as his name, "Brother Gregory," to cast his lot with the farm workers and become one of the full time volunteers for the union.

While some of these developments were taking place, many of the large growers were apparently taking stock of their position and evaluating their posture for the 1973 negotiations with UFWOC. The first major contract of that union was due to expire in the Coachella Valley in mid-April. Three factors apparently influenced the growers in their decision to try to oust the farm workers union from their fields.

Ranch foremen, some of whom were former labor contractors who had a vested interest in inflating anti-Chavez claims, reported that many of the workers were disillusioned with the new union. They pinpointed two major areas of grievances. The hiring hall where jobs were apportioned on a seniority basis rubbed some of the old "favored" workers the wrong way. UFWOC later conceded that some of its hiring hall practices were in need of correction. Also UFWOC's practice of requiring dues payments 12 months a year, even for seasonal workers, was the cause of considerable friction. This situation was later remedied at the union's convention, where the dues system was changed to provide for payments only in months of actual work.

Growers also apparently counted on the reports that the AFL-CIO hierarchy was disenchanted with Chavez and his union. Many of the old-line unionists were quoted as saying, "It's time that Chavez begins acting like a unionist, not a messiah." The combination of a union and a movement that characterized the new agricultural workers organization was largely alien to many in the labor movement. Top AFL-CIO officials, especially, were turned off by the union's independence in political matters and on foreign-policy matters. The movement aspect of the union was a source of constant complaint in some labor circles.

Having heard of the dissatisfaction in high labor circles with the boycott tactic, growers were led to believe that the AFL-CIO top leadership would not go again for a protracted boycott movement in support of UFWOC.

The Teamsters, who so many times before had appeared on the agricultural scene when growers were in need of a disruptive force to abort a potentially successful effort to organize farm workers, reportedly began meetings with growers during 1972. The public expression of Teamsters involvement came at a strange place—the national convention of the American Farm Bureau in Los Angeles, where Teamster's President Frank Fitzsimmons, in December, 1972, became the first labor official to address this traditional antilabor organization.

In rapid-fire order, Fitzsimmons, faced with a possible inner-union challenge by his predecessor James Hoffa, met with his officers in the Western Conference of Teamsters and with the growers from the Coachella Valley. The stage was set for a massive attack on the new farm-labor union.

In the Coachella Valley, more than 2,000 workers attended a mass UFWOC rally and voted to strike if necessary to maintain their contracts. In one election run by churchmen, the workers by secret ballot voted better than ten-to-one to remain with UFWOC. At the same time, four Teamsters Union organizers were circulating in the fields collecting signatures. (UFWOC later charged that many of these signatures were fraudulent.) The Teamsters Union claimed to have signed up over 4,000 workers. According to government a-gents in the farm area, this was more than the number then working in those fields.

Nevertheless, all but two Coachella growers on April 15, 1973, signed contracts with the Teamsters Union. This set the stage for one of the most turbulent periods in the tumultuous history of farm labor.

The AFL-CIO top leadership came out flatly in support of the striking farm workers union and in an unprecedented move made available $1.6 million for use in strike benefits. The Teamsters cal-led in many of its local officials to "guard" the workers in the fields, those that UFWOC called strikebreakers. The admitted cost to the Teamsters of this operation was over $300,000. The so-called guards were paid $50 a day plus $17 in expenses. So vehement was the public and labor reaction to this Teamsters tactic that the "guards" were removed from the fields after a relatively short period of time.

Coachella touched off a strike battle that raged throughout most of California's fields for six months. In the course of this struggle, UFWOC said that more than 4,000 of its members were arrested. Prominent political figures in the state and nation once again rallied to Chavez's cause. Among those arrested in the Fresno strike in 1973 was Dorothy Day, venerable editor of the *Catholic Worker*, published in New York City.

Brutal beatings were commonplace, and in one instance in Coachella the Reverend John Bank, publicity director for UFWOC, was sitting in a restaurant with a *Wall Street Journal* reporter when a Teamster "guard", Mike Falco, smashed him in the face, breaking his nose.

When the physical wounds were healed, UFWOC was a shadow of its former self. It had less than 6,000 dues-paying members, down from a high point of 55,000. At the same time, the Teamsters claimed that over 50,000 agricultural workers were under contract with their union. Once again the boycott was the main weapon of the farm workers, and they were trying desperately to recoup the gains that it had taken them more than ten years to win.

In August 1973 the fears of the Coachella Valley became the tragic realities of the San Joaquin Valley. On a Monday night, outside of a small tavern in the farming community of Lamont, eyewitnesses watched in disbelief as an active union member, Nagi Mohsin Daifullah, was struck over the head by a uniformed man wielding a large searchlight. Gilbert Cooper, the sheriff's deputy, later contended that Daifullah's fall to the ground while running from the deputy was responsible for his death. The autopsy performed by a pathologist for the county coroner, however, confirmed that the cause of the farm worker's death was a blow to the head. Chavez placed the cause of death in a social context in his speech at the funeral of the farm worker, who was among those Arabs who had migrated from Yemen to work in the California fields.

"The hand that struck Brother Nagi down trembles in fear," Chavez said. "It too is the victim of the climate of violence, racism and hatred created by those men who own everything and kill what they cannot own. We are faced with discrimination, exploitation, and even slaughter. The government represses our people, and millions of farm workers are trapped in poverty while the growers lavish in riches. . . . In the struggle to change these evils, Nagi gave his life."

On August 16, the atmosphere in and around Lamont was tense. Congressman Don Edwards (Democrat, California) had come to the area to meet with Chavez and others and to probe the union's charge of organized violence. A task force of Department of Justice agents, including at least one Black government employee, had come from many parts of the United States in an attempt to "cool it," as one agent who had been dispatched from Chicago put it. Meanwhile union representatives were desperately attempting to cut through the red tape to get the Kern County officials to release the body of Daifullah for the projected Delano funeral on the following day.

Several miles away on Wheeler Ridge, on the road beside the struck 6,000-acre Giumarra ranch, Juan de la Cruz and his wife Maximina were among the pickers. Sheriff's deputies, who were almost always on the scene where picketing was in progress, entered the fields and, according to pickets, conversed with some of the strikebreakers and then left the scene.

One of the strikebreakers who soon emerged from the fields was Bayani Bautista Advicula, 20, who was later charged with shooting his 22-calibre gun into the pickets as his car sped from the scene. One of the bullets hit Juan de la Cruz, 60, one of the original members of the farm-workers union who had been employed on the DiGiorgio Ranch, which was later sold to S. S. Camp and then to Hollis Roberts. When the union struck his employer, he joined the picket lines as he had done before.

Word of the shooting of de la Cruz came to the union hall in Lamont as they were preparing for the funeral of Daifullah, and to Chavez and Congressman Edwards in the Lamont Park where they had come to meet with farm workers. The Rev. John Bank, who was handling publicity for the union out of the Delano office, was called to the Kern County General Hospital in Bakersfield three hours later to administer the last rites to de la Cruz.

The next day in Delano, approximately 10,000 farm workers and union supporters, led by a delegation of hundreds of Arabs, carried the body of Daifullah through the streets. Noticeably absent from the funeral cortege were leaders of organized labor. Congressman Edwards was among the public figures who marched all of the four miles in the 100-degree heat. In front of the casket two Arab workers carried a huge photo of the late leader of Egypt, Gamal Abdul Nasser. Pictures of this procession, which were carried by wire services as well as local papers, created many difficulties for the union in later days when the farm workers tried to enlist support for the boycott in predominantly Jewish communities.

Four days later, on August 21, 5,000 marched through the streets of Arvin. It was a burial procession for Juan de la Cruz, who was born in Aguascalientes, Mexico, and who for the last 14 years of his life had lived with his family in Arvin, about 10 miles from the ranches on which he worked. The night before the burial, hundreds of farm workers marched through the small town in a candlelight procession, and throughout the long night they came from far and near to pay their last respects. His body lay in the recreation hall of DiGiorgio Park in Arvin, which had been converted for the occasion into a memorial chapel. Many spent the night in the park to be near their fallen comrade.

Three Catholic bishops came to celebrate the mass before the funeral. They were Bishop Hugh Donohue from Fresno, Bishop Patricio Flores from San Antonio, Texas and Auxiliary Bishop Juan Azurbe from Los Angeles. At the mass as well as at the graveside Joan Baez sang songs by that famous troubador of the farm workers, Woody Guthrie; and Taj Mahal, prominent Black artist, performed on his African harp.

In his eulogy, Chavez said that the thousands who had come to honor the memory of de la Cruz did so because his life was "an example of service and sacrifice." He also said that "Juan is a martyr in a just cause. We will give purpose and memory to his life by what we do. The more we sacrifice, the harder we work, the more life we give to the spirit of our brother Juan de la Cruz."

Thus the farm workers buried their dead. In a larger sense, the presence of the thousands at the two funerals within a four-day span was a referendum on the influence the union had with the farm workers in the San Joaquin Valley and elsewhere. There was little doubt among those present that the farm workers union had deeply touched the lives of the farm workers and had won their allegiance.

No sooner had the farm workers buried their dead than they moved ahead on two major programs: the boycott and preparations for the first constitutional convention of the AFL-CIO United Farm Workers of America in Fresno.

Feelings were running high among many of the rank-and-file leaders of the new union and also among its secondary officials, following the massive funeral processions in Delano and Arvin. The atmosphere was not conductive to the philosophy of non-violence. Chavez had ordered all picket lines removed from the fields following the death of the two union members and had initiated a three-day fast for August 20-23, 1973, in which he called upon union members and their supporters to "rededicate ourselves to the principles of non-violence."

On August 17, in Delano, following the emotion-packed funeral procession for Nagi Daifullah, one of the strike leaders angrily declared that he was through with non-violence and that he was among those who would press the union leadership for a more militant response to the attaaks in the fields and farm communities. Nevertheless, he was among those who attended the union's executive board meeting that very afternoon in Forty Acres and who reportedly concurred in the plans that were to do much to defuse the deep anger of the campesinos.

One of these plans included the immediate dispatch of hundreds of strikers to cities throughout the United States and Canada to prosecute the boycott of grapes coming from fields now under Teamsters Union contracts. Within days, workers were selling or renting their homes and household possessions and were en route to distant cities.

Later Dolores Huerta recalled that "the day the farm workers left the Forty Acres was pretty sad. We had pulled the picketlines down and said " 'we're going out on the boycott' and the reason it had to be done so fast was also because of the money. We just didn't have money to feed prople for very long." The $1.6 million that the AFL-CIO had donated for strike benefits had long since been used up by the strikers.

The scene in Delano in 1973 was, to Huerta, reminiscent of the early years of World War II when the Japanese on the West Coast were packed off to ten concentration camps. The difference being, of course, that the farm workers were leaving their homes voluntarily. In October, 1973, she related one significant episode. "I remember one lady asking me, 'What am I going to do about my rug?' I said to her, 'This is a war, this is a real war—all of the growers and the right-wing elements of the Republican Party are trying to crush the farm workers . . . we have to act like it's a real war.' This is the way our people responded."

In the very first caravan of strikers headed for Chicago, 22 cars broke down but the boycotters were thankful that none of the pregnant women in this contingent gave birth en route. In another caravan the following week, Rena Olivas, the child of a Delano striker, was killed in an auto accident when the family car was struck from the rear in Louisiana. Nevertheless, the caravans continued; grandmothers and grandchildren, sons and daughters of the original strikers in Delano in 1965 were, in 1973, once again on the same route, that of the boycott in the continuing battle for a farm workers union. The Delermente family had a father on the boycott in Los Angeles, a daughter in New York and a son in Ohio.

En route one caravan stopped at Ludlow, Colorado, where they paid tribute to martyred labor pioneers of another era at the scene of the historic April 20, 1914 massacre of the miners. The United Mine Workers Union has since established a memorial on the site. Hundreds of farm-union strike supporters joined the farm workers in Colorado at a rally in a union hall, and in St. Louis more than a thousand marched with them to a local cathedral where a bishop and 26 priests celebrated mass. In the Chicago area two state senators, two members of the city council, union leaders and a Catholic bishop greeted the caravan at a mass rally of 2,000 in South Chicago Heights, where United Auto Workers Union Local 588 hosted the boycotters from California.

Even as the caravans headed east, north and south, carrying farm workers to cities with cold climates unlike any that many of them had ever known, and where, in the main, only English was spoken, Cesar Chavez and his staff at the union's national headquarters were intensively preparing for the most unusual convention in the history of United States labor.

Being put together was a labor convention which encompassed much of the scope of the farm-union organizing movement. The sharp cutting edge of the struggle against the growers and their allies, the Teamsters, was depicted in a huge mural that dominated the large Selland Arena of the Fresno Convention Center. Using house paint, Carlos David Almaraz, a young Chicano artist, had in a period of less than one week created it in the style of the world-famous Mexican revolutionary artist David Sequeiros.

Delegates came from farms still under union contract, cities where boycotts and picket lines had taken place, and as far away as from Canada, Texas and New York. The 414 delegates, representing 60,000 members, formalized at this convention the establishment of the United Farm Workers of America, AFL-CIO. There were moments of great joy, touching scenes of sorrow and heated controversy during the September 21-23 session. Nationally prominent labor leaders shared the platform with local union leaders who had, over the years, displayed their devotion to the cause of the newly established international union.

Paul Hall, president of the Seafarer's International Union and representative of AFL-CIO President George Meany at the convention, had supported the re-election of President Nixon in the 1972 campaign, but this seemed to do little to diminish his stature in the eyes of the delegates. He told the delegates what they wanted to hear; that the attack on them by the growers and the Teamsters Union hierarchy was a "conspiracy on a grand scale" and that the ranchers were backed by "fink allies in the Teamsters Union." The delegates cheered as Hall said, "Let the boss know that if he thought it was hard to sell grapes before, it was easy compared to what's going to happen now." Despite his unqualified pledge of support for the boycott, AFL-CIO President George Meany did not come out in full with his endorsement of the boycott in the next seven months. In late April, 1974, Meany, speaking for the Executive Council, backed the lettuce and grape boycott on condition that the UFWA would not call on consumers to boycott stores selling the non-UFWA products.

"Your real enemy is still that god-damn boss who seeks to take your dignity away from you and keep you and your family down on the ground," Hall said, in trying to give the convention an anti-employer focus.

Leonard Woodcock, president of the United Auto Workers, presented Chavez with two checks of $10,000 each, part of the continuing weekly contribution by this union. He promised to stand by the new union of farm workers even it it put strains on the alliance between the UAW and the Teamsters.

This theme was also reflected by Jim Herman, president of Local 34 of the International Longshoremen's and Warehousemen's Union, who addressed the convention in behalf of his union. While conceding that the alliance between the ILWU and the Teamsters had been mutually beneficial, he said "that alliance be damned" if it had to be maintained at the expense of the UFWA. More than any other union the ILWU had backed the UFWA with job action on the docks, and Herman's local, above all others in the ILWU, was the most consistent in its support for the agricultural labor organizing drive.

Another local union leader, Bill Soltero from Arizona Laborers Local 838, also addressed the convention. It was his local that brought its entire Spanish-speaking staff to the Coachella valley in the spring of 1973 after the Teamsters Union had called in its "guards" from throughout southern California.

National and local politics were also reflected at the convention. Manuel Aragon, representing Los Angleles Mayor Tom Bradley, addressed the convention in Spanish and told them that the Black mayor had proposed to Secretary of State Henry Kissinger that Chavez be nominated for the Nobel Peace Prize. The long-time Kennedy family relationship with the farm workers was reflected in the presence at the convention of Senator Edward Kennedy and his wife Joan. It had all of the makings of a presidential candidate's appearance as the young Massachusetts senator made his first public appearance in the city of Fresno.

Politics of a different character were reflected in another convention speech and by a resolution at the convention. Dr. Stirling Cary, president of the National Council of Churches, brought forth a hearty round of applause when he denounced "the unholy alliance" which brought down the regime of Salvador Allende in Chile. Chavez, who was not a member of the resolutions committee, underscored the importance of this action by reading to the convention a resolution that urged the U.S. to withhold diplomatic recognition from the military junta which had seized power in Chile. Following its adoption, the convention stood, in memory of Allende, the martyred president of Chile.

While there was no opposition to the election of the top officers of the new union, Chavez, as it s first president and Gilberto Padilla its secretary, there were some disagreements over the election of other officers and the board members. Chavez's desire to have two women on the newly elected nine-member executive board was thwarted by some of the more militant young union members who were demanding representation. As a result of behind-the-scenes negotiations Dolores Huerta remained the only woman on the board. She was elected to the post of first vice-president.

While the membership of the union was predominantly Chicano, Chavez and othe union leaders put up a determined battle to elect a multinational leadership at the union's founding convention. This question was put to the test at the Fresno meeting in the vote for first vice-president. Chavez and those closest to him gave their backing to Philip Vera Cruz, long-time Filipino farm worker. Nominated to run against him was Al Rojas, one of the convention's "Young Turks." Vera Cruz, in an impassioned plea to the delegates, challenged them to elect one who is "a minority within a minority." The convention responded to this plea for the election of a Filipino in a largely Chicano union by electing Vera Cruz by a ten-to-one margin. Pete Velasco, another Filipino, was also elected as a vice-president.

Among its four executive board members, the new union chose Mack Lyons, a Black farm worker from the old DiGiorgio ranch; Marshall Ganz, an Anglo who came to the UFWA from the ranks of the Student Non-violent Coordinating Committee in 1965; Eliseo Medina, another one of the young militants in the union; and Richard Chavez, the outspoken and independent brother of Cesar.

At the convention's Sunday morning mass, which also took place in the convention hall, tribute was paid to the eight unionists who met death while performing duties in behalf of the union. Included among them was Roger Terronez, the first to die in an auto mishap in the early days of the strike; Nan Freeman who had her life literally squeezed from her on a UFWA picketline in Florida when a scab-driven truck pinned her to a retaining wall alongside the road; Daifullah and Juan de la Cruz. At the mass, noted folk singer Joan Baez, activist and long-time supporter of the UFWA, movingly rendered a song that she had composed in memory of the most recent casualty in the farm union's long series of battles, Juan de la Cruz.

Long-time unionists, who had come to the convention to observe and to demonstrate their support for the newest international union in the United States, watched in disbelief as the drama of the convention unfolded. In the course of three days and nights, the delegates were in session for 47 hours, more than some unions deliberate in the course of a two-week convention. They slept in the homes of supporters or other union members in the Fresno area during the few hours allotted between convention meetings. They were fed in the convention hall, as were many of the guests to the convention. The food had been prepared by strikers and union supporters.

None of the delegated got the customary per diem for meals and hotel expenses. Leading the convention was 46-year old Cesar Chavez, who, over the three-day span, got less than eight hours sleep. It was a convention that started from scratch. In the union's newspaper *El Malcriado*, in the issue preceding the convention, there was one major article entitled "What is a convention?" and another on "How do you write a resolution?", followed by a form to use in drafting a resolution and getting the necessary signatures to put it before the Fresno convention.

In addition to resolutions submitted to the convention arrangements committee ten days prior to the meeting, others, with the signatures of 25 delegates, were submitted to the convention committee during the sessions. It was one convention at which the resolutions were more than a mere formality. In the final hours of the Fresno convention a proposal was made to the weary delegates to refer some remaining resolutions to the incoming executive board. This stirred a heated debate and it was voted down. The UFWA's convention was also unusual in that the delegates voted on every one of the resolutions before it.

Twelve hours after the convention concluded, at 6:25 a.m. on Monday, September 24, in Fresno, a series of meeting began in La Paz, the union's national headquarters 140 miles south of the Central Valley convention city. The topic under discussion was the boycott of non-UFWA produce and many of the participants were convention-weary delegates.

In labor circles and elsewhere, many questions concerning the future of the United Farm Workers were being raised in the spring of 1974. Had this union, like so many of its predecessors, run its historical course? Had it successfully broken the ground in agriculture only to have the Teamsters harvest the fruit of its heroic backbreaking effort?

Only a single table-grape union contract was held by UFWA by April 15, 1974. It was with Lionel Steinberg, largest grape rancher in the Coachella Valley, who was a liberal Democrat favorably disposed to dealing with Chavez's union. Four years previous to this he had been among the table-grape growers who broke the ice with the UFWA. Other union agreements still maintained by the union included some with wine-grape companies, one with a Coca Cola subsidiary in Florida, covering citrus workers, and contracts with a number of lettuce companies.

Nevertheless, the United Farm Workers of America gave no indication of acting like an organization that was on the toboggan slide towards oblivion. Donations from unions, from churches and from other groups kept its income at almost the same level that it was at the peak of its membership. Locals 10 and 34 of the ILWU in the San Francisco area, for example, had within a 10-month period donated $6,044 to the cause of the farm workers' union and many of their members were participants in the $5. a month club which provided a steady source of income for the UFWA.

An estimated 500 full-time volunteer organizers constituted the union staffs in the fields, boycott cities, organizing offices and service centers. Its highly effective legal department was challenging the legality of actions by the Teamsters and growers, fully confident they would again be successful in voiding many of the current agreements between the companies and the Teamsters Union.

Nevertheless, it was a traumatic period for the leaders of the UFWA because the much-needed public support from the leaders of the AFL-CIO had not yet been forthcoming. This was reflected in a February 23, 1974, article in the *Los Angeles Times* headlined, "Meany Sees More Farm Strife, Raps Chavez, Teamsters." The account from Miami Beach, where the AFL-CIO Executive Council was then in session, said that the AFL-CIO president feared violence "when the Teamsters and growers bring in their goons and try to do everything in their power to beat down the farm workers." However, Meany also said the was "very pessimistic" about the new AFL-CIO union's ability to make immediate gains.

Displaying a lack of understanding of the forces at play in the fields, Meany said, "It was Chavez's own people who went to work behind picketlines in Coachella last year and that didn't indicate much support from the workers there for Chavez." In fact, the overwhelming number of strikers in Coachella in 1973 were imported from across the Mexican border, 100 miles south of Coachella.

This article, among others, gave rise to responses in the Teamsters Union publications such as one in the *Southern California Teamster*, which, on March 13, 1974, headlined its farm labor story, "Meany Changes Tune, Hangs Chavez, UFWA Out to Dry." Three weeks later, on April 3, the same Teamsters Union weekly newspaper, official organ of Teamsters Joint Council 42, featured a front-page article that reported on a meeting of food and drug unions in California. In it, John Henning, state AFL-CIO secretary, was reported as saying that "the Teamsters and other independent unions would eventually reunite with the AFL-CIO, presenting labor with a united front." The account went on:

"Declaring the Teamsters were the backbone of the labor movement in California during the 1930's, Henning said the current jurisdictional dispute between the Teamsters and the Farm Workers Union was no more serious than any other jurisdictional dispute which has marked the history of the labor movement."

One week later Meany announced that the AFL-CIO had endorsed the boycott of non-UFWA lettuce and grapes. In conjunction with this, the AFL-CIO announced that Chavez's union would not call on consumers to boycott the stores but they would be urged not to buy non-UFWA lettuce and grapes. Also, the AFL-CIO did not give its support to the Gallo and Franzia wine boycotts because some small AFL-CIO unions had contracts with these firms on the production end. The UFWA carried on these boycotts on its own. Meany in his letter to Chavez, which was well publicized throughout the labor movement, said:

"The entire AFL-CIO continues to fully support the UFWA and its struggle against the unconstrainable raid of the Teamsters and the collusive relationship between the Teamsters and the growers. We had hoped to resolve this dispute through the discussions and negotiations which were held. However, the Teamsters reneged on our agreement and the Teamsters and growers are jointly seeking to destroy the farmworkers. We urge the entire AFL-CIO membership to rally behind the Farm Workers and to support the boycott. . . ."[1]

[1]Charles Colson, one of the top Nixon administration officials indicted and convicted in the infamous Watergate case, was accused by Meany on April 16, 1974, of joining with Fitzsimmons in a "public relations ploy to erase from the public memory . . . the evidence that it was Teamster goons who were indicted for beating up aged strikers, including women; that it was Teamsters who conspired with the growers against the farmers."

AFL-CIO sources also accused Colson of being instrumental in torpedoing the tentative peace agreement reached by the AFL-CIO and the Teamsters in 1973. According to these sources, Colson, acting as an attorney for the Teamsters, advised Fitzsimmons to back off the already negotiated farm labor jurisdiction agreement with the AFL-CIO because Meany was, at that time, pushing the AFL-CIO position calling for the impeachment of President Nixon. Fitzsimmons was Nixon's chief labor support, having backed him strongly for reelection in 1972.

Yet the question still remained whether Chavez's claim that "the Teamsters have the contracts but we have the workers" was indeed an accurate description of the state of affairs in the fields in the early months of 1974.

A bus accident near Blythe, California, during the early morning hours of January 15, 1974, became the event that made it possible for Chavez to demonstrate that his estimate of the situation was an accurate one.

Nineteen farm workers died in that accident. They were being transported by Jesus Ayala, a labor contractor, in an old school-type bus from the Mexican border to the High and Mighty Farms, which was under contract with the Teamsters union. Chavez was then in Atlanta, Georgia, where on the previous day he was awarded the Martin Luther King, Jr. Nonviolent Peace Prize by Coretta King, the widow of the martyred civil rights leader. While he was there, the union was awarded a $1,000 donation by the movement that carried on the work of Dr. King, and the Atlanta Ford Assembly workers voted a $200-donation to the farm union.

From Atlanta, Chavez called the union's offices in California, and he flew directly to Calexico to meet the corps of lawyers, service-center personnel and others who had been summoned to the scene of the tragedy. The Teamsters Union, which had announced that it had set up its own Social Services Department for farm workers, was not visible at the scene. On both side of the Mexican border, farm workers were buried with the UFWA flag draped over their coffins. Those in need of medical care and legal aid were assisted by UFWA service center personnel.

The agitation among farm workers along the border mounted, and resentment against the Teamsters increased daily. On February 18, 1974, thousands of farm workers, estimated by the UFWA to number as many as 8,000, responded to the call of the union for a one-day "paro"—work stoppage. It was the UFWA's declaration of war on the growers and the Teamster Union officials. Chavez declared "this is the beginning of a whole series of strikes that will be taking place until such time as the growers and the Teamsters make up their minds that the workers are going to be represented by their own union." UFW organizer Ricardo Villalpando said, "We want to show them that the farm workers are united and that we can stop them at any hour we please."

For the first time in the history of agricultural labor in Imperial Valley, not a single worker was reported to have been fired following this "unauthorized" work stoppage. More than 1,000 workers signed cards calling on the UFWA to represent them through the union hiring hall.

Picket lines were set up at asparagus fields and 17 were arrested in the fields of grower Ben Abatti, one of the former UFWA companies that had switched to the Teamsters. They stayed in jail for three days because of high bail. They were later released on their own recognizance or at nominal bail.

The February 18 meeting of 500 asparagus workers addressed by Chavez was followed the next day by a strike in the asparagus fields. At first the asparagus growers threatened to bring in machines to replace the strikers. Four growers seeking an injuction against the UFWA contended that the walkout was costing them $50,000 daily. As in so many other struggles in Imperial Valley, violence was also part of this one. On February 21, eighteen farm workers, including UFWA organizer Manual Chavez, were arrested for allegedly violating the injunction, and a police attack on a peaceful picketline resulted in injuries to 35 workers, with three seriously hurt.

The showdown battle in the fields had begun, and the UFWA had started its own form of "guerilla warfare" to recapture the gains for which they had suffered untold hardships over a period of more than a decade. These workers had already made their mark in farm labor history. They were determined, however, to be more than a footnote in the history of agricultural labor. With the support of the labor and people's coalition that had strongly backed them in their earlier struggles, they set out with the same determination that had marked their earlier efforts to bring the growers back to the bargaining tables in California and elsewhere.

And the battle continues. . . .

Epilogue: New and
Dramatic Beginning

After having waged several major campaigns for the enactment of a farm labor law in California, the nation's key agricultural state, the efforts of the United Farm Workers were crowned with victory on June 5, 1975 with the adoption of the California Agricultural Labor Relations Act. It became effective on August 28, 1975.

Ever since the New Deal era, unions attempting to organize agricultural labor simultaneously campaigned for passage of legislation which would give farm workers rights comparable to those enjoyed by industrial workers. Passage of the California farm labor law, was the first such major breakthrough on continental United States.

Thereafter ensued one of the most intensive labor organizing campaigns in the nation's history. A total of 382 representation elections involving the UFW, the Teamsters Union and "no union" were conducted over a five month span. Represented in these elections were 59,856 farm workers. Of the 329 elections that were decided, according to a study by the UFW Research Department, 205 resulted in UFW victories. There were 30,804 workers represented on these ranches. In contrast, the Teamsters Union won a total of 102 elections with 11,179 workers. In 22 elections with a total of 2,778 workers the majority choice was for "no union."

On some ranches formerly under contract with the Teamsters, this union, which had been accused of consummating sweetheart agreements, could not get sufficient authorization cards even to get a place on the ballot.

On February 6, 1976 elections in California came to a sudden halt when the state legislature refused to vote additional funds for the Agricultural Labor Relations Board. Republican legislators were joined by rural Democrats in preventing the two thirds vote necessary for appropriations in California.

This came as a major blow to the UFW, which charged that the growers and Teamsters Union had ganged up on it because of the fact that so many farm workers were choosing the UFW as their representative. The UFW and Cesar Chavez had staked much on the election process. The militant union leader had walked 1,000 miles through all of the major California farm areas to mobilize support for the elections. Workers were urged to put their faith in the new legislation and many of them did so. When the new law became inoperative many of these same workers found themselves blacklisted.

From the outset of the election campaign there was a euphoric atmosphere in the UFW ranks. At the mid-August second convention of the UFW in Fresno, which came in the midst of Chavez's state-wide walk, hundreds of workers rode in from ranches then under contract with the Teamsters Union and took their places as UFW delegates. Representatives of the United Auto Workers, the International Longshoremen's and Warehousemen's Union and the national AFL-CIO were among those who pledged solidarity with the UFW.

At this convention the UFW called for "amnesty" for undocumented workers in the United States. The convention cheered delegate Epifanio Camacho who denounced "those on both sides of the border who exploit us and pit one against another." This was in marked contrast to the union's earlier position of cooperating with the Immigration and Naturalization Service in calling on the border patrol to seize undocumented workers who were strikebreaking. While the convention was essentially a rally for the forthcoming elections it also reflected certain independent positions, such as the one on undocumented workers, which ran counter to traditional AFL-CIO policy.

The UFW also pledged its support to the 1,200 Coca Cola workers in Florida who were in the midst of a protracted struggle for a new contract. As a result of the solidarity of West Coast farm workers with the Blacks from the East Coast this powerful Coca Cola management capitulated on November 4, 1975 and signed another three year agreement with the UFW.

Shortly after the convention and in the early stage of the elections there was dramatic new evidence that the UFW had won great public support. A nationwide poll by Louis Harris revealed that 12 percent had stopped buying grapes and 11 percent were boycotting lettuce. In addition to the millions represented by these figures there were also 8 percent, 11 million people, who were boycotting Gallo wines. As for union sympathy, this same poll showed 45 percent sided with the UFW and 7 percent with the Teamsters while 14 percent were neutral.

While the UFW was gaining support in the nation as a whole it was also concentrating on consolidating its ranks among those who were toiling in the fields. In one of the UFW's series of leaflets to all farm workers, Cesar Chavez called for unity of all workers, "whether they be citizens or immigrants." It spoke of many things including that "we have all committed errors." In a few short months the UFW had overcome much of the division between the UFW and the undocumented workers and on September 7, 1975 in Salinas, California an open letter to all farm workers was made public by seven undocumented workers. They were Armando Garcia, Gilberto Rojas, Ramiro Perez, Jesus Perez, Francisco Renan Catzin, Pablos P. Perez and Jose Moreno. They called on all workers to join with the UFW, a courageous act openly defying the border patrol which was deporting workers on an unprecedented scale.

When the legislature persisted in refusing to refund the farm labor board the UFW decided to go directly to the people of California with the issue. On April 1, 1976 they began circulating an initiative petition, which if passed by the electorate in November, 1976 would make the farm labor representation law a part of the state constitution. In 30 days the UFW collected 719,589 signatures. To qualify, the petition needed 312,404 valid signatures. Never before had any initiative movement collected so many signatures in so short a period of time.

May, 1976